The
Monongahela of Old

Or,
Historical Sketches of South-Western Pennsylvania to the Year 1800

By
James Veech

Reprinted with a New Index

CLEARFIELD

Originally published: Pittsburgh
1858 and 1892
and re-set in 1910

Reprinted from the 1910 Edition
With a New Index
by Genealogical Publishing Co., Inc.
Baltimore, Maryland, 1975

Reprinted from a volume in
the George Peabody Branch
Enoch Pratt Free Library
Baltimore, Maryland

Library of Congress Cataloging in Publication Data
Veech, James, 1808-1879.
    The Monongahela of old; or, Historical sketches of south-western Pennsylvania to the year 1800.
    Reprint of the 1858092 ed. published in Pittsburgh.
    Includes the author's pamphlet, Mason and Dixon's line, originally published in 1857.
    1. Monongahela Valley—History. 2. Fayette Co., Pa.—History. 3. Mason and Dixon's Line. I. Veech, James, 1808-1879. Mason and Dixon's line. 1975. II. Title.
F157.M58V5 1975   917.48'8'032   74-18048
ISBN 978-0-8063-0639-1

Copyright © 1975
Genealogical Publishing Co., Inc.
Baltimore, Maryland
All Rights Reserved.

Reprinted for Clearfield Company by
Genealogical Publishing Company
Baltimore, Maryland, 2002, 2011

Made in the United States of America

THE
MONONGAHELA OF OLD;

OR,

HISTORICAL SKETCHES OF SOUTH-WESTERN
PENNSYLVANIA TO THE YEAR 1800

BY

JAMES VEECH.

FOR PRIVATE DISTRIBUTION ONLY.

PITTSBURGH:
1858—1892

(This unfinished work of the author, which has been "in sheets" since 1858, is now issued for private distribution only. By the addition of pages 241-259, which were included in a pamphlet issued in 1857, entitled "Mason and Dixon's Line," the chapter relating to the boundary controversy between Pennsylvania and Virginia is completed.)

Copyright:
Mrs. E. V. Blaine.
1892.

Copyright re-issued to
James Hadden.
1910.

PREFACE

James Veech, the author of this work, was born in Menallen township, Fayette county, Pennsylvania, September 18, 1808.

He was graduated at Jefferson college, Cannonsburg, in 1827, and read law in Uniontown with James Todd who was appointed Attorney General of the State, 1835-'38. He was admitted to the bar of Fayette county in 1831, and was married to Maria Ewing, a sister of Hon. Nathaniel Ewing, in 1832, and practiced his profession in Uniontown until 1834, when he moved to Pittsburg, where in the same year he was appointed Assistant District Attorney for Allegheny county by Governor Ritner, which position he filled until 1838, when he returned to Uniontown and resumed his practice there.

In 1861 he accepted the appointment of paymaster in the army, and left Uniontown. Taking up his residence again in Pittsburg, in 1862, he opened a law office and became associated with D. T. Watson in the law firm of Veech and Watson.

He was for years a director in the Monongahela Navigation Company, and also in the Bank of Pittsburg. In 1855 he was a candidate for United States Senator, and in 1857 he was nominated for supreme judge, but was defeated by Justice William Strong. During this campaign the title of "judge" was popularly given to him, by which title he was ever afterwards known.

Judge Veech was a high minded gentleman of the old school; his dignified manner and profound legal ability commanded the respect of all. He retired from active life in 1872, and spent his later years in the congenial pursuits of history and literature in which he acquired fame.

In later years he made his home at Emsworth, on the Ohio river, six miles below Pittsburgh, on the Ft. Wayne road, where he died December 11, 1879, and his death was the occasion of marked sorrow and respect of the bar and public of Pittsburg as well as his many friends in Uniontown. He was buried in Union cemetery at Uniontown. He was survived by his wife and five daughters. His only son, David Henry Veech, having died in 1874, leaving a son, James Veech. This last named was an only son back through five generations, viz: James, of David Henry, of James, of David, of James.

The inception of this book dates from 1850, when Freeman Lewis, a competent surveyor of Uniontown, projected a history of Fayette county, and had already gathered some material for the purpose. The work soon grew to such proportions that Mr. Lewis was unable to handle it and proposed to transfer the undertaking to Mr. Veech, who immediately applied himself to collecting the necessary data, and in 1859, it was placed in the hands of the printer. The book was then printed, but was left in sheet form for several years, the manuscript having not all been furnished to the printer. In the middle of the chapter on the famous Mason and Dixon Line the history stopped short, and in this unfinished form a few copies were bound and furnished to a few of his personal friends as the work was originally intended for private distribution only.

In 1892, Mr. Veech's daughter, Mrs. E. V. Blaine, completed the chapter on Mason and Dixon's Line, and a supplement thereto and published a few copies of the still incomplete work.

It is ever to be regretted that Mr. Veech did not finish the work he had so ably begun and for which he was so amply fitted. The appointment as paymaster of the army, the duties of which compelled him to relinquish work on the history for the time, after which failing health compelled him to abandon it entirely.

The book as published, contains eight chapters and a supplement, which is not half of what the volume was originally intended to be. It will remain the standard history of Fayette county and will be referred to as such by all future histories of Western Pennsylvania.

THE MONONGAHELA OF OLD.

CHAPTER I.

ANTIQUITIES.

Ante-Indian Inhabitants—Old Forts; their forms; sites; localities—Mounds—Indian Towns—Indians Graves—Curious chain.

Of the original human inhabitants of the territory, of which Fayette county is a part, we know but little. When Anglo-Saxon traders and hunters first penetrated its wilds, it was the hunting ground of the Mingo Indians, or Six Nations; (a) the seat of whose power and chief population was Western New York. Delawares, whose original home was the western shore of the river of that name, and Shawnese, who, came from the Cumberland river, were also found. But that these were the successors of a race more intelligent, or of a people of different habits of life, seems clearly deducible from the remains of fortifications scattered all over the territory, and which are very distinct from those known to have been constructed by the tribes of Indians named, or any of their modern compeers.

These remains of embankments, or "old forts," are numerous in Fayette county. That they are very ancient is shown by many facts. The Indians, known to us, could give no satisfactory account of when, how, or by whom they were erected; or for what purpose, except for defense. While the trees of the surrounding forests were chiefly oak, the growths upon, and within the lines of the old forts, were generally of large black walnut,

---

(a) Called also the Iroquois. They were a Confederacy of the Mohawks, Oneidas, Onondagoes, Cayugas, Senecas and Tuscaroras. The Delawares and Shawnese were in league with them, but rather as conquered dependents.

wild cherry, and sometimes locust. We have examined some which indicated an age of from three to five hundred years, and they evidently of a second or third generation, as they were standing amid the decayed remains of their ancestors. How they got there, whether by transplanting, by deposits of floods, or of birds, or otherwise, is a speculation into which we will not go.

These embankments may have been originally composed of wood, as their debris is generally a vegetable mould. No stone was used in their construction; and among their ruins are always found some remains of old pottery, composed of clay, mixed with crushed muscle shells, even when far off from a river. This composite was not burnt, but only baked in the sunshine. These vessels were generally circular; and, judging from those we have seen, they were made to hold from one to three quarts.

These old forts were of various forms, square, oblong, triangular, circular and semi-circular. Their superficial areas range from one-fourth of an acre to ten acres.

Their sites were generally well chosen, in reference to defense and observation. And what is a very singular fact, they were very often, generally in Fayette county, located on the highest and richest hills, and at a distance from any spring or stream of water. In a few instances this was otherwise, whether being enclosed or contiguous, as they are generally in Ohio, and other more western parts of the Mississippi valley.

Having seen and examined many of these "old forts" in Fayette, and also those at Marietta, Newark, and elsewhere, in Ohio, we believe they are all the work of the same race of people; as are also the famous Grave Greek Mounds near Elizabethtown, Virginia; and if this belief be correct, then the conclusion follows irresistibly, that that race of people was much superior, and existed long anterior to the modern Indian. But who they were, and what became of them, must perhaps forever be unknown.

We will briefly indicate the localities of some of these "old forts" in Fayette county. To enumerate all, or, to describe them separately, would weary the reader and waste our space. The curious in such matters may yet trace their remains.

A very noted one, and of most commanding location, was at Brownsville, on the site of "Fort Burd," but covering a much larger area. Even after Col. Burd built his fort there, in 1759, it retained the names of the "Old Fort,"—Redstone Old Fort, or, Fort Redstone.

There was one on land formerly of William Goe, near the Mon-

ANTIQUITIES.

ongahela River, and just above the mouth of Little Redstone; where afterward was a Settler's Fort, called Cassel's or Castle Fort. And an old map which we have seen has another of these old forts noted at the mouth of Speers' run, where Bellevernon now is.

Two or three are found on a high ridge southwardly of Perryopolis, on the State road, and on land late of John F. Martin.

Another noted one is on the western bank of the Youghiogheny river, nearly opposite the Broad ford, on land lately held by James Collins.

There are several on the high ridge of land, leading from the Collin's fort above referred to, southwestwardly toward Plumpsock, on lands of James Paull, John M. Austin, John Bute and others; a remarkable one being on land lately owned by James Gilchrist and the Byers; where some very large human bones have been found.

There is one on the north side of Mountz's creek, above Irishman's run.

A very large one, containing six or eight acres, is on the summit of Laurel Hill, where the Mud pike crosses it; covered with a large growth of black walnut.

One specially noted, as containing a great quantity of broken shells and pottery, existed on the high land between Laurel run and the Yough river, on a tract formerly owned by Judge Young.

There are yet distinct traces of one on land of Gen. Henry W. Beeson, formerly Col. M'Clean, about two miles east of Uniontown.

There was one north-east of New Geneva, at the locality known as the "Flint Hill," on land now of John Franks.

About two miles north-east of New Geneva, on the road to Uniontown, and on land late of William Morris, now Nicholas B. Johnson, was one celebrated for its great abundance of muscle shells.

On the high ridge southwardly of the head waters of Middle run, several existed; of which may be named—one on the Bixler land—one on the high knob eastwardly of Clark Breading's—one on the Alexander Wilson tract—and one on the land of Dennis Riley, deceased, formerly Andrew C. Johnson.

These comprise the most prominent of the "Old Forts," in Fayette.

Of their cognates, Mounds, erected as monuments of conquest, or like the Pyramids of Egypt, as the tombs of kings, we have none.

Those that we have seen were of diminutive size, and may have been thrown up to commemorate some minor events, or to cover the remains of a warrior.

Our territory, having been an Indian hunting ground, had within it but few Indian towns or villages, and these of no great magnitude or celebrity. There was one on the farm of James Ewing, near the southern corner of Redstone, and the line between German and Luzerne townships, close to a fine limestone spring. Near it, on a ridge, were many Indian graves. Another was near where Abram Brown lived, about four miles west of Uniontown. There was also one on land of John M. Austin, Esq., formerly Samuel Stevens, near 'Sock. The only one we know of north of the Yough, was on the Strickler land, eastward of the Broad ford.

Piles of stones, called Indian graves, were numerous in many places in Fayette, generally near the sites of Indian villages. They were generally on stony ridges, often twenty or thirty of them in a row. In many of them have been found human bones indicating a stature of from six to seven feet. They also contained arrow heads, spear points and hatchets, of stone and flint, nicely and regularly shaped—but how done, is the wonder. On a commanding eminence, overlooking the Yough river, upon land now of Col. A. M. Hill, formerly Wm. Dickerson, there are great numbers of these Indian graves; among which, underneath a large stone, Mr. John Cottom, a few years ago found a very curious chain, consisting of a central ring, and five chains of about two feet in length, each branching off from it, having at their end, clamps, somewhat after the manner of hand-cuffs, large enough to enclose a man's neck—indicating that its use was to confine prisoners—perhaps to fasten them to the burning stake. The chains were of an antique character, but well made, and seemed to have gone through fire.

There are many other localities within our county limits, which may be justly ranked as antiquities; but we reserve them to be interspersed in our subsequent sketches of events, and localities of distinct classes, with which they are intimately connected. They will lose none of their interest by their associations.

CHAPTER II.

SETTLERS' FORTS.

Fayette territory exempt from Indian cruelties—Description of Settlers' Forts; their names and localities—An all-smoke incident.

We might refer these to our sketch of "Early Settlements;" but, as localities, we prefer introducing them immediately after the **old forts**, with which they are often confounded.

For reasons which will be unfolded in the sequel, the territory of Fayette County was, after the end of the old French war, in 1763, and during all the period of its early settlement, remarkably exempt from those terrific incursions of the savages which made forting so common and necessary in the surrounding country. Hence we had but few Settlers' Forts, and those few of but little note.

These forts were erected by the associated effort of settlers in particular neighborhoods, upon the land of some one, whose name was thereupon given to the fort, as Ashcraft's, Morris', &c. They consisted of a greater or less space of land, enclosed on all sides by high log parapets, or stockades, and cabins adapted to the abode of families. The only external openings were a large puncheon gate and small port-holes among the logs, through which the unerring rifle of the settler could be pointed against the assailants. Sometimes, as at Lindley's, and many of the other forts in the adjacent country west of the Monongahela, additional cabins were erected outside the fort, for temporary abode in times of danger, from which the sojourners could, in case of attack, retreat within the fort. All these erections were of rough logs, covered with clap-boards and weight poles, the roofs sloping inwards. A regular-built fort, of the first class, had, at its angles, block-houses, and sometimes a ditch protected a vulnerable part. These block-houses projected a little past the line of the cabins, and the upper half was made to extend some two feet further, like the over jet of a barn, so as to leave an overhanging space, secured against entrance by heavy log floors, with small port holes for repelling close attacks, or attempts to dig down, or fire the forts. These rude defenses were very secure, were seldom attacked, and seldom, if ever, captured. They were always located upon open, commanding eminences, sufficiently remote from coverts and wooded heights to prevent surprise.

The sites of the "old forts" already desribed were sometimes chosen for settlers' forts. This was the case with the site on the Goe land, just above the mouth of Little Redstone, where, as already stated, was a settler's fort, called Cassel's, or Castle Fort. How far Redstone Old Fort was so used cannot certainly be known, as, while it existed as a place of defense, after settlements began, it was a kind of government fort, for the storage of ammunition and supplies, guarded by soldiers. Its proper name, after 1759, though seldom given to it, was Fort Burd. And there is evidence that, besides its governmental purposes, it was often resorted to by the early settlers, with their families, for protection, though for that object it was less adapted than many of the private forts—a few of which, within our county limits, we will now notice.

One of the earliest erected forts of this kind was by John Minter, the Stevensons, Crawfords and others, on land of the former, since Blackiston, now Ebenezer Moore, about a mile and a half westwardly of Pennsville.

There was one on the old Thomas Gaddis farm, where Bazil Brownfield now lives, about two miles south of Uniontown; but what was its name we cannot certainly learn, or by whom or when erected,—probably, however, by Col. Gaddis, as he was an early settler, and a man of large public spirit.

Another, called Pearse's Fort, was on the Catawba Indian trail, about four miles north-east of Uniontown, near the residences of William and John Jones. Some old Lombardy poplars, recently fallen, denoted its site.

About one mile north-west of Merrittstown there was one, on land now of John Craft. Its name is forgotten.

Swearingen's Fort was in Springhill township, near the crossroad from Cheat river towards Brownsville. It derived its name from John Swearingen, who owned the land on which it stood, or from his son, Van Swearingen, afterward Sheriff of Washington County, a Captain in the Revolution and in the frontier wars, and whose nephew of the same name fell at St. Clair's defeat.

One of considerable capacity, called **Lucas' Fort,** was on the old Richard Brown farm, now Fordyce, near the frame meeting-house in Nicholson township.

M'Coy's Fort, on land of James M'Coy, stood where now stands the barn of the late Eli Baily, in South Union township.

SETTLERS' FORTS.

Morris' Fort, which was one of the first grade, was much resorted to by the early settlers on the upper Monongahela and Cheat, and from Ten Mile. It stood on Sandy Creek, just beyond the Virginia line, outside our county limits. It was to this fort that the family of the father of the late Dr. Joseph Doddridge resorted, in 1774, as mentioned in his Notes. The late Col. Andrew Moore, who resided long near its site, said that he had frequently seen the ruins of the fort and its cabins, which may yet be traced.

Ashcraft's Fort stood on land of the late Jesse Evans, Esq., where Phineas Sturgis lived, in Georges township. Tradition tells of a great alarm and resort to this fort, on one occasion, caused thus: On land lately owned by Robert Britt, in that vicinity, there is a very high knob called Prospect Hill, or Point Look-Out. To this eminence the early settlers were wont, in time of danger, daily to resort, to reconnoitre the country, sometimes climbing trees, to see whether any Indians had crossed the borders, of which they judged by the smoke of their camps. This hill commanded a view from the mountains to the Monongahela, and from Cheat hills far to the northward. On the occasion referred to, the scouts reported that Indians had crossed the Monongahela, judging from some smoke "which so gracefully curled." The alarm was given. The settlers flocked to Ashcraft's Fort, with wives and children, guns and provisions, and prepared to meet the foe—when lo! much to the vexation of some and the joy of others, the alarm soon proved to be "all smoke."

CHAPTER III.

INDIAN TRAILS, TRADERS' PATHS, ARMY ROADS, &c.

Indians had roads—Their night compasses—Catawba or Cherokee trail—Nemacolin's—Dunlap's path—Burd's road to Redstone—Fort Burd—Cresap—Mouth of Redstone—Turkey-foot roads—James Smith—Bullock pens—M'Culloch's path—M'Culloch caught—Sandy Creek road—Froman's road—Old County roads—Pack-horse business and travel—Prices.

At the risk of some infractions of chronological order, before we go into the eventful portion of these sketches, we prefer now to trace these old highways; and, to avoid repetitions, we must occasionally encroach upon subsequent narratives.

An erroneous impression obtains among many of the present day, that the Indian, in traversing the interminable forests which once covered our towns and fields, roamed at random, like a modern afternoon hunter, by no fixed paths, or that he was guided, in his long journeys, solely by the sun, moon and stars, or by the courses of streams and mountains. And true it is that these untutored sons of the woods were considerable astronomers and geographers, and relied much upon these unerring guide-marks of nature. Even in the most starless night they could determine their course by feeling the bark of the oak-trees, which is always smoothest on the south side and roughest on the north. But still they had their trails or paths, as distinctly marked as are our County and State roads, and often better located. The white traders adopted them, and often stole their names, to be in turn surrendered to the leader of some Anglo-Saxon army, and finally obliterated by some costly highway of travel and commerce. They are now almost wholly effaced and forgotten. Hundreds travel along, and plough across them, unconscious that they are in the footsteps of the red men, as they were wont to hasten, in single file, to the lick, after the deer and buffalo, or to the wigwams of their enemy, in quest of scalps.

The most prominent, and perhaps the most ancient of these old pathways across our county, was the old Catawba or Cherokee Trail, leading from the Carolinas, Georgia, Florida, &c., through Virginia and Western Pennsylvania, on to Western New York and Canada. We will trace it within our limits as well as we can. After crossing and uniting with numerous other trails, the principal one entered Fayette territory, at the State line, at the mouth of Grassy run. A tributary trail, called the Warrior Branch, coming from Tennessee, through Kentucky and Southern Ohio, came up Fish creek and down Dunkard, crossing Cheat river at M'Farland's. It run out a junction with the chief trail, intersecting it in William Gans' sugar camp, but it kept on by Crow's mill, James Robinson's, and the old gun factory,(a) and thence towards the mouth of Redstone, intersecting the old Redstone trail from the top of Laurel Hill, afterward Burd's road, near Jackson's, or Grace Church, on the National road. The main Catawba trail pursued "the even tenor of its way," regardless of minor points, which, like a modern grand rail road, it served by branches and turn-outs. After receiving the Warrior Branch junction, it kept on through land late of Charles Griffin, by Long's Mill, Ashcraft's Fort, Philip Rogers' (now Alfred Stewart's), the Diamond Spring, (now William James'); thence nearly on the route of the present Morgantown road, until it came to the Misses Hadden's; then across Hellen's fields, passing near the Rev. William Brownfield's mansion, and about five rods west of the old Henry Beeson brick house; thence through Uniontown, over the old Bank house lot, crossing the creek where the bridge now is, back of the Sheriff's house; thence along the northern side of the public grave-yard on the hill, through the eastern edge of John Gallagher's land, about six rods south of John F. Foster's (formerly Samuel Clarke's) house, it crossed Shute's run where the fording now is, between the two meadows, keeping the high land through Col. Evans' plantation, and passed between William and John Jones' to the site of Pearse's Fort; thence by the Murphy school-house, and bearing about thirty rods westward of the Mount Braddock mansion, it passed a few rods to the east of the old Conrad Strickler house, where it is still visible. Keeping on through land formerly of John Hamilton, (now Freeman,) it crossed the old Connellsville road immediately on the summit of the Limestone hill, a few rods west of the old Strickler distillery; thence through the old Lawrence Harrison land (James Blackiston's) to Robinson's falls of Mill run, and thence down it to the Yough river, crossing it just below the run's mouth, where Braddock's army crossed at Stewart's

---

(a) See memoir of Albert Gallatin, in "Early Settlers"—postea, Chap. VII.

Crossings. The trail thence kept through the Narrows, by Rist's, near the Baptist meeting-house, beyond Pennsville, passing by the old Saltwell on Green Lick run, to the mouth of Bushy run, at Tinsman's or Welshonse's mill. Thence it bore across Westmoreland county, up the Allegheny, to the heads of the Susquehanna, and into Western New York, then the empire of the Iroquois. A branch left the main trail at Robinson's mill, on Mill or Opossum run, which crossed the Yough at the Broad ford, bearing down across Jacob's creek, Sewickley and Turtle creeks, to the forks of the Ohio, at Pittsburg, by the highland route. This branch, and the northern part within our county, of the main route, will be found to possess much interest in connection with Braddock's line of march to his disastrous destiny.

This Cherokee or Catawba Indian trail, including its Warrior branch, is the only one of note which traversed our county northward and southward. Generally, they passed eastward and westward, from the river, to and across the mountains. To trace all these would be uninteresting. We will therefore confine our sketchings to those which have had their importance enhanced by having been adopted as traders' paths and as army or emigrants' roads.

Decidedly the most prominent of all these is Nemacolin's trail, afterwards adopted and improved by Washington and Braddock, the latter of whom, by a not unusual freak of fame, has given to the road its name, while its shrewd old Indian engineer, like him who traced for Napoleon the great road across the Simplon, has been buried in forgetfulness.

Nemacolin's path led from the mouth of Wills' creek (Cumberland, Md.) to the "Forks of the Ohio" (Pittsburgh). It doubtless existed as a purely Indian trail before Nemacolin's time. For when the Virginia, Maryland and Pennsylvania traders with the Indians on the Ohio, began their operations, perhaps as early as 1740,(b) they procured Indians to show them the best and easiest route, and this was the one they adopted. So says Washington. And when the "Ohio Company," hereafter to be noticed, was formed, in 1748, and preparing to go into the Ohio Indian trade on a large scale, they procured Col. Thomas Cresap, of Old Town, Md., to engage some trusty Indians to mark and clear the pathway. For this purpose he engaged Nemacolin, a well known Delaware Indian, who resided at the mouth of Dunlap's creek, which,

---

(b)There is some evidence that Indian traders, both English and French, were in this country much earlier.

in early times, was called Nemacolin's creek.(c) The commissioner and engineer, with the aid of other Indians, executed the work, in 1750, by blazing the trees, and cutting away and removing the bushes and fallen timber, so as to make it a good pack-horse path. Washington says that "the Ohio Company, in 1753, at a considerable expense, opened the road. In 1754, the troops whom I had the honor to command, greatly repaired it, as far as Gist's plantation; and, in 1755, it was widened and completed by Gen. Braddock to within six miles of Fort Du Quesne."(d) This is a brief history of the celebrated "Braddock's road." We will hereafter take the reader over it more leisurely. It was, until near its fatal termination, identical with Nemacolin's path, which, also, from Gist's northward, with a few variations, was identical with the old Catawba trail, or with its westward branch to the head of the Ohio. And we will see what Braddock lost by not following it implicitly to the end.

Dunlap's path, or road, was a very early one. It came from Winchester, by way of Wills' creek, to the mouth of Dunlap's creek. Dunlap was a trader, and, as Braddock did with the road, so he succeeded in wresting from Nemacolin the name of the creek, which now bears his name. From Wills' creek to the top of Laurel hill, near the Great Rock, the route of Dunlap's road was identical with that of Nemacolin or Braddock.(e) From that point Nemacolin's path bore north-east, along the crest of the mountain; while Dunlap's bore westwardly, descending the mountain a little south of the present National road, taking to Lick run about a mile from the foot of the hill. Thence it passed through the southern part of Monroe, by Isaac Brownfield's, past James McCoy's fort, near Samuel Hatfield's brick barn, crossing the Cherokee trail; thence to Coal lick or Jacob's run, on land now of N.

(c) In Gen. Richard Butler's journal of his expedition down the Ohio, in 1785, in company with Colonel, afterwards President Monroe, to treat with the Miami Indians, he speaks of an island called Nemacolin's, between the mouths of the Little Kanawha and Hocking, doubtless a subsequent abode of the same Indian.

(d) II. Sparks' Washington, 302, in an eloquent letter to Col. Bouquet, urging this route to be taken by Gen. Forbes, in 1758.

(e) Col. Burd, in the journal of his expedition to Redstone, in 1759, says: "At the foot of the hill [meaning the eastern base of Laurel hill] we found the path that went to Dunlap's place, that Col. Shippen and Capt. Gordon traveled last winter; and about a quarter of a mile from this we saw the Big Rock, so called." Dunlap's place, we believe, was where Wm. Stone now resides, on the Burnt Cabin fork of Dunlap's creek.

Brownfield (where a branch led off to Provance's bottom, or mouth of Big Whitley); thence passing by David Jennings', on Jennings' run, near Samuel Harris', and through the old John Woods' land, towards Jackson's or Grace church, near to which, in the head of Vail's sugar camp hollow, it united with the Redstone trail, or Burd's road, presently to be sketched. And were it not that a Virginia statute, hereafter to be cited, calls for this road as starting at Redstone Old Fort, we would make its western terminus at Crawford's ferry, to which it is certain a branch led. Perhaps the main path originally went from the fort up the river to the ferry or ford there, to connect with the road to Catfish's camp, (Washington, Pa.) which took to the river there to avoid the steep and rugged bluff opposite Brownsville.

When Virginia took it into her head to claim and exercise jurisdiction over this region of country,(f) she, by a statute passed in October, 1776, gave a temporary legal existence to Dunlap's road, by making it part of the dividing line between the counties of Monongalia and Yohogania. It is now as completely sunk in oblivion as most of her politicians wish the line of 36 deg. 30 min. to become.

The "road to Redstone," or Burd's road, as it was afterwards called, was originally an Indian trail, from the mouth of Redstone to the summit of Laurel hill, near the Great Rock and Washington's spring—the great focus of old roads—where it united with Dunlap's road and others. From Gist's to the Rock it seems to have been identical with Nemacolin's or Braddock's road. It was a much traveled path by the Indians, by early traders and adventurers, and by the French during the early part of the war of 1754-63. Captain Trent passed over it in February, 1754, on his way with men and tools and stores, to build a fort for the Ohio Company at the forks of the Ohio, and when he built the Hangard at the mouth of Redstone. By this path, also, came the French and Indians, under M. de Villiers, who attacked Col. Washington at Fort Necessity, and it was much used by them in their annoying excursions, during Braddock's and Dunbar's marches, in connection with canoe navigation up and down the Monongahela, of all which we will read further in subsequent sketches.(g)

We will also see hereafter,(g) that when Col. Washington, in June, 1754, found himself not strong enough to advance to Fort

---

(f) See postea—sketch of "Boundary Controversy, &c."—Chap. IX.
(g) See the next succeeding sketches—"French War—Washington and Braddock's Campaigns,"—Chaps. IV. and V.

INDIAN TRAILS, ARMY ROADS, &c.   29

Du Quesne, he determined to proceed by this path to the mouth of Redstone, and there erect a fort, and wait for reinforcements. Having come on to Gist's, (Mount Braddock,) he sent on a party, under Captain Lewis, to open a road to Redstone; that is, to widen and improve the Indian trail, so as to fit it for passing wagons; &c. This party had advanced with their work "about eight miles," when, alarmed at the approach of the enemy, they retreated, or were called back by Washington, to the incipient entrenchments at Gist's. The point at which the road was then stopped, was, we believe, at or near where it crosses Jennings' run, between John Gaddis' and B. Courtney's. It would seem that very little work was done on it; for, five years afterwards, Col. Burd had great difficulty to trace it.

In the latter part of the summer of 1759, Col. James Burd was sent out with two hundred men, by order of Col. Bouquet, then commanding the king's troops at Carlisle, to open and complete this road to the Monongahela river, at or near the mouth of Redstone, and there erect a fort. The English, under Gen. Stanwix, were, about the same time, commencing to build Fort Pitt, at the head of the Ohio, in lieu of Fort Du Quesne, from which the French had been driven by Gen. Forbes, and which they had burnt, the previous year. The great object of Col. Burd's expedition was to facilitate communications with this important fort from Maryland and Virginia, by using the river.(h) Col. Burd seems to have had no other authority for his road and fort than Col. Bouquet's orders. If he had, it was not from Pennsylvania, but from Virginia or the King, who doubtless provided the ways and means the more cheerfully, as the French were now effectually, and, as it turned out, permanently routed from this region of country. The Colonel came out by Braddock's road, from Fort Cumberland. Col. Thos. Cresap, the commissioner of Nemacolin's road, was with him; and the Rev. Francis Allison was his chaplain, preaching every Sabbath.

On the 12th of September, being encamped at Gist's place, he sent out parties to trace the route. His journal now reads thus: "At noon (13th) began to cut the road to Redstone, along some old blazes, which we take to be Col. Washington's. Began a quarter of a mile from camp, the course N. N. W. The course of

---

(h) Thus early was it seen that the route between Cumberland and Brownsville was the shortest and easiest land transit between the eastern and western waters. Alas! how rail roads have paled its glory.

Gen. Braddock's road N. N. E., and turns much to the eastward. Marked two trees at the place of beginning, thus: 'The road to Redstone, Col. J. Burd, 1759—The road to Pittsburgh, 1759.'" These trees stood near the beginning of Jacob Murphey's avenue, on the west side of the Connellsville road. The road followed the Indian trail, passing through the Rankin and Henshaw lands; thence nearly parallel with Bute's run, through the Carter lands, crossing the run and the creek near the run's mouth, and near Lucky's now Vance's mill, into Jacob Gaddis' land. It crossed Jennings' run near John Gaddis, or B. Courtney's, thence, in a pretty direct line, on through the old Hugh Crawford and Adams tracts, now Jacob B. Graham, Wm. Hatfield and others, until it came to a point a little north-west of where the Johnson or Hatfield stone tavern house stands. Here the old trail bore too much to the right, going through the old Grable place, the old Fulton place, (now William Colvin's), by the old Colvin house, the schoolhouse, Ayres Linn's and Isaac Linn's, to the mouth of Redstone. But Col. Burd left this trail at the point above indicated, and took along the high ridges, through the Colley and Hastings lands, near Brashears' and Eli Cope's, until he reached the site of his fort, "a hill in the fork of the river Monongahela and Nemacolin's Creek;" being on the south side of Front street, opposite where the fort-like mansion of N. B. Bowman, Esq., now stands. When completed, the road was found to be sixteen miles one quarter and sixteen perches, from the beginning, near Gist's, to the centre of the fort.

Col. Burd mentions a run which he calls "Coal Run," from being "entirely paved on the bottom with fine stone coal," which he crossed and where he encamped. By his journal he makes it only two and a half miles from the river. Were it not for this we would have said it was Jennings' Run. But it must have been the run which passes down by D. C. Colvin's to the paper mill.

Fort Burd was erected upon the site of "Redstone Old Fort;" but in common, or even official designation, could never supplant it, in its name. According to the science of backwoods fortifications in those days, it was a regularly constructed work of defense, with bastions, ditch and draw-bridge; built, however, wholly of earth and wood. The bastions and central "house," were of timbers laid horizontally; the "curtains" were of logs set in the ground vertically, like posts, in close contact—called a stockade, or palisades.

In XII Pennsylvania Archives, 347, we find the following plan

INDIAN TRAILS, FORT BURD, &c.

and dimensions of the fort, as found among the papers of Joseph Shippen, an Engineer, &c., who accompanied Colonel Burd: "The curtain, 97½ feet; the flanks, 16 feet; the faces of the bastions, 30 feet. A ditch, between the bastions 24 feet wide, and opposite the face, 12 feet. The log-house for a magazine, and to contain the women and children, 39 feet square. A gate 6 feet wide and 8 feet high; and a draw-bridge — feet wide."

From this description, we have constructed the following diagram:

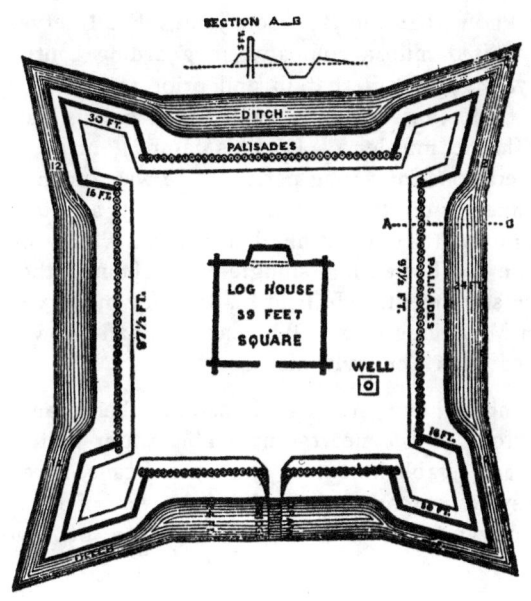

The gallant Colonel had rather a hard time of it, in constructing his fort. "I have," says he, "kept the people constantly employed on the works since my arrival; although we have been for eight days past upon the small allowance of one pound of beef and half a pound of flour, per man, a day; and this day we begin upon one pound of beef, not having an ounce of flour left, and only three bullocks. I am therefore obliged to give over working until I receive some supplies." He, however, soon got some supplies, and held on. The following is from his journal: "October 28—Sunday.—Continue on the works; had sermon in the fort." The last entry is—"November 4.—Sunday.—Snowed to-day—no work. Sermon in the fort. Dr. Allison sets out for Philadelphia."

The fort was not designed to be a place of great strength or danger. Col. Burd garrisoned it with one officer and twenty-five men. How long the garrison held it is unknown. But it seems to have been under some kind of military possession in 1774, during "Dunmore's War;" and during the Revolution and the contemporary Indian troubles, it was used as a store house and a rallying point for defense, supply and observation, by the early settlers and adventurers. It was never rendered famous by a seige or a sally. We know that the late Col. James Paull served a month's duty in a drafted militia company, in guarding continental stores here, in 1778. It is said that in and prior to 1774, Capt. Michael Cresap,(1) (who has unjustly acquired an odious fame by being charged with the murder of Logan's family), made this fort the centre of operations for a long period. He was a man of great daring and influence on the frontier. He early acquired a kind of Virginia right to the land around the fort, which he improved, erecting upon it a hewed log, shingle-roofed house—the first of that grade in the settlement. He held his title for many years, and sold out to John M'Cullough, or to Thomas, or Bazil Brown, to whom a Patent issued from Pennsylvania, in 1785.

The opening of the "road to Redstone," being an extension of Braddock's road to the nearest navigable water of the West; and the subsequent establishment of two other roads, hereafter noticed —the Pennsylvania road from Bedford, by way of Berlin, Connellsville, Uniontown, &c., and the combination of Braddock's and

---

(1)This Captain Michael Cresap was the son of Col. Thomas Cresap, of Old Town, Maryland, and father-in-law of the renowned Luther Martin of that State. He bore a very conspicuous part in the Indian troubles about Wheeling, Pittsburg, &c., in 1774. In June, 1775, he led a company of riflemen from Maryland to Cambridge, Mass., to join Gen. Washington's army. He soon took sick, and died on his way home, at New York, in October, 1775. His son, Michael, and John J. Jacob, (who married his widow,) of Allegheny Co., Md., were his executors, and as such, had some moneys to collect by suit in this county. His fame has been successfully vindicated from the murder of Logan's relatives, by his illustrious kinsmen, Martin and Jacob, who have proved most conclusively, not only that he did not do the deed, but that the name of Cresap was not in Logan's celebrated speech, as it was originally written, and that Logan never wrote or spoke it. See the evidence, &c., in II Craig's Olden Time, 44, 49, &c.

Dunlap's roads, called the Virginia road—soon caused the "mouth of Redstone," or, rather, the mouth of Dunlap's creek, to become a very notable place. It was the place of general embarkation by traders and emigrants to Kentucky and Ohio, or, as it was termed, "going down the river." It became the great place for shipping mill stones, made on Laurel Hill, to Kentucky and the West. "The writer has seen as many as thirty pairs lying at the mouth of Dunlap's creek at a time, from 1796 to 1808, waiting for boats and water to float off to Limestone. Kentucky and Southern Ohio were peopled from this point and the Lower Yough. John Moore, a very early settler on the farm now the residence of Johnson Vankirk, used to relate, that in the long cold winter of 1780—a prototype of those of 1856-'57—the snow being three or four feet deep and crusted, he saw the road from Sandy Hollow (Brubaker's,) to the verge of Brownsville, where William Hogg lived, lined on both sides with wagons and families, camped out, waiting the loosing of the icy bands from the waters, and the preparation of boats to embark for the West—the men dragging in old logs and stumps for fuel to save their wives and children from freezing."

Simultaneous with Braddock's march across the mountains, in June, 1755, an army road was being made by the colony of Pennsylvania, under the superintendence of Col. James Burd and others, from Shippensburg, by Raystown (Bedford,) to the Turkey Foot; thence to intersect Braddock's road at some convenient point, probably the Great Crossings (Somerfield.) Its purpose was to transport supplies to Braddock's army. It was opened, at great cost and labor, as far as the top of Allegheny mountain, within about eighteen miles of Turkey Foot; when the battle of Turtle creek having occurred, the laborers were alarmed and driven off by the French and Indians to Fort Cumberland. Thereupon the road was forsaken, until some years after Forbes captured Fort Du Quesne, when its opening was resumed and completed. It was called the Turkey Foot or Smith's road.(j) It crossed the three rivers at Turkey Foot, and passed a little south of Sugar Loaf moun-

---

(j)The name of Smith was given to the road, because while it was being made, a lad of about sixteen, James Smith, was captured by the Indians and carried to Fort Du Quesne, where he was on the eventful 9th of July, 1755, and witnessed the departure and return of the conquerors of Braddock, and the horrid orgies and tortures of prisoners which occurred that night. Mr. Smith afterwards became famous in the frontier and Revolutionary wars, in Westmoreland and Bedford counties, and held civil offices of honor. He subsequently removed to Kentucky, where he became a colonel and a member of the Legislature.

tain by Dunbar's Camp to Uniontown. It crosses Redstone where the National road now crosses it, and passing just north of the Methodist Graveyard, it fell into the route of the turnpike again, near Jennings' run; thence by the old Brownsville road to its junction with Burd's road, near Jackson's church, from which the two became identical.

The "Turkey Foot settlement" is one of the oldest west of the mountains. Hence roads to and through it were established very early; and every such road came to be called a "Turkey Foot road." Indeed, most of the early roads took the names of the localities to or through which they passed—as the Pennsylvania road, the Virginia road, Moorfield road, Sandy Creek road, &c. There was, however, one Turkey Foot road which was an important one, though it is now mostly abandoned, and much of it overgrown with bushes, or fenced in. It was established as a nearer route to Fort Pitt from Cumberland, than Braddock's road. It left the last named road somewhere in Maryland, east of the Great Crossings, and entered Fayette county, from Somerset, as it crossed the summit of Laurel Hill; thence, passing down Skinner's Mill run to near its entrance into Indian creek, crossing it a little above the junction, and the Mud Pike near where Springfield now is, it passed by Cornelius Woodruff's old place, descended the Chestnut ridge, and crossed Mountz's creek at Cathcart's, or Andrews' Mill, and crossed Jacob's creek about a mile below the old Chain Bridge, there leaving this county; and soon coming into the route of Braddock, it passed through the Sewickley settlement, &c., to Fort Pitt.

On this road, about the junction of Skinner's Mill run and Indian creek, were the well known "bullock pens." As early as 1776, if not earlier, Gen. George Morgan, afterwards Indian Agent in the Pittsburgh region, came out by this road with a lot of cattle, either on private account, or for the garrison at Fort Pitt, and finding fine range and natural meadow here, he stopped, had a large body of land, lying on both sides of the creek, enclosed with a rail fence, (some of which was visible within ten years past,) and kept the cattle there a long time. He afterwards had two warrants and surveys of the land in the names of George Morgan and John Morgan, which tracts he sold to some Germans, and they have since been known as land of Storman's heirs, and more recently of James Paull, Jr.

McCulloch's Path was an Indian and Traders' trail from Winchester and Moorfield, Va., westward. It came by way of Little

Yough, near the route of the Baltimore and Ohio Rail Road, crossing the Big Yough near the same point where that rail road crosses it, passing through Herrington's and Murley's Glades, and by the Crab Orchard. It entered Pennsylvania and Fayette county a little east of the summit of Laurel Hill, which it crossed at Wymp's Gap; thence passing a little north of Morris' Cross roads, it crossed the Monongahela into Greene county, between the mouth of Cheat and Neal's ferry.

McCulloch was an Indian Trader. His "camp" was just across the State line on the Monongahela river. He was in the habit of supplying the Indians, even in times of war, with knives, hatchets, powder, &c. The settlers complained of this, and threatened him, but he would not desist. At length they determined to enforce their threats. Learning that he sometimes returned by Sandy Creek and Braddock's road, a number of the settlers from about the Great Crossings and Turkey Foot, disguised themselves, and went in pursuit. They caught him at Jesse Tomlinson's, at the Little Crossings, or Castleman's river. They gave him to know that his contraband trade must cease. Mac. resisted and threatened and entreated. Tomlinson, it is said, sought to protect him as his guest. But the men were in earnest. Tom Fossit was one of them. Tom caught and held him in his giant grasp, while others, as the term used was, "deviled him," until he promised never more to transgress. After despoiling him of his ill gotten peltry and other pelf, they let him go, and he never was seen again in this region of country.

There were other old roads traversing the territory of Fayette, long before we had any County Courts, and consequently no record of them exists here, or in Bedford, or Westmoreland, except where they have been adopted in whole or in part as legalized highways. We will not attempt their enumeration, or location.(k)

(k) The very first petition for a road presented to the Court of Westmoreland, after its erection, was in April, 1773, by inhabitants of Springhill and west of the Monongahela river, setting forth their "difficult circumstance for want of a road leading into any public road where we can possibly pass with convenience," and therefore praying for "a public road to begin at or near the mouth of Fish Pot run, about five miles below the mouth of Ten Mile creek, on the west side of the Monongahela river, (it being a convenient place for a ferry [Crawford's Ferry,] as also a good direction for a road leading to the most western part of the settlement,) thence the nearest and best way to the Forks of Dunlap's path, and Gen. Braddock's road on the top of Laurel Hill." Viewers appointed—John Moore, Thomas Scott, Henry Beeson, Thomas Brownfield, James McClean, and Philip Shute.

There was, however, one called the Sandy Creek road, which was of considerable note. It came from the Ten Mile settlement, through Greene county, crossing the river at Hyde's Ferry, or mouth of Big Whiteley, passing by the south side of Masontown, through Haydentown, or by David Johns' Mill, up Laurel Hill, through the Sandy Creek settlement to Daniel McPeak's and into Virginia. It was by this road that the father and family of Dr. Joseph Doddridge, passed to Morris' Fort, in 1774, as related in his "Notes." This was the second road viewed and laid out by order of the Court of Fayette county, after its erection in 1783; a road from Uniontown to the mouth of Grassy Run, on Cheat, being the first.(1)

Another of these old roads we may refer to. It was called Froman's road, which led from Gist's, past Perryopolis and Col. Cook's to Pittsburgh.(m) It has been improperly called Washing-

---

At the same Court a petition was presented for a road from Washington's Spring to Sewickley, but the route is not designated.

At April Sessions, 1774, a petition was presented by inhabitants of Tyrone and Menallen, (see "outline of Civil History," &c. postea,) setting forth the "want of a road leading into Braddock's road, or any part of the mountain; and further we would observe, that from the natural situation of the country, we who at present live on the west side of the Monongahela river, are obliged frequently to carry our corn twenty miles to the mill of Henry Beeson, near Laurel Hill, and in all probability, at some seasons of the year, will ever have to do so; and therefore praying for a road from near Redstone Old Fort to Henry Beeson's mill, and thence to intersect Braddock's road near the forks of Dunlap's road and said road on top of Laurel Hill." Viewers appointed—Richard Waller, Andrew Linn, Jr., William Colvin, Thomas Crooks, Henry Hart, and Joseph Grayble. The road was reported and approved at January Sessions, 1784.

At January Sessions, 1783, a petition was presented for a road "from Beeson's Town, in the Forks of Youghiogheny to the Salt Works, and thence eastward to Bedford Town." The Salt Works referred to were those on Green Lick and Jacob's creek, in the vicinity of Tinsman's, or Welshonse's and Lobengier's Mills.

At January Sessions, 1784, of Westmoreland county, a road from Beeson's Town to Col. Cook's was reported and approved.

(1) Petitions for these roads had previously been acted upon in Westmoreland county, the latter one being at Stewart's Crossing. (Connellsville.)

(m) A petition for this road was presented to the Westmoreland Court at January Sessions, 1774, describing it as to lead "from Thomas Gist's to Paul Froman's mill near the Monongahela, (on Spear's run, near Bellevernon,) and thence to his other mill on Chartiers' creek," (a few miles west of Pittsburgh.) It seems that at that date a mill was a more important place than Pittsburgh. Froman's Mill, on Chartiers, was a prominent place in the boundary troubles of that year. This Paul Froman seems to have been a man of mills, for we find that Daniel M'Peak's or M'Peck's, named in the text, was, in 1783, on a road "from Froman's Mill."

ton's road. But he never passed over it, except in part, perhaps, when in 1770, and again in 1784, he went from Col. Crawford's, or Gist's, to look after his lands in the vicinity of Perryopolis. It was used to carry supplies to Fort Pitt, and as a nearer and safer route than Burd's or Braddock's roads.

We will here close our tracings of these primitive highways, by a brief recurrence to their early uses by the old settlers and traders. Besides the ordinary uses for milling, visiting, church going &c., their great use was for emigration and transportation of goods, even the most weighty and cumbrous, by pack-horses. To this end alone, they were fitted. None of the streams were bridged; and a five degrees' grade was not thought of. Except as to the Army roads, they were all mere paths through the woods, and among the laurel and rocks of the mountains. The two great emigrant and pack-horse routes, up to 1800, were the Pennsylvania and the Virginia roads, heretofore noticed. "The writer has seen as many as thirty pack-horses in a caravan, pass through Uniontown in a day—an occurrence so frequent as not to attract unusual notice. They were as common as droves of cattle or horses now-a-days. They were freighted with salt, sugar kettles, bar iron, nail rods, dry goods, glass, kegs of rum, powder, lead &c., &c. A good horse carried from two hundred to three hundred pounds, besides provisions and feed. These they would take up along the way, at places where they had dropped them in 'going down;' having no other heavy 'down loading' merely peltry, ginseng, feathers, &c. The provisions consisted generally, of poen, cheese and dried venison. A bear skin to each horse was an indispensable accompaniment, for a bed to the drivers, and to protect the cargo from rain. Each horse had his bell, silent by day, but let loose at night when browsing. Two men generally managed ten or twelve horses, one before and one behind each train, to guide them among the trees, and protect the loading from side contact. Strength was also needful to load and unload daily. Emigrants would have their little all swung across one, two, or more horses, according to their abundance, surmounted by their wives and children, or the old folk, with the little bag, or stocking of guineas, joes, or pistareens snugly, ensconced in the salt or clothes bag—after the manner of Joseph's brethren on their trip to Egypt for corn." In 1784, the freight on goods from Philadelphia to Uniontown, was Five Dollars per one hundred pounds. In 1789, thirty shillings, (Four Dollars,) from Carlisle—the beginning of the pack-horse transportation. We have before us a copy of the "Pittsburgh Gazette," of May

17, 1794, (Vol. VII.—measuring sixteen by twenty-two inches,) in which, among other antiques, is an advertisement offering $15 per month for pack-horse drivers, to all who may apply. James L. Bowman, Esq., has stated that the first wagon load of goods brought over the mountains, by the Virginia or Braddock's road, was in 1789, by John Hayden, (of whom more hereafter,) from Hagerstown to Brownsville, for his father, the late Jacob Bowman, Esq. With four horses he brought over two thousand pounds at $3 per hundred, making the trip in about a month.

This state of things made goods—even the necessaries of life, very high. The best of alum salt rated here at from $4 to $5 per bushel, of ninety-six pounds; ground alum salt, at from $3 to $3.50; coffee, 33 cents per pound; sugar, 25 cents; Jamaica spirits, $2.33 per gallon. In 1784, wheat sold for 67 cents per bushel; corn, 22 cents; rye, 50 cents. But flour at Natchez—if you could get it there, was worth $25 per barrel! A good two horse wagon and gears could be bought for two pack-horse loads of salt; or, a good tract of land, of four hundred acres, for a rifle gun and a horn of powder.

Having opened the ways, we are now prepared to introduce upon them actors and movements of a very different character from pack-horse drivers, and pack-horse loads of salt and emigrants. The war-whoop and the drum, are now, for a while, to precede the merry shout of the mover, and the glad greetings of the settler.

CHAPTER IV.

THE FRENCH WAR.—WASHINGTON'S CAMPAIGN, &c.

Origin of the War—First Bloodshed—Washington's Embassy in 1753—Gist—Ohio Company—Captain Trent—The Hangard—Ensign Ward—Colonel Washington at Great Meadows—at Gist's—his Forces—who were with him—Attacks Jumonville—Jumónville's Camp—The Half-King's Camp—Great Rock—De Villiers—Retreat to "Fort Necessity"—The Battle—Surrender—Retreat—Demolition—Garrison Drunk—Prayers—Fort Necessity described—Wants a Monument.

The nations were at peace. France held Canada on the north, and (a) Louisiana on the south and west. The Mississippi and its tributaries nearly united these possessions, which Louis XIV. with much show of right, claimed to hold by virtue of discovery and settlement. The Appalachian mountains seemed a natural boundary to the English colonies. The purpose of France was to make them such, in fact and forever:—by establishing a chain of forts from Lake Erie down the most western branch of the Allegheny, (French creek,) and thence, by that river and the Ohio, to Louisiana; and by these, and by securing the friendship and fears of the Indian tribes, establish an impregnable dominion. The movements to these ends rekindled the smothered jealousy of England and her Colonies, and led to the long and disastrous war of 1754—1763, as ruinous to the power of France in its results, as her conduct in the beginning was plausible and bold. The territory which at first appeared to be the prize of the contest, was that drained by the head waters of the Ohio. Each party claimed it, upon varied pretexts,—discovery, treaties, &c., but neither had any solid basis of claim,—the Indian was the rightful owner. The destinies of civilization were against the further continuance of the red man's occupancy; and the struggle was as to who should guide those destinies—the Anglo Saxon or the Gaul—the Jesuit and Jansenist, or the Puritan and Covenanter.

(a) Louisiana, as held by France, and ceded to the United States, in 1803, included all of the States and Territories now belonging to the United States west of the Mississippi, to the Rocky Mountains, embracing also those parts of Louisiana, Mississippi and Alabama which are east of the Mississippi river and south of north latitude 31 deg.

It is not proposed here to write the history of this eventful war. But Fayette county was by it made historic, nay, classic ground. From behind its Laurel Hill the star of Washington's fame first beamed. The first English army sent into the strife, traversed its territory. The first blood shed in the conflict moistened the rock-bottomed soil of its mountains; germinating seeds from which sprang the revolt and independence of the old thirteen colonies, and the horrors and triumphs of the French Revolution:—thus bringing upon both parties the visitations of retributive justice, for the wrongs done to the Indian, and to each other, in the inceptive strife. The reader of these sketches will therefore not regret to find even here recorded such of the events of this war as occurred in Fayette county.

The scene opens in November, 1753; when Major George Washington, then in his twenty-second year, crossed our mountains, by Nemacolin's trail, from Wills' creek, (Cumberland) as a special envoy, commissioned by Gov. Dinwiddie, of Virginia, to the French posts, between the head of the Ohio and Lake Erie, to spy out the French force and designs, to inquire of them why they came there, and to warn them off.

His party consisted of himself, John Davidson, an Indian interpreter, Captain Jacob Van Braam, as French interpreter,—a personage conspicuous the next year in the surrender of Fort Necessity,—Christopher Gist, as Guide, who in that year had settled at the place in Fayette, since known as Mt. Braddock,—Curran and McQuire, Indian traders, and Stewart and Jenkins,(b)—these four as "servitors." They left Wills' creek, November 15th, with horses, tents and baggage; and after seven days of toil over the mountains, amid snow and swollen streams, reached Frazier's trading post, at the mouth of Turtle creek; whence they proceeded, accompanied by some Indians, to the fulfillment of their mission. Washington, in his journal, says, they passed "Mr. Gist's new settlement," and that he, with Gist, returned by the same route. "We arrived," says he, "at Mr. Gist's,(c) at Monongahela, the 2d of January, (1754) where I bought a horse and sad-

---

(b) This Stewart is probably one of the family of that name who settled at, and gave name to "Stewart's Crossings." (Connellsville.) See Affidavit of William Stewart in note (u) to memoir of the Gist's in "Early Settlers,"—postea, Chapter VII.

(c) The reader must understand, that at this early day, Monongahela was a locality which covered an ample scope of territory. "Gist's Plantation" was about sixteen miles from the river, which, when Washington wrote this, he had never seen.

THE FRENCH WAR.—WASHINGTON'S CAMPAIGN, &c. 41

dle. The 6th, we met seventeen horses, loaded with materials and stores for a fort at the fork of the Ohio, and the day after, some families going out to settle."

These parties whom Washington met, were going out under the auspices of the "Ohio Company," an association formed in Virginia, about the year 1748, under a royal grant. Hitherto, the French and Pennsylvanians had enjoyed the trade with the Indians north of the Ohio, and around its head waters. The purpose of this Company was to divert this trade southward, by the Potomac route, and to settle the country around the head of the Ohio with English colonists from Virginia and Maryland. To this end, the king granted to the Company five hundred thousand acres of land west of the mountains, "to be taken chiefly on the south side of the Ohio, between the Monongahela and Kanawha, but with privilege to take part of the quantity north of the Ohio. Two hundred thousand acres were to be taken up at once, and to be free of quit rents, or taxes to the king for ten years, upon condition that the Company should, within seven years, seat one hundred families on the lands, build a fort, and maintain a garrison, to protect the settlement." It will be seen that this grant did not, in its terms, embrace Fayette county territory; yet, in the loose interpretations of that early period, the Company attempted settlements within our limits, which for many years afterwards were supposed not to be included in Penn's Charter; but to be part of the vast and undefined royal domain of Virginia.(d) The incipient movements of this Company provoked the French and Pennsylvania traders to jealousy, and to stir up the Indians to hostility; thereby at once raising a cloud upon its prospects, which eventually produced a torrent of blood which obliterated all its labors. Still, to this Company Fayette county is much indebted, not only for many scenes of historic interest, but to its early settlement, by means of the easy access, caused by the making of Braddock's road; which, as we have seen, was but an improvement of the Company's road, originally opened by Nemacolin.

It is said that Col. Cresap, of Maryland, the "Commissioner" of the Nemacolin road, was one of the Company. It is certain that Gen. Washington's brothers, Lawrence and John Augustine, were largely interested in it, and, as well as their more illustrious

---

(d)See further as to these matters, in the subsequent Sketches of "Boundary Controversy," and "Early Settlements"—Chaps. VI. and IX.

brother, were anxious for its success. Christopher Gist was the Company's agent to select the lands and conciliate the Indians.(e) The Company, having imported from London large quantities of goods for the Indian trade, and engaged several settlers, had established trading posts at Wills' creek, (the New Store,) the mouth of Redstone, (the Hangard,) the mouth of Turtle creek, (Frazier's,) and elsewhere; had planned their fort at the "Forks of the Ohio," (Pittsburgh) and were proceeding energetically to the consummation of their designs;—designs which, although they did not originate, yet served to hasten the great and decisive contest for supremacy over the land we now inhabit, between two very dissimilar branches of the great Teutonic race. The parties whom Washington met, were the pioneer heralds of the conflict.

The next movement in furtherance of the great end, was of a martial character; and it too traversed our territory. Early in 1754, Captain Trent was sent out from Virginia, with about forty men—intended to be recruited on the way—to aid in finishing the fort at the forks of the Ohio, already supposed to be begun by the Ohio Company. The captain's line of march was along Nemacolin's trail to Gist's, and then, by the Redstone trail to the mouth of that creek; where, after having built the store house called the Hangard,(f) he proceeded, probably by land and ice, to the forks of Ohio, where he arrived on the 17th of February, and went to work on the fort—which soon proved a vain labor.

Trent had returned to Wills' creek, and Frazier (Lieutenant of the forces,) was at his trading post, leaving Ensign Ward in command; when, on the 17th of April, he had to surrender to a large French force, which suddenly descended the Allegheny upon him; and, he, with his little party, thereupon retreated, by canoes, up the Monongahela to Redstone, and thence across the mountains. The French thereupon finished the fort, naming it Fort Du Quesne, in honor of the Governor-general of Canada.

The repulse of Ensign Ward was regarded as an overt act of war, for which preparations had before been made in several of the Colonies; and the loyal descendants of the old cavaliers in Virginia flew to arms. About the first of May, 1754, three companies of a regiment of Virginia provincials, commanded by Lieutenant-colonel George Washington, set out from Wills' creek

---

(e) See further as to Christopher Gist, in the memoir of him among "Early Settlers," postea,—Chap. VII.

(f) This ancient erection and its site, &c., will be particularly described hereafter.

THE FRENCH WAR.—WASHINGTON'S CAMPAIGN, &c. 43

to drive the French from Fort Du Quesne. They had to make the road which Braddock adopted the next year. By the 9th they reached the Little Meadows, (Tomlinson's) where more than two days were spent in bridging the Little Yough. On the 18th they arrived at the Great Crossings, (Somerfield) and remained there several days, while Washington, with five men in a canoe, descended the river to ascertain if it was navigable. His hopes and his voyage ended at the Ohio Pyle Falls. They crossed this river without bridging.

May 24th, the forces arrived at the Great Meadows, (Mount Washington) where, and in its vicinity, events of stirring and lasting interest were soon to be enacted. We must now ask to be more special in our details.

When Washington first encamped at the Great Meadows, he had but about one hundred and fifty men, soon after increased to three hundred, in six deficient companies, commanded by Captains Stephen, (to whom Washington there gave a Major's commission,) Stobo, Van Braam, Hogg, Lewis, George Mercer and Polson; and by Major Muse, who joined Washington, with reinforcements, and with nine swivels, powder and ball, on the 9th of June. He had been Washington's military instructor, three years before, and now acted as quartermaster. Captain Mackay, with the Independent Royal Company, from South Carolina, of about one hundred men, came up on the 10th of June, bringing with him sixty beeves, five days allowance of flour, and some ammunition, but no cannon, as expected. Among the subordinate officers, were Ensign Peyronie, and Lieutenants Waggoner and John Mercer.

Besides the illustrious commander, who became a hero, "not for one age, but for all time," several of these officers became, afterwards, sooner or later, men of note. Stephen was a captain in the Virginia regiment, at Braddock's defeat, and wounded. He rose to be a colonel in the Virginia troops, and to be a general in the War of the Revolution. Stobo was the engineer of "Fort Necessity," and he, with Van Braam, was at the surrender, given up as hostages to the French, until the return of the French officers taken in the fight with Jumonville. But the Governor of Virginia refusing to return them, the hostages were sent to Canada. Stobo, after many hair-breadth escapes, finally returned to Virginia in 1759, whence he went to England.(g) Van Braam was a Dutch-

---

(g)Neville B. Craig, Esq., of Pittsburgh, has made quite an interesting little book out of the "Life and Adventures of Captain Stobo."
Van Braam had been Washington's instructor in the sword exercise.

man, who knew a little French, and having served Washington as French interpreter the previous year, was called upon to interpret the articles of capitulation, at the surrender of "Fort Necessity;" and has been generally, but unjustly, charged with having wilfully entrapped Washington to admit that the killing of Jumonville, was an assassination. He returned to Virginia in 1760, having been released after the conquest of Canada by the English; but the capitulation blunder sunk him. Captain Lewis was the General Andrew Lewis, of Bottetourt, in the great battle with the Indians at Point Pleasant, in Dunmore's war of 1774, and was a distinguished general officer in the Revolution, whom Washington, it is said, recommended for commander-in-chief. He was a captain in Braddock's campaign, but had no command in the fatal action, and was with Major Grant at his defeat, at Grant's Hill, Pittsburgh) in September, 1758. Polson was a captain at Braddock's defeat, and killed. Of Captain Hogg, we know but little. Captain Mackay, was a royal officer, and behaved in this campaign with discretion, yet with some hauteur, as we shall see. Except that he afterwards aided Colonel Innes, of North Carolina, in building Fort Cumberland, nothing more is known of him. Peyronie was a French Protestant Chevalier, settled in Virginia, was badly wounded at "Fort Necessity," and was a Virginia captain in Braddock's defeat, and killed. Waggoner was wounded in the Jumonville skirmish, became a captain in Braddock's campaign, and behaved in the fatal action with signal good sense and gallantry. He escaped unhurt.

We may as well here mention other distinguished personages who figured about "Fort Necessity" while Washington's little army was there. Of these were Christopher Gist, already named, Dr. James Craik, the friend and family physician of Washington, until his death. Tanacharison, the half-king of the Senaca tribe of the Iroquois, a fast friend of Colonel Washington and the English; Monacatootha, alias Scarooyda, also a Six Nation Chief; Queen Aliquippa(h) and her son, and Shingiss, a Delaware Chief. Between the affair with Jumonville and the surrender, many

---

(h)Famous for her residence where M'Keesport now is, and for having taken offense at Washington for not having called to see her when on his outward trip to the French posts in November, 1753; which, however, he atoned for on his return, by paying her a visit and presenting to her a watch coat and a bottle of rum,—the latter of which, he says, she prized the most highly. No wonder. He should have given her a petticoat.

THE FRENCH WAR.—WASHINGTON'S CAMPAIGN, &c. 45

friendly Indians, with their families, in alarm, took refuge at the fort—in all about two hundred. Except the efficient aid of the half-king, and a few others as scouts, they were of no other service than to consume the scanty provisions at the fort. In the action of the 3rd of July they were wholly inefficient—though they did some execution in the attack on Jumonville's party. After the surrender they retreated with Washington to Virginia; but soon after took refuge in the interior of Pennsylvania, at Aughwick, and were for a while maintained by that Colony. Under the influence of Colonel Croghan, the Deputy Royal Indian Agent, their services were offered to General Braddock the next year; but he treated them so neglectfully that they gradually left him. The half-king died in October, 1754, at Harris's Ferry. We now return to the narrative of events in their order.

When Washington marched from Wills' creek with his little force, it was not his purpose, without strong reinforcements and artillery, to proceed to attack the French in their new Fort Du Quesne. From the first he designed only to make a road across the mountains, and to reach the Ohio Company's store house at the mouth of Redstone, and there to erect a fort; whence, when sufficiently reinforced, he could move to the attack, sending his artillery and heavy stores by water. To accomplish this was his aim throughout the campaign.

During his march, almost daily, reports were brought to him from the French Fort, by scouts, traders, Indians and deserters. He had also intelligence of parties of French and Indians coming towards him for various purposes, hostile and inquisitive. About the first of May, a party, under M. La Force, left their fort, as they represented, to hunt deserters. Washington sent a party to hunt them—but did not find them.

On the morning of the day of the arrival of Washington at the Great Meadows (May 24th,) the half-king sent him a letter saying that "the French army" was moving against him. He thereupon hastened to the Meadows, where, the same evening, the half-king's warning was confirmed by a trader, who told him the French were at the Crossings of the Youghiogheny (Stewart's) about eighteen miles distant, and that he had seen two Frenchmen at Gist's the night before. Washington immediately began to fortify. And three days afterwards, in the effervescence of youthful valor, as yet untried, he writes,—"We have, with nature's assistance, made a good entrenchment, and by clearing the bushes out of these meadows, prepared a charming field for an encounter."

This "French army" was the Jumonville party, commanded by M. La Force. Under date of May 27th, Washington writes,—"This morning Mr. Gist arrived from his place, where a detachment of fifty men was seen yesterday at noon, commanded by M. La Force. He afterwards saw their tracks within five miles of our camp. I immediately detached seventy-five men in pursuit of them, who I hope will overtake them before they get to Redstone, where their canoes lie." This latter idea seems to have been an error. If canoes were there they probably belonged to friendly Indians; for the French came by the Nemacolin path.

That same night (27th) the half-king, who, with some of his people and Monacatootha, were encamped about six miles from the Meadows, sent Washington an express, saying that he had tracked the Jumonville party to its hiding place, about half a mile from the path, in a very obscure camp, surrounded with rocks. Washington, with forty men, set out that dark and rainy night for the Indian camp; where, after council held, an attack was determined to be made at once. It was done early in the morning of the 28th. The French were surprised, Jumonville and others killed and scalped by the Indians, and M. La Force, M. Drouillon, two Cadets, and seventeen others made prisoners.(1) These were sent off at once to the Governor of Virginia, where most of them, especially M. La Force, "a person of great subtility and cunning," and who gave Washington a good deal of trouble at Venango the year previous, were detained a long time, contrary to Washington's agreement at the subsequent surrender.

This attack, and the killing of Jumonville, raised the ire of the French to a high degree, and have figured largely in the annals of that period. It was the first shedding of blood in this eventful war. The French made a hero of Jumonville, and called his killing an assassination. And amid the confusion of the surrender of the 3d of July, and the stupidity of Van Braam, Washington

---

(1)This,—not Fort Necessity, was really "Washington's first battle ground." Concerning it he wrote shortly after, "I fortunately escaped without any wound; for the right wing where I stood, was exposed to, and received all the enemy's fire; and it was the part where the man was killed and the rest wounded. I heard the bullets whistle; and believe me, there is something charming in the sound." The letter from which this is taken was written to his brother, and was published in the London Magazine; where George II. saw it; and thereupon dryly observed, "He would not say so if he had been used to hear many." So thought Washington himself in after years, when such music had lost its charm. Upon being asked if he had ever uttered such rodomontade, he answered gravely—"If I said so, it was when I was young."

was made to sign an admission, in the French language, which he knew not, of the truth of the charge;—a blunder which afterwards gave him no little uneasiness, but from which his fame has been fully relieved.

It was claimed by the French that Jumonville was a peaceful envoy, with a martial retinue for protection; and it may be that in some sense he was such. But his circumjacents were sadly against him. His party were acting as spies, and were in hostile array. Hostilities had begun by the repulse of Ensign Ward. Besides, this French party had been near to Washington's camp for several days without revealing themselves or seeking an interview; and they had chosen a singular locality for an ambassador's Court. Washington would have been greatly derelict had he not attacked them.

"Jumonville's Camp" is a place well known in our Mountains. It is near half a mile southward of Dunbar's Camp, and about five hundred yards eastward of Braddock's road—the same which Washington was then making. The Half-king's Camp was about two miles further south, near a fine spring, since called Washington's Spring, about fifty rods northward of the Great Rock.

The half-king discovered Jumonville's, or La Force's Camp by the smoke which rose from it, and by the tracks of two of the party who were out on a scouting excursion. Crawling stealthily through the laurel thicket which surmounts the wall of rock twenty feet high, he looked down upon their bark huts or lean-tos; and, retreating with like Indian quietness, he immediately gave Washington the alarm. There is not above ground, in Fayette County, a place so well calculated for concealment, and for secretly watching and counting Washington's little army as it would pass along the road, as this same Jumonville's Camp.

The discomfiture of La Force's party, and death of Jumonville, were immediately heralded to Contrecoeur at Fort Du Quesne by a frightened, barefooted fugitive Canadian; and vengeance was vowed at once. But it was not yet quite ready to be executed. Washington, however, knowing the impressions which this, his first encounter, would make upon the enemy, at once set about strengthening his defenses. He sent back for reinforcements, and had his fort at the Meadows palisadoed and otherwise improved. And, to increase his anxieties, the friendly Indians, with their families, and several deserters from the French, flocked around his camp, to hasten the reduction of his little store of provisions. Further embarrassments awaited him.

On the 9th of June, Major Muse came up with the residue of the Virginia regiment, the swivels and some ammunition; but it was now ascertained that the two independent companies from New York, and one from North Carolina, that were promised, would fail to arrive until too late. The latter only reached Cumberland after the surrender; while the fixed antipathies to war and propriety prerogative, of the Pennsylvania Assembly, had rendered all Governor Hamilton's entreaties for aid from that Colony ineffectual. In this extremity, Colonel Washington displayed the same energy and prudence which carried him so successfully through the dangers and disappointments of the Revolution. He hired horses to go back to Wills' creek for more balls and provisions, and induced Mr. Gist to endeavor to have the artillery, &c., hauled out by Pennsylvania teams—the reliance upon Southern promises of transport having failed, as it did with Braddock. But no artillery came in time, ten only, of the thirty four-pounder cannon and carriages, which had been sent from England, having been forwarded to Wills' creek, but too late. Washington also took active measures to have a rendezvous at Redstone, of friendly Indians from Logstown and elsewhere below Du Quesne; but in this he failed.

On the next day (the 10th,) Captain Mackay came up with the South Carolina Company; but as he bore a king's commission, he would not receive orders from the provincial colonel, and encamped separate from the Virginia troops; neither would his men do work on the road. To prevent mutiny, and a conflict of authority, Colonel Washington concluded to leave the royal captain and his company to guard the fort and stores, while he, on the 16th, set out with his Virginia troops, the swivels, some wagons, &c., for Redstone, making the road as they went. So difficult was this labor over Laurel Hill, that two weeks were spent in reaching Gist's a distance of thirteen miles.

On the 27th of June, Washington detached a party of some seventy men under Captain Lewis, to endeavor to clear a road from Gist's to the mouth of Redstone; and another party under Captain Polson, were sent ahead to reconnoitre. Meanwhile Washington completed his movement to Gist's.

Simultaneous with these detachments, something of a French army, on the 28th, left Fort Du Quesne to attack Washington. It consisted of five hundred French, and some Indians, afterwards augmented to about four hundred. The commander was M. Coulon de Villiers, half brother of Jumonville, who sought the command from Contrecoeur as a special favor, to enable him to avenge his kinsman's assassination." They went up the Monongahela in **periaguas** (big canoes,) and on the 30th came to the Hangard at the mouth of Redstone, and encamped on rising ground about two musket shot from it. This Hangard (built the last winter, as our readers will recollect, by Captain Trent, as a store house for the Ohio Company,) is described by M. de Villiers as a "sort of fort built with logs, one upon another, well notched in, about thirty feet long and twenty feet wide." It stood near where Baily's mill now is.

Hearing that the objects of his pursuit were entrenching themselves at Gist's, M. de Villiers disencumbered himself of all his heavy stores at the Hangard; and, leaving a sergeant and a few men to guard them and the periaguas, rushed on in the night, cheered by the hope that he was about to achieve a brilliant **coup de main** upon the young "buckskin Colonel." Coming to the "plantation" on the morning of July 2d, the gray dawn revealed the rude, half-finished fort, which Washington had there begun to erect. This, the French at once invested, and gave a general fire. There was no response; the prey had escaped. Foiled and chagrined, de Villiers was about to retrace his steps, when up comes a half-starved deserter from the Great Meadows, and discloses to him the whereabouts and destitute condition of Washington's forces. Having made a prisoner of the messenger, with a promise to reward, or to hang him, according as his tale should prove true or false, the French commander resolved to continue the pursuit. Upon this we leave him, while we post up Colonel Washington's movements.

Hearing of the French approach, Washington, being at Gist's on the 29th, began throwing up entrenchments, with a view there to make a stand. He called in the detachments under Captains Lewis and Polson, and sent back for Captain Mackay and his company. These all came, and upon council held it was determined to retreat. The imperfect entrenchment was abandoned, and sundry tools and other articles concealed, or left as useless. The lines of this old fortification have been long obliterated, but its position is known by the numerous relics which have been ploughed up. It was near Gist's Indian's hut and spring, about thirty rods east of Jacob Murphy's barn, and within fifty rods of the centre of Fayette County.

The retreat was begun with a purpose to continue it to Wills' creek, but it ended at the Meadows. Thither the swivels were brought back, and under the immediate device and supervision of

Captain Stobo, a ditch and additional dimensions and strength were given to the fort, now named "Fort Necessity." So toilsome was this hasty retreat, there being but two poor teams, and a few equally poor pack horses—that Washington and other officers had to lend their horses to bear burdens, and to hire the men to carry, and to drag the heavy guns. Captain Mackay's company were too royal to labor in this service, and the Virginians had to do it all. When they reached the Meadows on the 1st of July, their fatigue was excessive. They had had no bread for eight days; they had milch cows for beef, but no salt to season it. Arrived at the fort, they found some relief in a few bags of chopped flour, and other provisions from the "settlements,"(j) but only enough for four or five days. Thus fortified and provisioned, they hoped to hold out until reinforcements would arrive, but they came not.

After a rainy night, early on the morning of July 3d, the enemy approached, strong in numbers and in confidence, but fortunately without artillery. A wounded scout announced their approach. The French delivered the first fire of musketry from the woods, at a distance of some four or five hundred yards, doing no harm. Washington formed his men in the Meadow outside of the fort, wishing to draw the enemy into an open encounter. Failing in this, he retired behind his lines, and, after an irregular ineffective firing during the day, and until after dark, the French commander asked a parley, which Washington at first declined, but when again asked, granted. In this he behaved with singular caution and coolness; anxious lest his almost total destitution of ammunition and provisions should be discovered, yet betraying no fear or precipitation. The French and Indians had killed, or stolen all his horses and cattle, and thus his means of retreat were rendered as meagre as his means of defense. Yet with all these disadvantages, in numbers and resources, he obtained terms of surrender, highly honorable and liberal. Indeed, the French commander seems to have been a very fair sort of a man. The articles of capitulation were drawn and presented by him in the French language; and after sundry modifications in Washington's favor, were signed in duplicate, amid torrents of rain, by the dim light of a candle, by Captain Mackay, Colonel Washington and M. de Villiers.

The French commander professed to have no other purpose

(j) See notice of "Wendell Brown and family," in sketch of "Early Settlers," postera, Chapter VII.

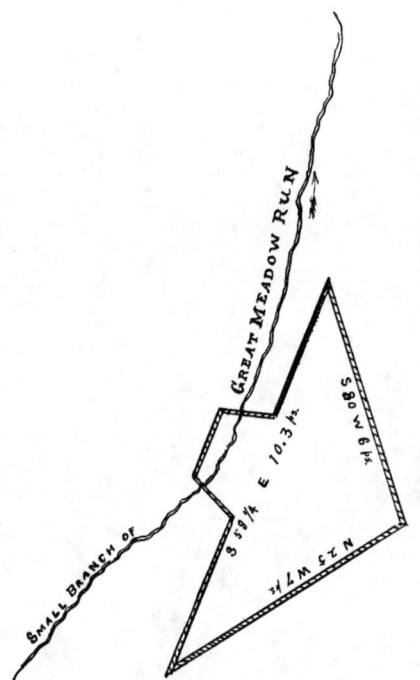

THE FRENCH WAR.—WASHINGTON'S CAMPAIGN, &c.   51

than to avenge Jumonville's "assassination" and to prevent any "establishment" by the English upon the French dominions. Hence, the articles of capitulation agreed on, allowed the English forces to retire without insult or outrage from the French or Indians, to take with them all their baggage and stores, except artillery, the English colors to be struck at once, and at day-break next morning (July 4th,) the garrison to file out of the fort and march with colors flying, drums beating, and one swivel gun. They were also allowed to conceal such of their effects, as by reason of the loss of their oxen and horses they could not take with them, and to return for them hereafter, upon condition that they would not again attempt any establishment there, or elsewhere west of the mountains. The English were to return to Fort Du Quesne the officers and cadets taken at the "assassination" of Jumonville, as hostages for which stipulation, Captains Van Braam and Stobo were given up to the French, as we have before related.

Such was, in substance, the terms of the surrender of "Fort Necessity." But so powerless in all the **physicale** of military movement had Washington become, that nothing could be carried off but the arms of the men, and what little of other articles were indispensible for their march to Wills' creek. Even the wounded and sick had to be carried by their fellows. All the swivels were left. These were the "artillery," which the French required to be given up. It is said that Washington got the French commander to agree to destroy them. This was not done as to some of them—perhaps they were only spiked; for in long after years, emigrants found and used several of them there. Eventually they were carried off to Kentucky to aid in protecting the settlers of the "bloody ground."

The French took possession of the fort, and demolished it on the morning of the 4th of July, a day afterwards to become as gloriously memorable in the recollections of Washington, as now it was gloomy.

Washington's loss in the action, out of the Virginia regiment, was twelve killed and forty-three wounded. Captain Mackay's losses were never reported. The French say they lost three killed and seventeen wounded.

The French, apprehensive that the long expected reinforcements to Washington might come upon them, hastily retired from the scene on the same day, marching "two leagues," or about six miles. On the 5th they passed Washington's abandoned entrenchment at Gist's, after demolishing it and burning all the contiguous houses. At 10, A. M. next day, they reached the mouth of Redstone, and after burning the Hangard, re-embarked on the placid Monongahela. On the 7th they accomplished their triumphant return to Fort Du Quesne, "having burnt down," says M. de Villiers, in his Journal, "all the settlements they found."

Washington returned, sadly and slowly, to Wills' creek, and thence to Alexandria; and now the French colors float over the entire Mississippi Valley.

The historian of "Braddock's Campaign" (W. Sargent) asserts, upon what authority is not stated, that at the time of the surrender, "half the garrison was drunk." Be this true or not, it seems the material was there, for M. de Villiers records that when he took possession of the fort he very considerately executel the "Maine law" upon sundry casks of liquor, to prevent Indian excesses. And it may be, that in accordance with the "spirit of the age," the half-starved and rain-drenched soldiers were allowed to season their slow beef and dry their powder and clothes with rum, the only article they seem to have had a surplus of.

There is cotemporary testimony to a much more pleasing fact: that Washington caused prayers to be said in the fort daily; probably read by himself (for he had no Chaplain,) from the ritual of the English Episcopal Church, then the legal religion of Virginia. His friend, Lord Fairfax, suggested this observance to influence the Indians. But Washington was doubtless "moved thereunto" by higher and holier considerations.

If both these facts be facts, what an incoherent medley of order and confusion, of staid solemnity and swaggering courage, did the old Meadow fort present on that memorable day! And who knows but that both contributed to avert the horrors of an Indian onslaught, and to assuage the anguish of the surrender. Nor must we either wonder at the strange association of influences, or censure Washington for their allowance. Two years afterward, when Dr. Franklin played General on the Lehigh, he had for his Chaplain the Rev. Charles Beatty, a very worthy Presbyterian Minister, and a pioneer of religion in Western Pennsylvania, who, as Franklin records, served also as "Steward of the Rum," dealing it out just after the prayers and exhortations, to secure the soldiers' attendance, "and never," says he, "were prayers more generally or more punctually attended."

The engraving and description of "Fort Necessity" given in Sparks' Washington (vol. 1, p. 56, and vol. 2, p. 457,) are inaccurate. It may have presented that diamond shape, in 1830. But in 1816, the senior author of these sketches made a regular survey of it with compass and chain. The accompanying engraving exhibits its form and proportions.(k) As thereby shown, it was in the form of an obtuse angled triangle of 105 degrees, having its base or hypothenuse upon the run. The line of the base was, about midway, sected or broken, and about two perches of it thrown across the run, connecting with the base by lines of about the same length nearly perpendicular to the opposite lines of the triangle. One line of the angle was six, the other seven perches; the base line eleven perches long, including the section thrown across the run. The lines embraced in all about fifty square perches of land, or nearly one-third of an acre. The embankments then (1816,) were nearly three feet above the level of the Meadow. The outside "trenches," (in which Captain Mackay's men were stationed when the fight began, but from which they were flooded out,) were filled up. But inside the lines were ditches or excavations, about two feet deep, formed by throwing the earth up against the palisades. There were then no traces of "bastions," at the angles or entrances. The junctions of the Meadow, or glade, with the wooded upland, were distant from the fort on the south-east about 80 yards,—on the north about 200 yards, and on the south about 250. North-westward in the direction of the Turnpike road, the slope was a very regular and gradual rise to the high ground, which is about 400 yards distant. From this eminence the enemy began the attack, but afterwards took position on the east and south-east, nearer the fort. One or two field pieces skillfully aimed and fired would have made short work of it.

A more inexplicable, and much more inexcusable error than that in Mr. Sparks' great work, is the statement of Colonel Burd, in the Journal of his expedition to Redstone in 1759. He says the fort was round! with a house in it! That Washington may have had some sort of a log, bark-covered cabin erected within his lines, is not improbable; but how the good Carlisle Colonel could meta-

---

(k) The lithographed view of "Fort Necessity," which forms the frontispiece of this book, varies a little, but not materially, from the description here given. The design of the young artist (David Shriver Stewart, son of Hon. Andrew Stewart, of Fayette,) is to represent the Surrender, on the morning of July 4, 1754. Washington is shown upon the only poor horse left capable of locomotion. In every respect, the picture is not only topographically, but historically correct; losing, however, much of its force and beauty by having to be lithographed upon a much reduced scale. (This frontispiece was never used.—Hadden.)

morphose the lines into a circular form is a mystery which we cannot solve.

The site of this renowned fort is well known. Its ruins are yet visible. It stands on Great Meadow run, which empties into the Youghiogheny. The "Great Meadows," with which its name associates in history, was a large natural meadow or glade, now highly cultivated and improved. The place is now better known by the name of "Mount Washington," on the National Road, ten miles east of Uniontown, the old fort being about 300 yards southward of the brick mansion, or tavern house. In by-gone days thousands of travelers have stopped here, or rushed by, without a thought of its being or history; while a few have thrown a reverential glance upon the classic spot. Washington, in all his afterlife, seems to have loved the place. As early as 1767 he acquired from Virginia a preemption right to the tract of land (234 acres), which includes the fort; the title to which was afterwards confirmed to him by Pennsylvania. It is referred to in his last will, and he owned it at his death. His executors sold it to Andrew Parks of Baltimore, whose wife, Harriet, was a relative and legatee of the General. She sold it to the late General Thomas Meason, who sold it to Joseph Huston, as whose property it was bought at sheriff's sale by Judge Ewing, who sold it to the late James Sampey, Esq., whose heirs have recently sold it to a Mr. Fasenbaker. An ineffectual effort was made some years ago to erect a monument upon the site; it is hoped that it will yet be done. The "first battle ground of Washington" surely deserves a worthier mark of commemoration than mouldering embankments surmounted by a few decaying bushes.

CHAPTER V.

BRADDOCK'S CAMPAIGN.

War in earnest—Albany Council—Indians join the French—Braddock's march—His Forces, Officers and Attendants—Slow movements—His Encampments—Division of Army—River fordings—The Battle—Terrible defeat and losses—Retreat—Drought—Gist's Plantation—Washington—N. Gist—Dunbar's division—Dunbar's camp—Flight—Ancient tavern—Braddock's death—Grave—Who killed Braddock?—Tom Fossit—Career and Character of Braddock—Apology for Dunbar—Consequences of the Defeat—Forbes' conquest—No more battle on Fayette territory.

By the acts of both parties a state of war now existed between England and France; and the wilds of America became the arena and the prize of the conflict. Hence the expedition of Washington in 1754 was followed in the next year by Braddock's campaign, "an enterprise," says Mr. Sparks, "one of the most memorable in American history, and almost unparalleled for its disasters, and the universal disappointment and consternation it occasioned." It was heralded with great preparation and promise, conducted with great show and expenditure, and ended in unprecedented loss of life and treasure. We purpose not to write its history, but only to record such of its events as transpired upon Fayette territory; noticing briefly other matters which seem needful for their being rightly understood.(a)

While Washington, in June, 1754, was wending his toilsome march from the Great Meadows to Gist's, a convention or council was sitting in Albany, composed of Commissioners from the colonies of New York, Pennsylvania, Maryland, Virginia and the

---

(a) In the preparation of this sketch, we have drawn largely from that most valuable recent publication by the "Pennsylvania Historical Society," entitled "The History of an Expedition against Fort Du Quesne, in 1755, under Major General Edward Braddock, Generalissimo of H. B. M. forces in America. Edited from the original manuscripts, by Winthrop Sargent, A. M., member of the Historical Society of Pennsylvania." Octavo, 1855. This is the most minute and interesting detail of the events of that expedition, and history of the French war in America generally, which has appeared. Every Fayette reader should peruse it. Its chief basis is the Journal of Captain Orme, one of General Braddock's Aids. But this has served only as a nucleus around which the author has gathered with unwonted labor and research, a full narrative of the causes and achievements of that eventful war.

four New England colonies, of the one part; and chiefs and warriors representing the Mingoes or Six Nations, of the other part. Among its results was a treaty or deed, by which the Indians named ceded to the Penns a very considerable portion of territory, calling for the southern and western limits of the province of Pennsylvania, but really, by the descriptive terms used, not extending to either. This ambiguity, if such it could be called, and the ever encroaching spirit of the colonists, led to disputes and to jealousies on the part of the Indians. The Delawares and Shawanese, with considerable justness, asserted a right to the territory claimed to have been ceded, which the Six Nations could not alienate, and which the latter asserted with equal justness that they had not ceded, or did not intend to cede. The two allied tribes named were greatly dissatisfied, and complained that the cession, if as claimed, "did not leave them a country to subsist in." Of these difficulties the French, who now held possession and power in the west, availed themselves with great ease and effect to the prejudice of the English pretensions. These Indian tribes and confederacy of tribes gradually and generally became hostile to the Anglo-Saxon colonists. And even the few who had adhered to Washington in 1754, wavered, and finally and almost wholly attached themselves to the French. As heretofore stated, these friendly Indians, after having retired with Washington's retreating forces for a while to Virginia, soon took refuge at Aughwick, in Pennsylvania. But the outside influences were, in 1755, against the continuance of their friendship. The Half-king, their Nestor and Achilles, died in October, 1754, at Harris' Ferry; and in April, 1755, the Pennsylvania colony refused longer to support them and their destitute families.

This adverse state of the colonial relations with the lords of the soil, told with terrible effect upon the fortunes of Braddock and his army; and when to it is added the neglect and maltreatment by Braddock of the few who evinced a willingness to uphold his standard, we have the key to his fate. But eight,—among them Monacatootha, or Scarooyada, followed his colors up to the fatal day; whilst, with other advantages, the French brought hundreds to their aid, led, it is said, by the afterwards renowned Pontiac.

On the 7th, 8th and 10th of June, 1755, the army of Major General Sir Edward Braddock marched from Fort Cumberland, or the mouth of Wills' creek. It consisted of the 14th Regiment of (English) Infantry, Colonel Sir Peter Halket, the 48th, Colonel Thomas Dunbar, sundry Independent (colonial) companies, a company of horse, another of artillery, a company of marines, &c., in all 2150, "besides the usual train of non-militants, who always accompany an army, women who could not fight, Indians who would not, and wagoners who cut loose their horses and fled, at the first onset." The other field officers were Lieutenant Colonels Burton and Gage (of Bunker Hill notoriety); Majors Chapman and Sparks; Major Sir John St. Clair, Deputy Quarter Master General; Matthew Leslie, his assistant; Francis Halket, Brigade Major; William Shirley, Secretary; and Robert Orme, Roger Morris and George Washington, Esquires, aids-de-camp to the General. We have, in the preceding sketch, named some of the Captains—Stephen, Lewis, Polson, Hogg, Peyronie, Mercer and Waggoner. These commanded provincial troops, chiefly from Virginia. The New York Independent companies were commanded by Captains Rutherford and Horatio Gates, the General Gates to whom Burgoyne surrendered at Saratoga. Christopher Gist and his son Nathaniel, accompanied the army as guides; George Croghan, the Indian Agent, of Aughwick, with Montour, interpreter, were also about, trying to be useful in the Indian department, aided by Monacatootha and Captain Jack, the "wild hunter of the Juniata."

Among the Virginia surgeons, were Doctors James Craik and Hugh Mercer, men of imperishable fame.(b) They were both Scotchmen, the latter having fled to Virginia from the service of the Pretender on the fatal field of Culloden. Dr. Craik had followed Washington in his campaign of 1754, was his companion in his journey to the west in 1770, and was his physician at his

---

(b) Both these distinguished men became owners of land in what is now Fayette County. Dr. Craik owned the two tracts called "Boland's camp," and "Froman's Sword," on Boland's and Bute's Runs, in Franklin township, which are warranted in the name of James Craig. General Douglas, as his attorney in fact, sold them to Samuel Bryson. They have since been owned by the late James Paull, Jr., John Bute, the Allens and others.

Dr. Mercer's lands were two tracts near Braddock's road in Bullskin township, patented to him by the Penns in 1771. His executors sold them to Colonel Isaac Meason. See note (m,) to "Early Settlements," Chapter VI. Dr. Mercer was badly wounded at Braddock's Field; and being unable to escape in the general flight, concealed himself for a while behind a fallen tree, where he witnessed the plundering and scalping of the dead and dying. At night he set out alone; and guided by the stars and streams, after several days of painful, half starved wandering, reached Fort Cumberland in safety. A like misfortune befel him when serving as Captain in Colonel John Armstrong's expedition against the Indians at Kittanning in 1756, from which he again returned a wounded wanderer to Fort Cumberland. He had a great life, which was reserved as a sacrifice in a nobler cause.

death. Dr. Mercer became a field officer in the Revolution, and fell at Princeton in January, 1777.

One month was spent in the march from Fort Cumberland to the fatal field. The route, as far as Gist's, was that of Washington the year before; and although Washington had marched from Wills' creek to the Meadows in twenty-three days, making the road as he went, yet it took Braddock eighteen days to "drag his slow length along" over the same distance, and Colonel Dunbar eight days longer. Truly did Washington say that "instead of pushing on with vigor, without regarding a little rough road, they were halting to level every mole-hill, and erect bridges over every brook." This needless delay, like everything else in this campaign, contributed its share of adversity to the disastrous result. For while Braddock was halting and bridging, the enemy was acquiring a force of resistance and attack which three days' quicker movement would have anticipated.

At the Little Meadows (Tomlinson's) a division of the army in the march was made; the General and Colonel Halket, with select portions of the two regiments, and of the other forces, lightly incumbered, going on in advance, being in all about 1400. Colonel Dunbar, with the residue, about 850, and the heavy baggage, artillery and stores, were left to move up by "slow and easy marches;" an order which he executed so literally as to earn for himself the soubriquet of "Dunbar the tardy." When, on the 28th of June, Braddock was at Stewart's crossings, (Connellsville) Dunbar was only at the Little Crossings. Here, Washington, under a violent attack of fever, had been left by Braddock, under the care of his friend Dr. Craik and a guard, two days in advance of Dunbar, to come on with him when able; the gallant Aid requiring from the General a "solemn pledge" not to arrive at the French fort until he should rejoin him. And as Washington did not report himself until the day before the battle, this pledge may be some apology for Braddock having consumed eighteen precious days in marching about eighty miles.

According to Captain Orme's journal, the encampments, &c., of Braddock in Fayette were as follows:

On the 24th of June he marched from Squaw's fort (near Somerfield,) six miles to a camp east of the Great Meadows, near the "Twelve Springs." He crossed the Yough without bridging, about half a mile above where the national road now crosses it. In this day's march they passed a recently abandoned Indian camp, indicating by the number of huts that about 170 had been there. "They had stripped and painted some trees, upon which they and the French had written many threats and bravadoes, with all kinds of scurrilous language." This encampment of Braddock was between Mt. Augusta and Marlow's, south of the National Road.

June 25th.—The army moved about seven miles, and encamped in what is now the Old Orchard, near and northwest of "Braddock's Grave," called then two miles west of the Great Meadows:—the General riding in anticipated triumph over the very spot which in twenty days was to be his last encampment. The army seems to have passed the ruins of Fort Necessity without a halt or a notice It is singular they did not encamp there; for Orme says they were late in getting to their ground, because that morning, about a quarter of a mile after starting, they had to let their carriages down a hill with tackle. In this day's march three men were shot and scalped by the enemy; and the sentinels fired upon some French and Indians whom they discovered reconnoitering their camp—an annoyance now become so frequent, that on the next day Braddock offered a bounty of five pounds for every scalp that his Indians or soldiers would take.

June 26th.—They marched only about four miles, by reason of the "extreme badness of the road," arriving at what Orme calls Rock Fort, on Laurel Hill, a place now known as the Great Rock, near Washington Spring, and the Half-king's old camp, being a little over two miles southward of Dunbar's camp. We quote here from Orme's journal: "At our halting place we found another Indian camp, which they had abandoned at our approach, their fires being yet burning. They had marked in triumph upon trees the scalps they had taken two days before, and many of the French had written on them their names and sundry insolent expressions. We picked up a commission on the march, which mentioned the party being under the command of the Sieur Normanville. This Indian camp was in a strong situation, being upon a high rock, with a very narrow and steep ascent to the top. It had a spring in the middle, and stood at the termination of the Indian path to the Monongahela at Redstone.(c) By this pass the party came which attacked Mr. Washington last year, and also this which attended us. By their tracks they seem to have divided here, the one party going straight forward to Fort Du Quesne, and the other returning by Redstone creek to the Monongahela. A captain's detachment of

---

(c) See preceding sketch of "Indian Trails, &c."—Chap. III.

94 men marched with guides, to fall in the night upon the latter division. They found a small quantity of provisions and a very large batteau, which they destroyed, but saw no men; and the Captain joined the General next day at Gist's."

June 27th.—"We marched,' says Orme, "from the camp at Rock Fort to Gist's plantation, which was about six miles, the road still mountainous and rocky. Here the advance party was relieved, and all the wagons and carrying horses with provision belonging to that detachment joined us." This advanced party consisted of about 400, under Lieut. Col. Burton, who, with Sir John St. Clair, had been sent in advance to cut and make the road, taking with them two six-pounders, with ammunition, three wagons of tools, and thirty-five days' provisions, all on pack horses.

June 28th.—The army marched from Gist's, where the encampment was near Washington's of the previous year—to a camp near to, and west of, Stewart's crossing(d) of the Yough, a short half mile below New Haven, on land now of Daniel Rogers, formerly Col. William Crawford.

It has been commonly supposed that a division of the army in the march here took place—the English troops, &c., here crossing the river and bearing northward; while the Virginia, or colonial forces, went down the river and crossed at the Broad-ford, thence bearing more to the west, crossing Jacob's creek at Stouffer's mill —the two divisions re-uniting at Sewickley, near Painter's salt works. There may be error in this idea. Orme's journal has no notice of any such division. The Broad-ford route may be that which was traversed by the detachments, or convoys of provisions, &c., from Dunbar's division, which were from time to time sent up to the main army; one of which, Orme says, came up Thicketty run, a branch of Sewickley, on the 5th of July. Another detachment of 100 men, with pack horse loads of flour, and some beeves, according to Washington's letters, left the camp west of the Great Meadows on the 3d of July, with which he went, joining the army on the 8th, the day before the battle, "in a covered wagon." This convoy took up the one hundred beeves which were among the losses in the defeat. It is a noticeable fact, that Washington, enfeebled by a consuming fever, was so invigorated by the sight of the scenes

---

(d)So called from the name of an early settler and Indian trader, who was drowned in the Yough at or near the fording which for more than a century has commemorated the event. He probably had a temporary abode near the same place. See Affidavit of William Stewart in Note (1,) to Memoir of the Gists, in "Early Settlers"—postea, Chap. VII.

of his discomfiture the previous year, as to sieze the opportunity of celebrating its first anniversary by hastening on to partake in an achievement which, as he fondly hoped, would restore to his king and country all that had been lost by his failure. How sadly was he disappointed!

June 30th.—The army to-day crossed the Yough at Stewart's Crossing or Ford, in strict military style, with advanced guard first passed and posted There is here a little confusion in Captain Orme's journal. Not only does he make the west to be the east side of the Yough, but he says, "We were obliged to encamp about a mile on the west (east) side, where we halted a day, to cut a passage over a mountain! This day's march did not exceed two miles." It would seem the halt was on the 29th, before crossing the river; for the march is resumed on the 1st of July. This "mountain" is the bluff known as "the narrows," below Davidson's mill. The camp is not certainly known; probably on land late of Robert Long, deceased;—maybe it was south of the narrows on Mr. Davidson's land.

July 1st.—Says Orme, "We marched about five miles, but could advance no further by reason of a great swamp, which required much work to make it passable." The course was north-eastward. This swamp can be no other than that fine looking champaign land about the head waters of Mountz's creek and Jacob's creek, north and east of the old chain bridge, embracing lands formerly of Col. Isaac Meason, now Geo. E. Hogg and others.

July 2nd.—The army moved in the same direction (east of north) about six miles, to "Jacob's Cabin."

The localities of this and the last preceding camp cannot be precisely fixed; and the curious reader and topographer is left to his own conclusions from the data given. Jacob's Cabin was doubtless the abode of an Indian, who gave his name to the creek on which he trapped and hunted.

July 3d.—"The swamp being repaired, we marched about six miles to Salt-lick creek. This(e) Salt-lick creek is Jacob's creek, and the camp at the end of this day's march was near Welshonse's mill, about a mile and a half below Mount Pleasant.

Although now beyond the confines of Fayette, we may as well follow the army route to its end. From Welshonse's mill the

---

(e) What is now known as Indian creek, a tributary of the Yough above Connellsville, was also called Salt-lick creek—whence Salt-lick township. Both derived their common name from the salt licks in the vicinity of their head springs.

course was northward, passing just to the west of Mount Pleasant; thence crossing Sewickley ("Thicketty run") near Painter's salt works; thence, bearing a little westward, it crossed the present tracks of the Pennsylvania Rail Road and Turnpike, west of Greensburg, to the Bush fork of Turtle Creek. Here Braddock abandoned his wise design to approach the French fort by the ridge route, or Nemacolin's path, being deterred by the difficulties of crossing the deep and rugged ravines of the streams. Turning, at almost a right angle, westward, he got into the valley of Long run at or near Stewartsville, and went down it past Samson's mill, encamping on the night of the 8th of July, where Washington joined him, about two miles east of the Monongahela. The army moved from this encampment early next morning, turning into the valley of Crooked run, which they followed to its mouth, and crossed the river at "Braddock's upper ford," below McKeesport; thence down the river on the west side, about three miles, to Braddock's lower ford, just below the mouth of Turtle creek and Dam No. 2, where they recrossed to the fatal encounter of the 9th of July. This double crossing of the river was to avoid the intervening narrows.

It does not come within our design to rehearse the oft-told tale of Braddock's Defeat, which for more than a century has been a word of horror. Braddock had conducted the march hitherto with most commendable care and with signal success; and now, as he neared the object of his labor and ambition, he took all the precautionary measures to avoid surprise and disaster which his military education called for. But, unfortunately, he knew nothing of Indian gunnery and backwoods tactics. He was sensible that his near approach was known to the French fort, and that all his movements were closely and secretly watched. Hence, at the crossings of the river he had his advance guards well posted, and having caused his soldiery to be well appareled and their arms brightened, he made a display well calculated to strike terror into the enemy's spies, and to inspire his men with a feeling very variant from a presage of the sudden discomfiture and death which in a few hours awaited them. Washington was wont to say that he never saw a more animating sight than the army's second crossing of the Monongahela. Coming events cast no disheartening shadow before them. Yet it was known that Sir Peter Halket, Mr. Secretary Shirley and Major Washington, were not without anxious forebodings.

Controcoeur, the commandant at the fort, frightened at the exaggerated reports of the numbers and gun-power of the English, had prepared to surrender, or to fly, as his successor did before

BRADDOCK'S CAMPAIGN. 63

Forbes in 1758. Indeed he reluctantly yielded assent to any resistance. And when, on the 8th, M. M. Beaujeau, Dumas and De Ligueris sought a detachment of regulars and Indian aid, it was merely to dispute the river passes and to annoy and retard the march of the English. They had caused the ground to be thoroughly examined, and knew well the ravines, or natural trenches, which so well served them for attack and protection in the conflict. But the English knew them not. Herein was Braddock's decisive deficiency.

To comprehend the nature of the action and the inevitableness of Braddock's defeat, one must visit the field. He will there, even yet, see two ravines, dry, with almost perpendicular banks, just high enough to conceal, protect and fire from, capable of containing an army of 2,000 men, putting down across the gently sloping second bank of the river towards it, one on each side of the line of Braddock's march, converging towards the high hill which overlooks the scene. And if he will imagine this second bank to be densely wooded, and covered with a thick and tangled web of peavine and other undergrowth, with a newly cut road, twelve feet wide, passing about midway between the ravines, and at no place more than eighty yards distant from one or the other, he will have fully before him the scene of the disaster.

The French and Indians were about 900 strong, the latter being more than two-thirds of the force. They arrived on the ground too late to dispute the passage of the river. The army had crossed, formed its line of march, and was moving—marching into the snare—when the enemy appeared right in front and near the heads of the ravines. As if by magic, at a preconcerted silent signal from M. Beaujeau, the chief in command, the Indians at once disappeared right and left into the excavations, leaving only the little French line visible. These were engaged with spirit and success by Lieut. Col. Gage, and until the Indians began to pour in their invisible deadly shots, the poise of battle favored the English*. It soon changed, and no efforts could restore it. Even tree fighting could not have saved the doomed English soldiery, who held their ground, fought well, and obeyed their officers as long as they had officers to command them. They were in the jaws of death, and nothing could have delivered them, except, perhaps, a timely charge of

---

*Beaujeau was mortally wounded and carried back to Fort Du Quesne where he died on the 12th—the day before the death of General Braddock—Pittsburgh Gazette, July 5, 1858.

dragoons into the ravines, or a raking fire of grape or round shot, up or down their paths. The excuse for not essaying these expedients, is, that the ravines were unknown and invisible. Even yet, when all is clear around them, you do not discern them until you are almost ready to step into them. If the arch demon of Death had been commissioned to fit up an arena for surprise and overthrow, he could not have made it more complete.

The further stages of the encounter, which lasted from about one to five, P. M., need not be here noted. Of the 1460, besides women and other camp followers, who on that bright morning crossed the Monongahela, 456 were killed, and 421 wounded, many of them mortally. Out of 89 commissioned officers, 63 were killed or wounded. Among the killed were the brave Sir Peter Halket and the gallant young Secretary Shirley. All the artillery and ammunition, baggage, provisions, wagons, and many horses, were lost. The General lost his military chest, containing, it is said £25,000 in specie ($125,000), and all his papers. Washington also lost many valuable papers. In short, the officers and soldiers who escaped the carnage lost nearly everything, except the clothes on their backs and the arms in their hands; many abandoning even these. Captain Orme saved his journal, now almost the only authentic continuous record of this most disastrous campaign.

Braddock displayed, in the perplexing circumstances of the action, great activity and courage. His only shortcomings were those already noticed. He had four horses killed under him; and, after having mounted a fifth, while in the act of issuing an order, near the head of one of the ravines, and near the end of the conflict, he received a mortal wound, the ball shattering his right arm and passing into his lungs. He fell to the ground, "surrounded by the dead and almost abandoned by the living," And had it not been for the devotedness of his Aid, Captain Orme, and the almost obstinate fidelity of Capt. Stewart, of Virginia, who commanded the light horse, the fallen General would have had his wish gratified —that the scene of his disaster should also witness his death. He was borne from the ground at great risk, at first in a tumbril, then on a horse. Every officer above the rank of captain was now either killed or disabled, except Washington, who escaped unhurt, though two horses were shot under him and his clothes pierced with balls. So feeble and emaciated was he that day that he had to ride upon

---

(f)Letter of Hon. Wm. Findley, of Westmoreland, relating Washington's own account of this disastrous day, in Niles' Register, Vol. XIV., page 179.

a pillow.(f) The drums had beat a retreat just before Braddock fell, and now Washington undertook to give to it whatever of order it was susceptible of,—for it was a headlong flight. The retreat was by the same route as the advance, crossing the river at the same fording.(g) The enemy did not pursue, but remained to riot in scalps and plunder.

Braddock was carried with the little remnant of the army that could be held together. It is not probable that the panic-stricken fugitives all returned to Gist's by the same path;—many, through fear of pursuit, betaking themselves to the woods and by-ways. The Pennylvania wagoners, it is said, escaped to a man, astride their fleetest horses. Certain it is that by ten o'clock next morning several of them were in Dunbar's camp on Laurel Hill, nearly forty miles distant, with the tiding's of Job's messengers. And one or two wounded officers were carried into the camp before noon of that day.

After crossing to the west side of the river in the flight, a rally was effected of about 100 men, with whom were Braddock, Burton and Washington. From this point Washington was sent to Dunbar for aid, and wagons to convey the wounded. The road was then new and hard to find in the night. There had been a coldness between the General and Dunbar; hence it was deemed necessary, to ensure obedience, that Washington, as an aid-de-camp, should go with orders. Weak and exhausted as he was, he shrunk not from the duty. He set out with two men in a night so wet and dark that frequently they had to alight from their horses and grope for the road. Nevertheless, they reached Dunbar's camp about sunrise.(h) Braddock and his few followers reached Gist's about ten o'clock that evening. What a dismal scene did "Gist's plantation" present on that warm summer night, as the dying General and his few hungry and wounded adherents lay postrate and sleepless around the Indian's spring, waiting for food and surgical aid to come from the camp of "Dunbar the tardy!"

(g)It is probable the river was then uncommonly low. In the Pennsylvania Colonial Records, Vol. VI., under date of June 6th, 1755, a Fast is proclaimed, because of "there having been no rain for two or three months, and all sorts of grain near perishing, and as the General was beginning his march." The Allegheny was so low that the French had great difficulty in getting down from their upper forts This fact, not, we believe, before noticed in any account of this campaign, may in some degree explain the difficulties of Braddock's and Dunbar's marches—the weakness of their horse power and the scarcity of flour and other provisions—there being no steam mills in those days.

(h)Letter of Hon. Wm. Findley in XIV. Niles' Register, 179, before cited.

Nathaniel Gist,(i) son of Christopher, with "Gist's Indian," were dispatched from the battlefield to Fort Cumberland, with tidings of the overthrow, but with instructions to avoid passing by, or disturbing the repose of Dunbar. They traveled a-foot, and through unfrequented paths, to avoid the Indians. While snatching some repose during the darkness of the first night of their journey, in a thicket of bushes and grape-vine, on Cove run, a branch of Shute's run, within view of the camp fires of Dunbar, they mistook the noise of the movement of some bird or beast for Indians, and run with heedlessness of alarm. They thus became separated. But each wended his way cautiously and alone. When nearing their destination, upon emerging from the bushes into the open road, Gist saw a few rods ahead his long lost Indian, who had also just taken the highway! Like two soothsayers, they had to laugh at each other for their causeless alarm and separation.(j)

Although the sufferings of Braddock, in mind and body, were intense, he was not unmindful of his dismayed and wounded soldiers. Upon the arrival, on the morning of the 11th, at Gist's, of some wagons and stores from Dunbar, he sent off a convoy of provisions for the relief of those supposed yet to be behind, and ordered up more wagons and troops from the camp, to bring off the wounded. It is probable these humane provisions were available to but few. Except as to the general officers, and perhaps a few others, all the badly wounded were left on the bloody field to the merciless cruelties of the savages, or perished in its vicinity. In after years human bones were found plentifully all around, some as far off as three miles.

Having made these arrangements, had their wounds dressed, and taken some food, Braddock and his adherents, on Friday, the 11th, moved up to Dunbar's camp. We now go back a little, to trace the movements of Col. Dunbar.

We left him at the Little Crossings on the 20th of June, with about 850 of the army, and the heavy artillery and stores. On the 2d of July he passed the Great Meadows, and on the 10th is found at his camp on the top of Laurel Hill. How long he had lain there is uncertain—several days.

It is, perhaps, ample apology for the slow movements of Dunbar, that, besides the rugged and steep passes of the mountains, the

---

(i) More of him hereafter, in memoir of the Gists, among "Early Settlers," Chap. VII.

(j) I had this story from old Henry Beeson, the founder of Uniontown, who had it from Gist himself.—F. L.

troops he had with him were the refuse of the army, very many of whom sickened and died on the way, with the flux, and for want of fresh provisions. The Indians and French constantly annoyed his march and beset his camps; and, having got in his rear, cut off much of his scanty supplies. But the great cause of delay was the want of horse power to move his heavy train. After one day's toil at half the wagons and other vehicles, the poor jaded beasts had to go back the next day and tug up the other half,—often moving not more than three miles a day, and consuming two days at each encampment. It was with more ease and rapidity that they moved down hill by block and tackle, than to ascend, by all their motive power of man and beast. So exhausted were the horses that an officer of the train estimated it would require twenty-five days for Dunbar to overtake Braddock, from the Great Meadows. And in the council of war held by Braddock at Jacob's creek on the 3d of July, to consider Sir John St. Clair's suggestion to halt, and send back all their horses, to bring up Dunbar's division, it was adjudged that with this aid he could not be brought up in less than eleven days, so weak were all the horses. Besides, it was never designed that Dunbar should overtake Braddock until the fort was captured. And this setting apart of him, his officers and soldiers to an ignoble service—making it a "forgone conclusion" that they were not to share the honors or spoils of victory, soured their tempers and relaxed their exertions

Dunbar's Camp is situated south-east of the summit of Wolf hill, one of the highest points of Laurel Hill mountain, and about three thousand feet above the ocean level. It is in full view of Uniontown, to the eastward, about six miles distant, and is visible from nearly all the high points in Fayette, and the adjacent parts of Greene and Washington counties. The camp was about three hundred feet below the summit, and at about half a mile's distance, on the southern slope. It was then cleared of its timber, but is since much overgrown with bushes and small trees. It is, however, easily found by the numerous diggings in search of relics and treasure, by the early settlers and others even in later times. Near it are two fine sand springs, below which a dam of stones and earth, two or three feet high, was made, to afford an abundant supply of water. This dam is still visible, though much overgrown by laurel. Into this spring, pool, or basin, it is said, when Dunbar's encampment was broken up, fifty thousands pounds of powder, with other material of war, were thrown, to render them useless to the enemy. Old Henry Beeson, the proprietor of Uniontown, used to relate that when he first visited those localities, in 1767, there were some six inches of black, nitrous matter visible all over this spring basin. The locality of Jumonville's hiding place, the Half-king's camp, the Great Rock, and Washington's spring, in reference to Dunbar's camp, have been heretofore noticed. The Turkey Foot, or "Smith's road," from Bedford, crossed Braddock's, or Nemacolin's road just at this camp. Both are yet plainly visible; and the remains of an old stone chimney near this cross-roads indicate the site of an ancient tavern,(k) where many a pioneer halted, and many an old emigrant and settler took his "ease in mine inn." It is now a lonely spot.

When the remains of Braddock's division rejoined Dunbar here, on the 11th of July, the camp was found in great consternation and disorder. Many had fled the day before, on the first tidings of the slaughter of the 9th. And, as had been the case upon that disaster, the wagoners and pack-horse drivers were among the first to fly, and were the earliest messengers of the defeat to Governor Morris of Pennsylvania, then at Carlisle, superintending the forwarding of supplies. From their depositions, taken before him on the 17th, they left about noon on the 10th. They say nothing of Washington's arrival that morning, but say that Sir John St. Clair and another of the wounded officers had been borne into camp on sheets, and others of Braddock's men, wounded and whole, before they left. They all represented Braddock as killed—some qualifying it by saying he had been wounded, put into a wagon, and afterwards "fell upon and murthered by the Indians."

Orders still continued to be issued in Braddock's name, though his life was fast ebbing away. Retreat became inevitable. The camp was abandoned on the 12th. All the stores and supplies, artillery, &c., which had been brought hither at such great labor and expense, were destroyed. Nothing was saved beyond the actual necessities of a flying march. These included two six-pounders, and some hospital stores, horses and light wagons for the sick and wounded, of whom there were over three hundred. The rest of the artillery, cohorns, &c., were broken up, the shells bursted, the powder thrown into the spring basin, the provisions and baggage scattered, and one hundred and fifty wagons burned. A few days afterwards some of the enemy came up and completed the work of destruction.

(k) This must not be confounded with Fossit's, afterwards Slack's, "Hotel," which was further south, near the Great Rock and Washington's spring, where sundry old roads united.

BRADDOCK'S CAMPAIGN.   69

It has been a current tradition, based upon cotemporary statements,(1) that some of the field pieces and other munitions of war, and even money, were buried or concealed near the camp; and much time and labor have been spent in their fruitless search. This story, it seems, reached the ears of Dunbar while on his retreat from Wills' creek through Pennsylvania; and he and all his officers, in a letter to Governor Shirley,(m) dated August 21, 1755, expressly contradict it in these words: "We must beg to undeceive you in what you are pleased to mention of guns being buried at the time General Braddock ordered the stores to be destroyed; for there was not a gun of any kind buried." However, such things as cannon balls, bullets, brass and iron kettles, crow-bars, files, some shells, irons of horse gears and wagons, &c., &c., have been found by the early settlers and other explorers.

The remains of the re-united army encamped on the night of the 13th of July at the Old Orchard camp, "two miles west" of Fort Necessity. Here Braddock died—having, before he expired, it is said, but rather apocryphally, bequeathed to Washington his favorite charger and his body servant, Bishop. Mr. Headley has endeavored to give to Braddock's funeral the romantic interest of the burial of Sir John Moore, "darkly, at dead of night," by the light of a torch, instead of "lanterns dimly burning," and with the addition of Washington reading the funeral service. But he was buried in daylight, on the morning of the 14th, in the road, near the run and Old Orchard, and the march of the troops, horses and wagons passed over the grave to obliterate its traces, and thus prevent its desecration by the enemy. The tree labeled "Braddock's Grave" indicates the place, nearly, where were re-interred,

---

(1) It is not improbable that this belief originated from a letter of Col. Burd to Governor Morris, dated, Fort Cumberland, July 25th, 1755, in which the Colonel relates in detail a dinner conversation at that place with Dunbar, then on his retreat, after which he adds:—"Col. Dunbar retreated with 1500 effective men [effective?—at least 300 sick and wounded, and as many more scared to death]. He destroyed all his provisions, except what he could carry for subsistence. He likewise destroyed all the powder he had with him, to the amount, I think, of 50,000 pounds. His mortars and shells he buried, and brought with him two six-pounders. He could carry nothing off for want of horses."

So fully impressed was Col. Burd with this belief, that, when on his march out to cut the "road to Redstone" and build Fort Burd, in September, 1759, he stopped at Dunbar's camp—"the worst chosen piece of ground for an encampment I (he) ever saw"—and spent a day there. "Reconnoitered all the camp, and attempted to find the cannon and mortars, but could not discover them, although we dug a great many holes where stores had been buried, and concluded the French had carried them off."

(m) VI. Colonial Records, 593.

in 1812 some of the bones of a man supposed to be Braddock. They had been dug out of the bank of the run, in 1812, in repairing the old road. They may, or may not, have been the bones of Braddock. The military accompaniments, said to have been found with them, indicate that they were. Several of the bones were carried off before the re-interment at the tree, many of which, it is said, were afterwards collected by Abraham Stewart, Esq., (who was the road supervisor when they were dug out,) and sent to Peale's Museum at Philadelphia, as curiosities! We doubt this tale. But it is a lasting stigma upon the British Government that it made no effort to reclaim the reliques of this brave but unfortunate commander, and that "not a stone tells where he lies." Col. Burd says he found the spot of his interment, about "twenty rods from a little hollow," &c., when he came out in 1759. But Washington says(n) that when he buried him, "he designed at some future day to erect a monument to his memory; which he had no opportunity of doing till after the Revolutionary war, when he made (in 1784) diligent search for his grave, but the road had been so much turned and the clear land so extended, that it could not be found."

Who killed Braddock?—has been made a grave question in tradition and history. For at least three-quarters of a century the current belief has been that he was shot by one Thomas Fossit, an old resident of Fayette county. The story is therefore entitled to our notice. Mr. Sargent, in his interesting "History of Braddock's Campaign," devotes several pages (144—252) to a collation of the evidence upon the question, and arrives very logically from the evidence at the conclusion that the story is false, got up by Fossit and others to heroize him, at a time when it was popular to have killed a Britisher. Nevertheless, the fact may be that Fossit shot him. There is nothing in the facts of the case, as they occurred on the ground, to contradict it,—nay, they rather corroborate it. Braddock was shot on the battle field by somebody. Fossit was a provincial private in the action. There was generally a bad state of feeling between the General and the provincial recruits, owing chiefly to his obstinate opposition to tree fighting, and to his infuriate resistance to the determined inclination of the backwoodsmen to fight in that way, to which they were countenanced by the opinions of Sir Peter Halket and Washington. Another fact is that much of the havoc of the English troops was caused by the firing of their

---

(n) Letter of Hon. Wm. Findley, before referred to, in XIV. Niles' Register, 179.

own men—whenever they saw a smoke. But Braddock raised no smoke, and when he was shot a retreat had been sounded. If, therefore, Fossit did shoot him, he must have done it purposely. And it is said he did so, in revenge for the killing of a brother for persisting in firing from behind a tree. This is sustained by the fact that Tom had a brother, Joseph, in the action, who was killed. All these circumstances, with many others, seem to sustain the allegation. Against it are the inconsistencies and falsities of other parts of the testimony of the witnesses adduced, and even of Fossit's own narrations.

"I knew Thomas Fossit well.(o) He was a tall, athletic man, indicating by his physiognomy and demeanor a susceptibility of impetuous rage, and a disregard of moral restraints. He was, moreover, in his later years, somewhat intemperate. When Fayette county was erected, in 1783, he was found living on the top of Laurel Hill, at the junction of Braddock's and Dunlap's roads, near Washington's spring, claiming to have there, by settlement, a hundred acres of land, which by deed dated in April, 1788, he conveyed to one Isaac Phillips. For many years he kept a kind of tavern, or resting place, for emigrants and pack-horse men, and afterwards for teamsters, at the place long known as Slack's, now Robert McDowell's. His mental abilities by no means equaled his bodily powers. And, like a true man of the woods, he often wearied the tired traveler with his tales about bears, deer and rattlesnakes, lead mines and Indians. I had many conversations with him about his adventures. He said he 'saw Braddock fall, knew who shot him —knew all about it,' but would never acknowledge to me that he aimed the deadly shot. To others it is said he did, and boasted of it.

"I once kept a country school in Fayette county. One day, when the children were at noon play, I heard a cry of 'there's old Fossit, the man who killed Braddock.' The children feared him, his appearance and noisiness, especially when intoxicated, being rather terrifying. I knew him, and got him to sit down by a tree, which soon dissipated the alarm of the children. He at once began fluttering his fingers over his mouth to imitate the roll of a drum. This amused them. He soon got at his old rigmarole, which ran about thus:—'Poor fellows—poor fellows—they are all gone— murdered by a madman—Braddock was a madman—he would

---

(o) The reader will understand that it is the senior of the dual authors who now speaks, as elsewhere in these sketches in like cases.

not let us tree, but made us stand out and be shot down, when we could see no Indians:—yes, Braddock was a madman—he said "no skulking, no treeing, but stand out and give them fair English play;"—if he had been shot when the battle begun, and Washington had taken the command, we could have licked them,—yes, we'd a licked 'em.' 'How could you have done that?' I asked. 'Why, we'd 've charged on them, and driven them out of the bushes and peavine—then we would have seen their red skins, and could have peppered them—yes, we'd 've peppered their red skins!' He would then repeat his 'boo-oo-oo—my old Virginia Blues—poor fellows—all gone,' &c., &c.—and tears would roll over his rough cheeks.

"The last time I saw him was in October, 1816. He was then a pauper at Thomas Mitchell's, in Wharton township. He said he was then 104 years old, and perhaps he was. He was gathering in his tobacco. I stayed at Mitchell's two days, and Fossit and I had much talk about old times, the battle, and the route the army traveled. He stated the facts generally, as he had done before. He insisted that the bones found by Abraham Stewart, Esq., were not the bones of Braddock, but of a Col. Jones;—that Braddock and Sir Peter Halket were both buried in one grave, some fifty rods north-eastwardly of the place since marked as the place—That Braddock died at Dunbar's camp in the night, and his body was brought on to the next encampment, and buried in the camp, and that if he could walk to the place he thought he could point it out so exactly—near a forked appletree—that by digging, the bones could yet be found.

"There are parts of this story wholly irreconcilable with well ascertained facts. There was no Col. Jones in Braddock's army. Sir Peter Halket and his son, Lieut. Halket, were killed and left on the field of battle. Braddock did not die at Dunbar's camp, but at the first camp eastward of it, and it is nowhere said that Braddock was buried in the camp,—but that might be true. Fossit died, I believe, in 1818, and was, consequently, according to his own statement, about 106 years old."

The reader will naturally wish to know something of the previous history of Braddock and what was his military and private character.

It is said he was an Irishman, but of Anglo-Saxon descent. His father bore the same name, and was an officer in the Coldstream Guards, in which the son received his military training. The General was the only son, and left no issue. His two sisters also died unmarried. This destitution of any near kindred may aid in accounting for the utttter neglect of his remains and grave; and for the absence of any attempt to vindicate his character from the aspersions which his appalling defeat rendered popular in England and America.

At the early age of fifteen, Edward Braddock the younger entered service as Ensign in the second regiment of the Coldstream or Foot Guards, a very aristocratic division of the army, the body guard of Royalty, from the restoration of Charles II. to, perhaps, the present day—deriving its name from the place of its quarters. He rose rapidly through the grades of promotion without any signal achievements, and in 1745 became Lieut. Colonel. Yet it is recorded that his regiment, under his command, behaved well at the battles of Fontenoy and Culloden. His patron and commander was the renowned Duke of Cumberland. In 1746 he was made a Brigadier-General and sent on duty to Gibraltar. In March, 1754, he was gazetted a Major-General, and in September following was appointed Generalissimo of the forces to be sent to, and raised in, America, against the French.

The appointment was a bad one, considering the country and the service he was to be employed in. He had too exalted an opinion of the universal efficiency of old European modes of warfare and of the regular army, and too low an estimate of provincial troops and backwoods tactics. He was, moreover, haughty and imperious. Little was said of his private character prior to his death; but when gone to his last account, his reputation was blackened with almost all the crimes of the Decalogue, and many more—save that of cowardice;—his most cancorous defamers admit his bravery. No doubt much that was said against him was truly said, but there is as little doubt that great injustice has been done to his memory. That he was a gamester and a duellist is no doubt true; but these were vices of his times and profession, of which better men than he were equally guilty. Says Horace Walpole, who delighted in the use of strong terms, "Desperate in his fortune, brutal in his behavior, obstinate in his sentiments, he was still intrepid and capable." His secretary, the lamented young Shirley, wrote of him before the defeat: "We have a General most judiciously chosen for being disqualified for the service he is in, in almost every respect. He may be brave for aught I know, and he is honest in pecuniary matters." Bravery and honesty are very strong redeeming qualities. Dr. Franklin, whose sagacity and accuracy in estimating men was unsurpassed, says of him, that "he was a brave man, and might probably have made a figure as a good officer in some European war. But he had too much self-confidence, too high an opinion of the validity of regular troops, and too mean a one of both Americans and Indians." But the opinion of Washington, given of him, in mature years, after he had passed through the Revolution, is doubtless nearer the truth than any other. "I mentioned(p) (to Washington) the bad impression I had received of Gen. Braddock as an officer. 'True—true,' said he, 'he was unfortunate, but his character was much too severely treated. He was one of the honestest and best men of the British officers with whom he had been acquainted; even in the manner of fighting he was not more to blame than others;—for, of all that were consulted, only one person (himself, probably,) objected to it.' And looking around seriously to me, he said, 'Braddock was both my General and my physician. I was attacked with a dangerous fever on the march, and he left a sergeant to take care of me, and James' fever powders, with directions how to give them, and a wagon to bring me on when I would be able,' &c." It is very manifest that many of the idle traditions which have so needlessly sought to exalt that truly great and just man at the expense of the fallen General, could have received no frame-work upon which to be woven, from him.

Much opprobrium and censure was heaped upon Col. Dunbar, for not making a further effort to accomplish the object of the campaign, or at least making a stand until reinforced. But when it is recollected that great numbers of the troops with him, say 800 —at best none of the best(q)—were sick;—that half of his accessions from the crushed remains of Braddock's division, say 400, were wounded, and all half naked and panic-stricken—we must be satisfied that such an army was not the kind with which either to stand or advance, in a wilderness with hostile surroundings flushed with spoil and victory, without horses to move, or a prospect of obtaining them. The best justification of Dunbar is in the fact, that with all the efforts and resources of crown and colonies for

---

(p) Hon. Wm. Findley's Letter relating a conversation with Washington while President, in XIV. Niles' Register, 179, before cited.

(q) The two regiments—the 44th and 48th, of the Irish Establishment, which formed the main body of Braddock's army, had been recruited for the campaign in Ireland and London by enlistments "of the worst class of men, who, had they not been in the army, would probably have been in Bridewell."— Sargent's "History of Braddock's expedition," &c., 135.

three succeeding years, and until Forbes' great army came in 1758, nothing was accomplished towards driving the French from Fort Du Quesne. Great talk and some effort was made even that year (1755) in Virginia, under the influence of Col. Washington and Governor Dinwiddie, but nothing was done. The Virginia Governor proposed to the Governors of Pennsylvania and Maryland, to raise a force, cross the mountains, and build, and garrison with 800 men, a fort at the Great Crossings, (Somerfield,) or at the Great Meadows. But the proposal was the end of it.

For a long period succeeding the defeat of Braddock, the territory of Fayette, in common with its adjacents, was given up entirely to the French and Indians, who seem to have used it for the subsistence of the forests, and as a field of transit for their predatory and warlike excursions further to the east and south;—which indeed they had begun before the defeat. For these purposes Braddock's road and the other ancient trails were much used. Says Washington, in a letter of May, 1756, to Gov. Dinwiddie, "The roads over the Allegheny Mountains are as much beaten as they were last year by Gen. Braddock's army." No white man not leagued with the new confederacy of French and Indians, could find a resting place in all the West. "You cannot conceive," wrote Gov. Morris of Pennsylvania to Gen. Johnson, in November, 1755, "what a vast tract of country has been depopulated by these merciless savages. I assure you that all the families from Augusta county in Virginia (of which we were then considered a part) to the river Delaware, have been obliged to quit their plantations, on the north side of that chain of mountains that is called the 'Endless Hills.'(r) Indeed the desolation seems to have extended further eastward. In November, 1756, the Provincial Council of Pennsylvania was credibly informed that in Cumberland county (then embracing all Pennsylvania west of the Susquehanna, except what is now York and Adams) there were not left 100 men fit to bear arms, whereas a year before there had been over 3000. The colonies of Virginia, Maryland and Pennsylvania sought to shut themselves up behind a chain of forts far to the east of their western limits,—the nearest to us being Forts Cumberland and Ligonier. Things remained thus, until, upon the accession of William Pitt, "the great commoner," to the Prime Ministry of England, new life and energy were in-

---

(r)The range which separates Franklin county from Bedford, and Huntingdon and Juniata from Perry.

fused into the civil and military arms. Thereupon in 1758, General Forbes was sent out with an army of foreign and provincial troops, in all about 7000, who, in November of that year, frightened the French from Fort Du Quesne, and re-established the English power around the head of the Ohio:—thus ending forever the struggle for supremacy here between the Gaul and the Saxon. Fayette county had no part in this expedition. The conquering army came by a new road from Bedford, through Westmoreland county, though strongly urged by Col. Washington, who commanded the Virginia levies, to take Braddock's road.

The French party which came up to spoil the camp of Dunbar is the last hostile invasion that has ever pressed the soil of Fayette. In the perilous times which intervened, up to Wayne's great victory and treaty in 1794-5, Fayette territory was never, so far as known to history or tradition, the scene of any considerable fight, or Indian atrocity, of any kind. We shall have occasion frequently hereafter to notice this peculiar exemption, its reasons and results. Except when our citizens were promptly going forth to do, or were honorably returning after having done, yeomen's service in defending their own or invading the enemy's country, all the subsequent military movements within our borders have been upon the Peace Establishment. May it ever be so; for

"Peace hath her victories, no less than war."

CHAPTER VI.

EARLY SETTLEMENTS.

A large Field—Penn's Charter—Quaker regard for the Indian—Dunkards and the Youghiogheny—Dunkards in Greene—First Settlers—The Browns—Gists—Gist's neighbors—The Ohio Company—French dominion—Col. Burd's Expedition—Military Permits—Titles about Brownsville and Bridgeport—Era of Settlement—Non-intervention—Pontiac's War—First Settlers from Virginia and Maryland—The West—Settlements trouble the Indians—Kingly and Colonial Anxieties—Names of Settlements—Settlers warned, and driven off by the Military—Indian Titles—Bald Eagle—Indian Stephen—Burnt Cabin—Bloody Law against Settlers—Mission of Rev. Steel to warn them—Names and Number of Inhabitants in 1768—Indian Treaty—Settlers let alone—Indians sell out to the Penns—Titles begin—Surveys—Prices of Lands—Devesting Act—Proprietary Patents—Slavery abolished—Our Slave-owners—Migration to Kentucky—New Settlers—Quakers—Presbyterians—Dr. McMillan's Journal—Mount Moriah—The Baptists—Methodists—Associate Reformed — Episcopalians — Catholics — German Churches —Others—Country Churches—Old Schools—Country Academies—Dunlap & Littell's High School—Character of our Early Settlers.

We now enter upon a large and diversified field. And if any of our readers shall recollect some rugged prominences, or little flowered nooks, which we do not sketch, we beg them, although our ignorance may be the true cause of their omission, to set down their absence to the want of room upon our canvas, and our inability to group them, consistently with the **tout ensemble** of the picture. Our effort shall be, faithfully and intelligibly to present to view all the strong features of the subject, and so to animate the sketch as to give to it, if not the reality, at least the semblance, of life and interest.

Whoever has been curious enough to peruse the Charter for Pennsylvania, granted in 1681, by Charles II. of England, will have seen that His Majesty, assuming the territory to be the "king's own," conveyed it to William Penn, his heirs and assigns, to hold in free and common socage, as of the Castle of Windsor, yielding and paying the yearly rent of two beaver skins and one-fifth of all gold and silver ore, and reserving unto the crown the sovereignty of the colony and the fealty and allegiance of its inhabitants. The Governors were to be appointed by the proprietaries, "by and with the advice and consent of" the king and council. To them, and to the freemen of the colony in Assembly, were committed all the powers of legislation and government, save that of making war,—subject to the revisal and approbation of their laws by the king and council, and to appeals from the provincial to the king's courts. But the appointment of all subordinate officers and the disposal of lands to settlers or others, were committed to the proprietaries only, or their deputies or Governors, in their names; without any interference or control by the Assembly, or by the king or parliament.

This absolute power over the lands gave to the proprietaries, indirectly, a control over the settlers thereon, and enabled them to enforce their peculiar, peaceful and just policy towards the Indian nations. Indeed, one of the principal specified objects for which Penn sought the grant, was "to reduce the savage native, by gentle and just manners, to the love of civil society and the Christian religion." This cardinal purpose was steadfastly kept in view by the colonial government during its entire existence, and brought it often in conflict with the adverse purposes and conduct of settlers. The Penn policy was never to grant lands, or to allow any settlement upon them, until after they had been purchased from, and formally ceded by, the Indian owners. Immediate or direct purchases by individuals from the Indians were strictly forbidden. And so scrupulously just and conciliatory were the proprietaries, that when they found that the Indians did not comprehend the import and extent of the terms used in the deed of cession signed at Albany in 1754, to which we have before referred, they relinquished all beyond certain limits, to which the Indians admitted they meant to go.

This unyielding deference to aboriginal title by the Penns became ingrafted into the character of the province, and was transmitted to the commonwealth. It was however not a characteristic of its neighbor, Virginia; who put it on, only as an outward profession, when the king commanded or self-interest demanded it. We shall presently see something of these antipodal courses of policy, and much more, when we come to the "Boundary controversy."

When, as early as 1751, as related by Croghan and Montour, at a council of the Six Nations and Delaware and Shawnee tribes of Indians, held at Logstown on the Ohio, some sixteen miles below Pittsburgh," a Dunkard from Virginia came to town and requested leave to settle on the Yogh-yo-gaine river, a branch of the Ohio; he was told that he must apply to the Onondaga council, and be recommended by the Governor of Pennsylvania." This little item of history reflects the peculiar non-intrusive Indian policy of the Penns, and is also the earliest recorded design (except that of the

Ohio Company, which did not recognize Pennsylvania proprietorship,) of effecting an orderly settlement within the bounds of our county. It failed of accomplishment from some cause. Doubtless the applicant was one of the Eckerlin brothers who, a few years afterwards, located their little colony at the mouth of Dunkard creek in our neighbor, Greene; whence, after giving their name to the stream, they soon removed to Dunkard's bottom on Cheat river, and thence to the south branch of the Potomac, where their history is as tragical as their character was peaceful and holy. They were in advance of the spirit of the times, and of the localities which they sought to people.

We believe the first actual white settlers within our present county limits were the Browns—Wendell Brown and his two sons, Maunus and Adam, if not a third one, Thomas. They came in 1751 or '52. Their first location was on Provance's bottom, a short distance below the mouth of little Jacob's creek. But soon after, some Indians enticed them away from that choice alluvial reach, by promises to show them better land, and where they would enjoy greater security. They were led to the lands on which, in part, the descendants of Maunus now reside, and erected their cabin upon the tract now the home of his grandson, Emanuel Brown, really among the best in the county. They came as hunters, but soon became herdsmen and tillers of the soil. It has been said that Frederick Waltzer was contemporary with the Browns. We think this an error. He did not come for some years afterwards.

The next settler within our bounds was Christopher Gist; and 1752 has been generally stated to be the date of his settlement. But we think he did not acquire a local habitation here until 1753. In the Virginia Commissioners' certificate, given in 1780 to his son, Thomas Gist, for the land on which his father first settled, 1753 is fixed as the year of his settlement. Washington's embassy to the French posts, when he speaks of having passed "Mr. Gist's new settlement," was in November of that year. His agency for the Ohio Company brought him here. His cabin was, we believe, on that part of the Mount Braddock lands now owned by Jacob Murphy, contiguous to the spring near his barn. By this early settlement he and his sons were enabled, in after years, to acquire the largest and finest body of lands ever owned by any one family in this county embracing not only the Mount Braddock estate, now owned by Isaac Beeson, but also the fine farms of Isaac Wood, Jacob Murphy and P. C. Pusey;—a domain which many a German prince might give his kingdom for.

We have seen it stated somewhere that "Gist induced eleven families to settle around him, on lands presumed to be within the Ohio Company's grant." This may be so. But the late Col. James Paull, whose father, George Paull, was an early settler in that vicinity, and intimately acquainted with the Gists, said he never heard of these settlers. What gives great probability, however, to the statement, is the fact, stated by de Villiers, the French commander of the expedition against Washington at Fort Necessity, in 1754, that on his return, he not only ordered the houses at the entrenchment at Gist's to be burnt down, but detached an officer "to burn the houses round about." He also took several prisoners at Gist's. It is certain that grants of lands within our county limits were made by the Ohio Company. These were prior to 1755, and were chiefly, if not wholly, in the Gist neighborhood. The Stewarts, who settled in the vicinity of, and gave name to, "Stewart's crossings," (Connellsville,) were unquestionably in this class of settlers.(a) William Cromwell, son-in-law of Gist, set up a claim, under the Ohio Company, to a part of the Gist lands, "in the forks of the roads to Fort Pitt and Redstone," including Isaac Wood's farm, asserting, somewhat inconsistently, a gift of it to his wife from her father, and a settlement thereof in 1753. He sold his claim to one Samuel Lyon, between whom and the Gists a long controversy was waged for the title, wherein the Gists prevailed. It may be that others of the early settlers, in that part of the county had grants from this Company which, as the French war blasted the Company's prospects in this region, proved useless, and obliged them thereupon to secure their lands under Virginia and Pennsylvania. Such indeed was the case with the Gists. It is not unlikely that William Jacobs, who settled in 1761 at the mouth of Redstone, where the Hangard was built by the Ohio Company in 1754, claimed under that Company.

The repulse of Washington in 1754, and still more decisively the defeat of Braddock in 1755, put an end, for some time, to all efforts by the English colonists to settle west of the mountains; and all that were here at and before those events, were forced to retire for a time to the eastward, or south. The French never attempted any permanent settlements in this part of the country, and during their sway universal desolation reigned. Many of the old settlers returned after the expulsion of the French in 1758, and

---

(a)See note (a) to Memoirs of the Gists, in Chapter VII.

resumed their possessions. Among these were the Browns and the Gists, whom we will further notice in the sequel.

The expedition of Col. James Burd, in 1759, to open the "road to Redstone" and erect Fort Burd, led to some settlements in that vicinity, between that year and 1764, by persons who had been connected with the expedition, and by others. Of these were William Colvin, whose settlement right, acquired in 1763, to lands now of Eli Cope and others, he sold to Thomas Brown. It is probable that such was the origin of the titles of John and Samuel M'Culloch to the land where Brownsville now is, extending from creek to creek, and whose rights, together with Cresap's, became vested in Thomas and Bazil Brown, to whom patents issued. Capt. Lemuel Barrett held the land where Bridgeport now is, under a "military permit from the commander at Fort Pitt, in 1763, for the purpose of cultivating lands within the custom limits of the garrison then called Fort Burd." He was a Marylander. In 1783 he conveyed his title to Rees Cadwallader, the town proprietor. The land just above Bridgeport, on the river, embracing some three or four hundred acres, was, in early times, the subject of long and angry controversies—from 1769 to 1785—between adverse claimants under "military permits." It was well named, in the official survey, which one of the parties procured of it under a Pennsylvania location, "Bone of Contention." One Angus M'Donald claimed it, or part of it, under a military permit from Col. Bouquet, dated April 26th, 1763, and a settlement on it. In March, 1770, he sold his claim to Captain Luke Collins, (a) describing the land as "at a place called Fort Burd, to include the field cleared by me where the sawpit was above the mouth of Dunlap's creek." Collins conveyed it to Captain Michael Cresap (of Logan's speech celebrity) on the 13th of April, 1772, "at half past nine in the morning,"—describing it as situate between "Point Lookout and John Martin's land,"—recently owned, we believe, by the late Mrs. John S. Krepps. Cresap's executors, in June, 1781, conveyed to one William Schooly, an old Brownsville merchant, who conveyed to Rees Cadwallader. The adverse claimants were Henry Shryock(b) and William Shearer, assignee of George

---

(a) Of some celebrity in the "Boundary Controversy," and as the friend and correspondent of Col. George Wilson, which see—Chap. IX.
(b) Of Frederick county, Md. We find the name of Henry Shryock among the members of the Maryland Convention to ratify the Constitution of the United States, in April, 1788—probably the same person.

Andrew. Their claim reached further southward towards the creek, and further up the river, covering the John Martin land. They sold out to Robert Adams and Thomas Shain. Although they had the oldest permit (in 1762) their title seems to have been overcome by the settlement and official location and survey of their adversary.

One Robert Thorn seems also to have been a claimant of part of the land, but Collins bought him out. This protracted controversy involved many curious questions, and called up many ancient recollections. No doubt the visit to this locality of Mr. Deputy-Sheriff Woods, of Bedford, in 1771, was parcel of this controversy.(c) Many of these early claims were lost, or forfeited, by neglect to settle the land, according to law, and thus were supplanted by others. They were valued by their owners at a very low mark, and often sold for trifling sums.

These settlements, by virtue of military permits, began about this period—from 1760 to '65, to be somewhat numerous in the vicinities of Forts Pitt and Burd, and along the army roads leading thereto.(d) They were subsequently recognized as valid by the Penns, even before they had bought out the Indian title. This was a departure from their general policy, required to maintain those forts and keep up access to them. They were indeed regarded as mere appendages to the forts, and as accessories to the trade and intercourse with the Indians, and not as permanent settlements for homes and subsistence. The Monongahela river below Fort Burd, being in fact an army highway, came in for a share of these favors. Their aggregate was few, and they were often far between.

It was not until about 1765-'6, that settlements, in the true and legitimate sense of the term, came to attract notice in what is now

---

(c) See his Affidavit in sketch of "Boundary Controversy,"—Chap. IX.

(d) Even these military settlements would seem to have been contrary to the plighted faith of the English to the Indians, as given by Sir Jeffry Amherts, Commander-in-Chief of the British in North America, who at an Indian treaty held at Fort Pitt, in August, 1760, told them that "no part whatever of their lands joining to the forts should be taken from them, nor any English people be permitted to settle upon them," without their consent, and being paid therefor. These military permits were generally issued by Col. Bouquet, who commanded at Fort Pitt in 1762-'3, &c., and by Capt. Edmondstone, and the king's proclamation of October, 1763, referred to hereafter, wore the semblance of forbidding them. See a reference to Col. Bouquet's proclamation of 1762, in a subsequent note (f). These royal and military flourishes of supreme regard for Indian sovereignty had very much the consequence of the modern doctrine of "non-intervention," viz—to encourage irresponsible individuals to violate it; the "poor Indian" being the victim in the one case, as the honest settler is in the other.

South-Western Pennsylvania. And it is a well-ascertained fact that the earliest of this class of settlements, for homes and subsistence, were in what is now Fayette County. This was the result of several co-operating causes, some of which have been alluded to in a preceding sketch. The great abundance of game, the general immunity from Indian aggression, the fertility of the land, its fine springs and water-courses; but, above all, its short and easy access from the Atlantic slope by Braddock's road;—these were the combined causes, which now near a century ago, planted all over our county territory, in almost every valley, whether large or small, in both mountain and lowland, the seeds of a rude but hardy civilization.

Although the French were expelled from this region in 1758, yet the Indians were not quieted until 1764; so long did it require for the waves raised by the storm of '54-'5 to subside. This was effected by two very dissimilar agencies—conciliatory intercourse, and the military expeditions of Colonels Bouquet and Bradstreet, of that and the previous years. The reduction of Canada had led to hopes of peace with the Ohio Indians, but French influence was still at work. Added to this, the progress of the English in their career of conquest, and the establishment of lines of Forts all over the Indian territory, alarmed the natives, and led to that powerful Indian confederacy for war and rapine, designated in the bloody annals of that period as Pontiac's War,—planned and executed by that Napoleon of savage warfare. This was in 1763; and while it raged, "the frontiers of Pennsylvania, Virginia and Maryland were overrun by scalping parties, marking their way with blood and devastation." Nearly all the English forts—Detroit, Niagara, Presque Isle, Le Boeuf, Venango, Pitt, Ligonier, &c., were vigorously attacked. And it was not until the decisive but costly victory of Bouquet, at Bushy run, between Ligonier and Pitt, and his bloodless subjugation of the Indians on the Muskingum in the ensuing year, that peace and safety were restored. Although our county territory enjoyed its usual impunity during these bloody years—the inhabitants never flying, as they had to do from neighboring territory—yet the terror which was inspired prevented the influx of settlers. But when this barrier was removed, the tide of immigration rolled in with rapid and steadily-augmenting force, so that 1765 may be set down as the era of the settlement of Fayette county.

The first settlers, almost without an exception, came from the frontier counties of Virginia and Maryland, chiefly from the former. The events in this region, of the preceding French War, had, more than any knowledge of the boundaries, served to create the general belief, among the people of those counties, that this was Virginia territory. Yet it may be assumed that the first settlers came, without knowing, or caring to know, whether this belief was well founded or not. They knew they were coming into that vast and perilous, but fertile domain denominated the West, where land was cheap, and liberty as exuberant as the soil. They had perhaps heard that Virginia claimed all the West, from the then undefined Western limits of Maryland and Pennsylvania to the Mississippi, and from the Lakes on the North, to 36 deg. 30 min. on the South; and supposed that the only adverse jurisdiction was that of the Indians—for as yet there existed here no organized government —no officers of the law. Although nominally embraced within Cumberland county, Pennsylvania, or Augusta county, Virginia, yet, as the county-seat of the former was Carlisle, and of the latter Stanton, with vast mountain wastes intervening, these dependencies were too remote to be reached by the civil arm: and for a while the settlers were unheeded and unmolested by the government of either colony. Hence the tide flowed fast and free. Says a letter from Winchester, Va., dated April 30, 1765—"The frontier inhabitants of this colony and Maryland are removing fast over the Allegheny Mountains in order to settle and live there." And Geo. Croghan, the Deputy Indian Agent, under date of Fort Pitt, May 24, 1766, says, "as soon as the peace was made last year (by Col. Bouquet,) contrary to our engagements to them (The Indians) a number of our people came over the Great Mountain and settled at Redstone creek, and upon the Monongahela, before they had given the country to the King their Father." Concurrent with this is all the testimony of that period. And so imposing did these settlements soon become, that they threatened to bring both the Governments and people of Pennsylvania and Virginia into trouble with the Indians. For this reason, and this alone, they now attract the notice of the civil and military powers.

After the definite treaty of peace between France and England, signed at Paris, in February, 1763, which terminated the French War, had given to England, Canada and the Floridas, and ended the French power and possessions on the American Continent, except in Louisiana, England began to make a great show of care for the Indians. On the 7th of October of that year, the King issued a proclamation regulating the bounds and affairs of his newly acquired possessions, and dealing out, in large profusion, his tender regard for the Indian tribes;—declaring that they must not be molested in their hunting grounds, and forbidding any governor or commander-in-chief, in any colony, to grant warrants of survey, or patents, for any lands beyond the heads of rivers which fall into the Atlantic, or which had been ceded by the Indians. This was an interdict to all settlements and surveys in what is now South-Western Pennsylvania, as well as in all the West. Yet, as its violations were visited by no specified penalties, it was disregarded by settlers, and even, to some extent, by the Government of Virginia, though never by that of Pennsylvania. It was by some of the best men in the "Old Dominion," even by Washington,(e) looked upon as a mere ruse, or pretense, to keep down or quiet the apprehensions of the natives. They, however, did not so regard it. They claimed its enforcement, and were as clamorous and tenacious of their reserved rights to their lands and hunting-courses as has been the Virginia of the present century for the doctrines of the "Resolutions of '98," and threatened resistance as vociferously as did the chivalry of Carolina in 1832. It was the opinion of those most conversant with the Indians, among whom were the British Commander-in-Chief in America, General Gage, Sir William Johnston, the Indian Agent General and his Deputy, Croghan, that unless the intruding settlers were speedily removed, a general Indian war would be the inevitable result. Indeed, it was to the actual and threatened encroachments upon their lands in this region, by the English, that General Gage attributed the loss of the Indian's affections in 1754-'55, which led them to throw themselves into the arms of the French for protection, and brought on the disasters of those years, and subsequent hostilities. A remedy was imperatively demanded.

The documentary history of 1765-'6-'7, indeed, of all that decade, speaks of no other settlements in Western Pennsylvania, or the West generally, than those within, or immediately bordering upon, the Monongahela, upon Cheat, upon the Yough, the Turkey-foot and Redstone;—the first and last being the most prominent, and the last the most extensive, covering all the interior settlements about Uniontown. Georges creek settlers were referred to Cheat; those about Gist's to the Yough; while Turkey-foot took in all the mountain districts. All these settlements seem to have been nearly cotemporaneous; those on the Redstone and the Monongahela border being perhaps the earliest, those on the Yough and Turkey-foot the latest, while those of Georges creek and Cheat occupy an

---

(e)See his letter to Colonel Wm. Crawford, dated 21st Sept., 1767, copied into subsequent Sketch of "Washington in Fayette"—Chap. XIV.

intermediate date, blending with all the others. They all range from 1763 to 1768, inclusive.

The earliest efforts to dispossess, or drive off these early settlers, were of a military character.(f) In June, 1766, Captain Alexander Mackay, commanding a part of the 42d Regiment,* was sent from Fort Pitt by Major Murray, the commandant there, to Redstone creek, at which place, meaning doubtless Fort Burd, he, on the 22d of that month, issues "to all whom it may concern," a Notice, stating that the commander-in-chief, "out of compassion to your ignorance, before he proceeds to extremity," had sent him there to collect them together, inform them of their lawless behavior, and to order them all to return to their several provinces without delay, upon pain of having their goods and merchandise made lawful prize by the Indians, of having their persons and estates put out of the pale of protection; and if they disobeyed, or remained, of being driven from the lands they occupy by an armed force.

This martial demonstration was quickly followed by proclamations from the civil arm. On the 31st of July, 1766, Governor Fauquier, of Virginia, made proclamation of like requirements and penalties. And on the 23d of September, Governor Penn issues a similar fulmination, wherein he specially forbids "all his Majesty's subjects of this, or any other province, or colony, from making any settlements, or taking possession of lands, by marking trees, or otherwise, beyond the limits of the last Indian purchase (that of 1754 at Albany as subsequently restricted) within this province, upon pain of the severest penalties of the law, and of being excluded from the privilege of securing such settlements should the lands, where they are made, be hereafter purchased of the Indians."

Both these proclamations are declared to have been made by virtue of instructions from his Majesty, given in October, 1765, from which it is inferred that the settlements had become alarming to

---

(f)Even before the King's proclamation of Oct. 1763, Col. Henry Bouquet, then commanding at Fort Pitt, had, in the latter part of 1762, issued a proclamation forbidding "any of his majesty's subjects to settle or hunt to the west of the Allegheny mountains, on any pretense whatever, unless upon leave in writing from the General or the Governors of their respective provinces produced to the commander at Fort Pitt," requiring all such persons to be seized, and sent, with their horses and effects, to Fort Pitt, there to be tried by court-martial and punished accordingly. Though often violated. we read of no case of seizure or punishment. The policy of this period was by fair pretenses, to counteract the insinuations of the French, that the English were really seeking to supplant, not to protect the Indians, in the possession of their lands. Hence these repeated "springes to catch wood-chucks."

*This regiment was a part of Col. Bouquet's force that marched to the relief of Fort Pitt in 1763. V. Bancroft, 129, note 3. Ibed 339. VI. Do. 353.

the Indians, or rather the provincial authorities, so early in that, or the previous year, as we have reached the royal councils at that date. Indeed, Governor Fauquier writes to Governor Penn, in December, 1766, that he had issued two previous proclamations of like import, but that all had been disregarded. Governor Penn, however, says, in January, 1767, that the efforts had been partially successful, that many families had withdrawn, but some had since returned.

This co-operative action by the two Governors, seems to have been rendered necessary by the unsettled state of the boundaries between the two provinces. So thought Governor Penn; and Governor Fauquier joined in the effort very cordially but without intimating any claim, on the part of Virginia, to the territory intruded upon. Its value had not yet been weighed—the horns of the strife were not yet grown.

Despite all these threats and warnings, the current of intrusive settlement still rolled on, expanding with time, and growing stronger by resistance. In the mean time the Indians are becoming more and more restive and complaining, especially those of the tribes owning the lands, who had their habitations and rovings at some distance off: for, as is often the case with civilized men, those most remotely concerned utter the earliest and loudest complaints. The settlers generally contrived to keep themselves at peace with the Indians here, trading and hunting with them, and even buying settlement rights from them. This was not an unfrequent mode of acquiring rights to squat upon some of the choicest lands. Indeed, nearly all the earliest settlers resorted to it,—Gist, the Browns, and others already named. And it is said that the ancestral Provance in this way got possession of Provance's Bottom, and James Harrison of the lands on Brown's run, surveyed in the names of John and Robert Harrison, including where James Wilson now resides; also the Michael Debolt and Adam Sholly tracts, on Catt's run, now owned by David Johnson and James S. Rohrer, late George Rider. These, and many others of like origin, were purchased and settled about 1760. By the Indian treaties made between that year and 1765, they bound themselves not to sell lands to any others than the King, or the provincial proprietors, an obligation which was not, perhaps, always kept inviolate. Such purchases had no validity as titles; they only enabled the purchasers to acquire thereby, and by their subsequent improvements thereon, some of the best lands. They gave a kind of conventional right, and were looked upon as a grade higher than mere "tomahawk settlements."

This increasing contact and intercourse of pioneer settlers, with the Indians led, as might be expected, to many disorders; and as the jealousies of the latter grew stronger, occasional personal conflicts, and even homicides, occurred, which added to the animosities by the whites, and to the causes of complaint by the natives. Many Indians were killed on the frontiers of Virginia and Pennsylvania, and occasionally a white trader or hunter met a corresponding fate. But within the territory of Fayette few such outrages are known to have been perpetrated. Of these was the murder of "Bald Eagle," on the Monongahela,(g) the killing of Indian Stephen at or near Stewart's Crossings, (h) and the shooting, and burning the cabin of the two stranger hunters and settlers near Mendenhall's dam, on the Burnt Cabin fork of Dunlap's creek.(i) When this case occurred is not so certainly known, but the two

---

(g) "Bald Eagle" was an inoffensive old Delaware warrior. He was on intimate terms with the early settlers, with whom he hunted, fished and visited. He was well-known along our Monongahela border, up and down which he frequently passed in his canoe. Somewhere up the river, probably about the mouth of Cheat, he was killed—by whom, and on what pretense, is unknown. His dead body, placed upright in his canoe, with a piece of corn-bread in his clenched teeth, was set adrift on the river. The canoe came ashore at Provance's Bottom, where the familiar old Indian was at once recognized by the wife of William Yard Provance, who wondered he did not leave his canoe. On closer observation, she found he was dead. She had him decently buried on the Fayette shore, near the early residence of Robert McClean, at what was known as McClean's Ford. This murder was regarded, both by whites and Indians, as a great outrage, and the latter made it a prominent item in their list of unavenged grievances.

(h) This offense was committed by one Samuel Jacobs, aided and abetted by one John Ingman, an "indented servant" of Capt. Wm. Crawford—probably a negro slave. The provocation and other circumstances of the case are unknown. The case acquired importance from the fact that the Governor of Virginia, contrary to the claim of that province to the territory embracing the locality of the killing, had sent one of the offenders back from Virginia to Pennsylvania to be tried for the offense.—See "Boundary Controversy."

(i) This case, as related by Joseph Mendenhall, an old soldier, and settler at the place known as Mendenhall's Dam, in Menallen township, was thus:—About three and a half miles west of Uniontown, on the south side of the State, or Heaton Road, which leads from the Poor-House, through New Salem, &c., and within five or six rods of the road (on land now of Joshua Woodward) are the remains of an old clearing of about one-fourth of an acre, and within it the remains of an old chimney. Two or three rods south-eastward is a small spring, the drain of which leads off westward into the "Burnt Cabin fork" of Dunlap's or Nemacolin's creek; and still further south, some four or five rods is the old trail, or path called Dunlap's road, which we have heretofore traced. The story is, that in very early times—perhaps about 1767, two men came over the mountains by this path to hunt, &c., and began an improvement at this clearing, and put up a small cabin upon it. While asleep in their cabin, some Indians came to it, and shot them, and then set fire to the cabin. Their names are unknown. So far as known, this is the only case of the kind that ever occurred within our county limits.

Indians were killed in 1766. Great efforts were made to apprehend and punish the offenders, but except as to an alleged accomplice in the case of Stephen, they were fruitless. "At this," writes Governor Fauquier, "I am not surprised, for I have found by experience that it is impossible to bring any body to justise for the murder of an Indian, who takes shelter among our back inhabitants, among whom it is looked upon as a meritorious action, and they are sure of being protected."

The Indian murmurs grew louder, and their threats of vengeance more earnest and alarming. So far as concerned Pennsylvania, the great burden of complaint was the settlements upon their lands along the Monongahela, Redstone, the Youghiogheny and Cheat. They complained also of the murder of their people, and to these the more sober and discreet of their tribes, as a distinct grievance, the increasing corruption of the young men and warriors by Rum. They had, however, thus early learned to discriminate between the people of the two rival colonies, and charged nearly all their grievances to the people of Virginia. But, as the localities were in Pennsylvania, it behooved the Penn Government to devise and execute a remedy for the wrongs complained of, so as thereby to prevent the savage retaliation which impended over the border inhabitants.

In the summer of 1767, another military effort was made to remove the settlers by the garrison at Fort Pitt, but as no other punishment ensued than a temporary removal, no sooner was the soldiery withdrawn than the settlers returned with reinforcements.

The running of Mason & Dixon's line, our Southern boundary, in 1767, showed that the new settlements were all within Pennsylvania; and Virginia, under the Governorships of Fauquier and Botetourt, did not pretend to gainsay it. In January, 1768, Governor Penn called the special attention of his Assembly to this newly ascertained jurisdiction, and after rehearsing the fruitless efforts hitherto made to remove the settlers, invoked their aid to devise a remedy for the alleged wrongs, and thus if possible, avert the threatened war. The Assembly appear to have been as badly frightened as the Governor. A perusal of the historical memoirs of the period does not lead to the conclusion that the danger was either very apparent or very imminent. Nevertheless, the Governor and Assembly go to work, and enact a most terrifying law to drive off the settlers. It is dated February 3d, 1768. After reciting that "many disorderly people, in violation of his Majesty's proclamation, have presumed to settle upon lands not yet purchased from the Indians, to their damage and great dissatisfaction, which may be attended with dangerous and fatal consequences to the peace and safety of this province," it proceeded to enact that if any settlers after being required to remove themselves and families, by personal notice or proclamation sent to them, should not so remove within thrity days thereafter; or, if after having removed, they should return; or, if any should so settle after such notice, every such persons "being thereof legally convicted by their own confession, or the verdict of a jury, shall suffer death without benefit of clergy." And if any persons thereafter should enter upon such unpurchased land, to make surveys, or should cut down, or mark trees thereon, "every person so offending shall forfeit and pay, for every such offense, the sum of fifty pounds, and suffer three months imprisonment without bail, or mainprize." And, to make trials more grievous, and convictions more certain, the offenders were to be taken to Philadelphia, and there tried by courts and juries of that county.

This law savors more of the fourteenth than of the eighteenth century; and, as might have been expected, its sanguinary character rendered it inefficient—a mere **brutem fulmen.** Its only effect was to increase the irritations between the settlers and the Indians, and to ease the treasury of some of its funds, to pay for sending sundry persons and proclamations among the settlers to warn them.

There were, however, specially exempted from the operations of this law, all settlers, past, present or future, upon the main, or army roads to Fort Pitt, or in the neighborhood of that post, by virtue of military permits, and settlers in George Croghan's settlement, "above the said fort." These exemptions saved many of our settlers, along Braddock's and Burd's roads, and around Fort Burd, from the terrors of the law. If others feared, yet they fared no worse than these.

In February, 1768, Governor Penn commissioned the Rev. John Steele, of Carlisle, a Presbyterian clergyman of some celebrity, and three other citizens of Cumberland county, to visit the obnoxious settlements, distribute proclamations embodying the bloody act, and warn the settlers to quit. These envoys set out early in March, and traveled by way of Fort Cumberland and Braddock's road. Our readers will pardon us for copying their Report entire:

"April 2d, 1768.

"We arrived at the settlement on Redstone on the 23rd day of March. The people having heard of our coming, had appointed a meeting among themselves on the 24th, to consult what measures to take. We took advantage of this meeting, read the Act of Assembly and Proclamation—explaining the law and giving the reasons of it as well as we could, and used our endeavors to persuade them to comply; alleging to them that it was the most probable method to entitle them to favor with the Honorable Proprietors when the land was purchased.

"After lamenting their distressed condition, they told us the people were not fully collected; but they expected all would attend on the Sabbath following, and then they would give us an answer. They, however, affirmed that the Indians were very peaceable, and seemed sorry that they were to be removed, and said they apprehended the English intended to make war upon the Indians, as they were moving off their people from the neighborhood.

"We labored to persuade them that they were imposed upon by a few straggling Indians; that Sir William Johnston, who had informed our Government, must be better acquainted with the mind of the Six Nations, and that they were displeased with the white people's settling on their unpurchased lands.

"On Sabbath, the 27th, of March, a considerable number attended (their names are subjoined,) and most of them told us they were resolved to move off and would petition your Honor for a preference in obtaining their improvements when a purchase was made. While we were conversing we were informed that a number of Indians were to come to Indian Peter's. We, judging it might be subservient to our main design that the Indians should be present, while we were advising the people to obey the law, sent for them. They came, and, after sermon, delivered a speech, with a string of wampum, to be transmitted to your Honor. Their speech was—'Ye are come, sent by your great men, to tell these people to go away from the land, which ye say is our's; and we are sent by our great men, and are glad we have met here this day. We tell you, the white people must stop, and we stop them till the treaty, and when George Croghan and our great men talk together, we will tell them what to do.' The Indians were from Mingo town, about eighty miles from Redstone (a little below Steubenville).

"After this the people were more confirmed that there was no danger of war. They dropped the design of petitioning, and said they would wait the issue of the treaty. Some, however, declared they would move off. We had sent a messenger to Cheat River and to Stewart's Crossings of Youghiogheny with several proclamations, requesting them to meet us at Gist's place as most central for both settlements. On the 30th of March, about thirty or forty met us there. We proceeded, as at Redstone, reading the Act of Assembly and a Proclamation, and endeavored to convince them of the necessity and reasonableness of quitting the unpurchased land; but to no purpose. They had heard what the Indians had said at Redstone, and they reasoned in the same manner, declaring they had no apprehensions of a war, that they would attend the treaty, and take their measures accordingly. Many severe things were said of Mr. Croghan; and one Lawrence Harrison treated the law and our Government with too much disrespect.

"On the 31st of March we came to the Great Crossings of Youghiogheny, and being informed by one Speer that eight or ten families lived in a place called the Turkey Foot, we sent some proclamations thither by said Speer, as we did to some families nigh the Crossings of Little Yough, judging it unnecessary to go amongst them.

"It is our opinion that some will move off in obedience to the law; that the greatest part will await the treaty, and if they find the Indians are indeed dissatisfied, we think the whole will be persuaded to remove. The Indians coming to Redstone, and delivering their speech, greatly obstructed our design.
"We are, &c.

John Steel,
John Allison,
Christopher Lemes,
James Potter.

"To the Honorable John Penn, Esquire,
Lieutenant-Governor, &c., &c."

"The Indians names who came to Redstone, viz:
Captains Haven, Hornets, Mygog Wigo, Nogawach, Strikebelt, Pouch, Gilly and Slewbells.

The names of the inhabitants near Redstone:
John Wiseman, Henry Prisser, William Linn, William Colvin, John Vervalson, Abraham Tygard (Teagarden), Thomas Brown, Richard Rodgers, John Delong, Peter Young, George Martin, Thomas Downs, Andrew Gudgeon (Gudgel), Philip Sute (Shute), James Crawford, John Peters, Henry Swats, James McClean, Jesse Martin, Adam Hatton, John Verval, Jr., James Waller, Thomas Douter (Douthitt), Captain Coburn, Michael Hooter, Andrew Linn,

EARLY SETTLEMENTS. 93

Gabriel Conn, John Martin, Hans Cack (Cook), Daniel McKay, Josias Crawford, one Provence (William Yard, or John William), (j).

Names of some who met us at Guesse's (Gist's) place.

One Bloomfield, (Thomas or Empson Brownfield), James Lyne, (Lynn or Lyon), Ezekiel Johnson, Thomas Guesse (Gist), Charles Lindsay, James Wallace (Waller), Richard Harrison, Phil. Sute (Shute), Jet. (Jediah) Johnson, Henry Burkon (Burkham), Lawrence Harrison, Ralph Higgenbottom.(j)

Names of the people at Turkey Foot:

Henry Abrams,(k) Ezekiel Dewitt, James Spencer, Benjamin Jennings, John Cooper, Ezekiel Hickman, John Enslow, Henry Enslow, Benjamin Pursley."

In a supplemental report to the Governor by Mr. Steel, he says: "The people at Redstone alleged that the removing of them from the unpurchased lands was a contrivance of the gentlemen and merchants of Philadelphia, that they might take rights for their improvements when a purchase was made. In confirmation of this they said that a gentleman of the name of Harris, and another called Wallace, with one Friggs, a pilot, spent a considerable time last August in viewing the lands and creeks thereabouts. I am of opinion, from the appearance the people made, and the best intelligence we could obtain, that there are but about an hundred and fifty families in the different settlements of Redstone, Youghiogheny and Cheat." We suppose this estimate included all the settlers in what is now Fayette county and Turkey Foot. The names of Harris, Wallace and Frigg do not appear in our early land titles, so far as we know. They were perhaps agents for others.

The treaty referred to so often in the foregoing report was to be held at Fort Pitt in the ensuing April and May, by George Croghan,

---

(j)Several of these persons resided at considerable distances from the mouth of Redstone, or from Gist's—as Philip Shute and James McClean, who lived in N. Union township, near the base of Laurel Hill; Thomas Douthitt on the tract where Uniontown now is; Captain Coburn some ten miles southeast of New Geneva; Gabriel Conn probably on Georges creek, near Woodbridgetown. The Provances settled on Provance's Bottom, near Masontown, and on the other side of the river, at the mouth of Big Whiteley. The Brownfields located south and southeast of Uniontown. Ralph Higgenbottom resided on the Waynesburg road, in Menallen township, a little west of the Sandy Hill Quaker graveyard. The others, so far as we know, resided near the places to which they came. It is singular that the Commissioners did not visit the upper Monongahela, or Georges creek and Cheat settlements. We infer that they were discouraged by their ill success at Redstone.

(k)Grandfather of Ex-Judge Abrams, of Brownsville.

Deputy Indian Agent, with the Six Nations, Delawares, Shawnese, and other tribes of western Indians. It came off accordingly. Pennsylvania had two commissioners in attendance, Messrs. John Allen and Joseph Shippen. Its purposes were to learn the minds of the Indians, and, by presents and fair speeches, to appease their irritations on account of the intrusions upon their lands and the killing of several of their people by the whites. Between 1000 and 2000 Indians attended, upwards of £1000 worth of presents distributed, and sundry talks, belts and wampums delivered. Although not so recorded, yet doubtless many of the obnoxious settlers were also in attendance, plying the requisite influences to accomplish their purposes. The only complaint uttered by the Indians against the settlements was by a Six Nations' Chief, who said—"Some of them are made directly on our war path, leading to our enemy's country, and we do not like it." The numerous other Indian speakers were silent as to this grievance. Indeed the Pennsylvania Commissioners manifested much more anxiety than the Indians, to have the settlers driven off; complaining most vehemently of the Indians' interference and speech at Redstone, as related by Messrs. Steel and others, and remonstrating against their breach of faith in selling their lands to others than the Proprietaries. So palpable was this play of cross purposes between the Indians and the Government agents, that when the latter solicited the former to send some of their chief men to the settlements to co-operate with two white men selected by them, for the purpose of again warning off the settlers, the representatives of the Six Nations, after at first consenting to do so, upon "sober second thought" refused.

They put their refusal upon two grounds: first, that their delegated powers did not extend to this extra duty; (a precedent for modern "strict constructionists,") and second, that they didn't like to engage in the business of driving off the white people, believing it most proper that the English should do that kind of work themselves. Kayashuta, an old Senaca (Six Nations') chief, made the following very sensible speech to the Penn agents, on this head:—
"We were, all of us, much disposed to comply with your request, and expected it would have been done without difficulty, but I now find that not only the Indians appointed by us, but all our other young men are very unwilling to carry a message from us to the white people, ordering them to remove from our lands. They say they would not choose to incur the ill will of those people; for, if they should be now removed, they will hereafter return to their set-

tlements, when the English have purchased the country from us; and we shall be very unhappy, if, by our conduct towards them at this time, we shall give them reason to dislike us, and treat us in an unkind manner when they again become our neighbors." A rare example of prudent forecast and wise moderation.

This brought to an abrupt termination all efforts to enforce the non-intrusion law. Henceforth the settlers were let alone. But upon a review of these and other schemes to dispossess the early settlers in our country, while we do not condemn the anxiety of the Government to preserve inviolate the faith of Indian treaties, we must censure its too easy alarm, and too vindictive efforts and enactments. These, and the occurrences at this Fort Pitt "treaty" produced two very natural consequences. First, they served to alienate the affections of the settlers from the Pennsylvania Government, and hence to carry them the more devotedly into the embraces of Virginia in the Boundary Controversy which now soon begun; and second, they contributed, with other co-operating influences, to promote and maintain a good feeling between our early settlers and the Indians; which, as we have more than once remarked, was a striking characteristic of our early history.

The speech of the old Senaca chief, which we have quoted, foreshadowed coming events. The Indians' title to the lands intruded upon was soon to cease forever; and although they were not to be forcibly removed, as has been the rule in modern times, yet soon henceforth they were to become mere tenants by sufferance, their camp-fires gradually to go out, and fences spring up across their war paths and hunting courses.

No doubt the project, so necessary to peace and the fulfillment of "manifest destiny," of purchasing this region of country from the native proprietors, had been agitated for some time; and the Indians looked to its accomplishment as anxiously as did the whites. It will be remembered that all of Western Pennsylvania belonged to the Mingoes or Six Nations of Indians, and to their allies and dependants, or "nephews," the Shawnese and Delawares; composing then a numerous and powerful body, now almost extinct. The seat of their power and their chief home was in Western New York. There, at Fort Stanwix (Rome,) near the head of the Mohawk Valley, a Grand Council or Conference of the Six Nations, convened under the auspices of Sir William Johnston, was soon to assemble to agree upon a boundary between their dominions and the settlements of the Middle Colonies. Thither the tribes repaired in September, 1768, and to their councils came Gov. Penn and his agents, and representatives from Virginia and New York, to negotiate and make purchases. The result was that in November the Indians made large cessions to those Colonies, the Penns procuring a deed from the Six Nations, for the consideration of £10,000 conveying to them all of South-western, and much of Northern and Middle Pennsylvania. This was the first treaty of Fort Stanwix, in contradistinction to that of 1784, at which the State bought out all the remaining Indian title within her limits; the Delawares and Shawnese assenting to it by the treaty of Fort McIntosh, (Beaver,) in 1785. Their express assent to the cession of '68 was never given, but they acquiesced.

The way was now clear to settlers and for the acquisition of rights to land.(1) The tide of immigration now rolled high and unresisted; and when on the 3d of April, 1769, the Proprietaries' Land Office was opened for receiving applications for land in the "New Purchase," there was a perfect rush. It was found necesary to put them in a box as received, and then, after being shaken or well stirred up, to draw them out, lottery fashion, and number them as drawn, so as to determine preferences where there was more than one applicant for the same land. Not many such collisions occurred, and after August this plan was abandoned, and warrants substituted. In the first month the number of applications exceeded 3,200. The surveys in what is now Fayette County, then Cumberland, began August 22, 1769, by Archibald McClean and Moses McClean, elder brothers of Col. Alexander McClean, who was with them, and succeeded them as Deputy Surveyor, in 1772. In the remaining five months and ten days of that year (1769) seventy official surveys were executed upon Fayette territory, and in 1770 eighty more besides great numbers, by the same surveyors, in adjacent parts of Westmoreland, and a few in Washington, Allegheny and Somerset, which are found entered in our first Survey Books.

---

(1)The only instance we find of a direct grant of right to land in Fayette (other than the military permits and army road settlements) prior to April 3, 1769, is, what is called a "grant of preference," dated January 22, 1768, given by Governor Penn for 500 acres, to Hugh Crawford, who had been "Interpreter and conductor of the Indians" in the running of the western part of Mason & Dixon's Line in 1767. The order of survey was withheld until January, 1770, in which year he died, and his administrator, Wm. Graham, sold the land for payment of debt, by order of the Orphans' Court of Cumberland county, to Robert Jackson. This is now a part of Col. Samuel Evans' estate; and it and one of the Gist tracts are the only instances in the county of a grant for more than 400 acres. We find a Hugh Crawford, an Indian trader of prominence, in the Ohio country and eastward, about 1750, who was probably the same man.

The number then fell off rapidly—in 1771, twelve; in '72, fourteen; in '73, eleven; in '74, seven; and in '75, two, when official surveys entirely ceased until '82 and '83, in each of which years only three were executed. This suspension was owing in part to the Boundary Controversy, and in part to the Revolution, during which the Land Office was substantially closed, and was not opened for new sales until July 1, 1784. This caused another great rush to vent the accumulation of the last ten years. In 1784, twenty surveys were executed upon Fayette lands; in '85, two hundred and fifty-eight; in '86 one hundred and fifty, in '87 eighty-eight, in '88 sixty-two, in '89 twenty-eight, and in '90 nineteen, after which they progressed with a more equable pace, increasing somewhat after 1792.

Despite the threats to the contrary, preferences were from the first given to those settlers who had made improvements on the lands applied for, regardless of whether they were made before or after the Indian purchase, except that settlements made after that purchase and before April 3, '69, were disregarded, thus discriminating in favor of what the Proprietors had before fiercely denounced. Settlements made under military permits were also preferred. The price of lands in this region was £5 per 100 acres, and one penny per acre per year quit rent, under the Proprietary Government, and until 1784, when it was reduced to £3, 10s. and no quit rents, but with interest from the date of the improvement. In 1792 the price was further reduced to 50s. per 100 acres and interest, at which it continued until the flush times of 1814, &c., when it was put up to £10 per 100 acres and interest from date of settlement. In 1835 the Graduating Act was passed, by which the payment of interest is regulated.

On the 27th November, 1779, was passed by the Commonwealth "An Act for vesting the estates of the late Proprietaries (the Penns) in this Commonwealth." The late Chief Justice Tilghman called this "a high-handed measure—an instance that might made right," but it was a necessary act of Revolution. The State paid them therefor £130,000 sterling in annual payments of from £15,000 to £20,000, without interest, beginning one year after the close of the Revolutionary war; and reserved to them their private and manor property, which was worth perhaps £130,000 more. They prudently took the money, and thus confirmed the questionable legislation.

Very few patents for lands, within the limits of Fayette county, were issued under the Proprietary Government, or before the

Revolution.(m) For this there were several reasons;—the scarcity of money—the validity, as against all but the Proprietors, of settlements, and of official surveys and returns; but especially the uncertainty whether we were in Virginia or in Pennsylvania. Indeed there are, in Fayette county, many tracts of land worth from twenty to fifty dollars per acre, and settled from seventy to ninety years, which are yet unpatented. The rich reckonings of interest which these, from time to time, yield up to the State Treasury, make its insatiate coffers smile.

Thus much we thought we might safely here say as to our land titles. To go further into them would be an unwarrantable digression from our main purpose—to which we now return.

Although the boundary troubles, the Revolutionary and subsequent Indian wars until 1794, operated greatly to retard the growth of our settlements, still they did progress during that period, slowly, but steadily. Indeed during the Revolutionary war, Pennsylvania adopted the recommendation of Congress to States having wild lands, not to grant them to settlers, lest by so doing they might hinder enlistment. This, however, did not hinder, but only discouraged immigration, and postponed the lawful acquisition of titles, as already stated. The great hindrances to settlements here were the difficulties of getting here, the privations when here, and the fear of the Indians. The latter cause, however, had comparatively with other neighboring territory, little influence. No bloody Indian forays ever crossed our lines after '55. Our inhabitants never fled, except sometimes to their noteless private forts upon groundless alarm. Often did our sturdy yeomen and youth go over our borders to the relief of their more exposed neighbors of Washington

---

(m)The only Proprietary Patents for Fayette lands which we know of are the following:

John Penn, Governor, &c., to John Paull, July 7, 1770, for a tract called "Walnut Level," in now Nicholson township, on the river below New Geneva, sold by Paull's executors to Philip Pierce, owned once, in part, by Hon. John Smilie, and since by Jacob and James Biffle, and Thomas W. Nicholson.

Thomas and Richard Penn to William Robertson, January 12, 1771, for a tract on or near Braddock's road, and on both sides of Jacob's Creek, between Lobengier's and Tinsman's (Snyder's) Mills, in part in Bullskin township—the scene of the old quarrels and lawsuits between Robertson and Ralph Cherry.

Thomas and Richard Penn, March 2, 1771, to Doctor Hugh Mercer, of Fredericksburg, Virginia, (the General Hugh Mercer, of the Revolution, who fell at Princeton, N. J., Jan. 3, 1771, for three tracts in Bullskin township, above the Chain Bridge ford, and near Braddock's road. General Mercer's executors sold them to Col. Isaac Meason.

In September and November, 1766, John Penn and John Penn, Jr., granted Patents for a number of tracts in now Wharton and H. Clay townships, and in contiguous parts of Somerset county, to B. Chew and ―――― Wilcocks.

and Westmoreland. Indeed this impunity from the terrors of the times conduced to our increase of population, and caused our county to far outstrip its neighbors in this particular. From 150 families in 1768, say 700 persons, our population rose in 1790 to 12,995 free whites and 282 slaves.

As already stated, the earliest settlers came from Virginia and Maryland, chiefly the former. About 1770-'2 a few came from the Eastern counties of Pennsylvania, bordering on Maryland. There were occasional instances before and after that period, up to '84, when Pennsylvania immigrants began to preponderate. The old settlers had, as they thought, come to Virginia territory, many of the better sort bringing with them their slaves and their attachments to Virginia rule and manners. In 1780 Pennsylvania passed her celebrated "Act for the gradual abolition of Slavery," declaring that all colored persons born on her soil after March 1, 1780, should be free, subject to such as would otherwise have been slaves, being servants until twenty-eight years of age, if duly registered. The act required a registry in the office of the Courts of all slaves. How many were registered by inhabitants of Fayette we do not certainly know, as it was until 1783 part of Westmoreland, where the Register is common to what is now several counties.(n) But, under the Act of March 1788, requiring a registry of those born of slave mothers after March 1, 1780, we find there were registered in Fayette, 354, between the 5th of February, '89, and January 12th, 1839.

The passage of this law, and its becoming a "fixed fact" about the same time that this was Pennsylvania territory, combined to induce many of our early settlers to sell out and migrate to Kentucky, which about this date had opened her charms to adventure, settlement and slavery. Fayette gave to that glorious State many of her best pioneer settlers—among whom were her Popes, her

---

(n) Among the largest slave owners, as shown by the Registers, were Robert Beale, 18; Van Swearingen, 13; William Goe, 11; Walter Brisco, 9; Margaret Hutton, 9; Isaac Meason, 8; Edward Cook, 8; James Cross, 8; Nacy Brashears, 12; Rev. James Finley, 8; Andrew Linn, 7; Benoni Dawson, 7; Sarah Hardin, 7; Richard Noble, 7; Benjamin Stephens, 6; James Dearth, 6; Thomas Brown, 6; John Stevenson, 5; Samuel Kincade, 5; Peter Laughlin, 5; Wm. McCormick, 5; John McKibben, 5; Edmond Freeman, James Blackiston, Isaac Pierce, Auguetine Moore, Benjamin Davis, Hugh Laughlin, James Hammond, each 4; Providence Mountz, Margaret Vance, John Minter, Thomas Moore, William Harrison, Joseph Grable, Dennis Springer, John Wells, Robert Harrison, Isaac Newman, each 3; Zachariah Connell, Mark Hardin, John Hardin, Theophilus Phillips, Philip Shute, John Mason, Robert Ross, John Laughlin, Otho Brashears, Rezin Virgin, Jonathan Arnold, Richard Stephenson, each 2; and many others, one.

Rowans, her Metcalfs, her Hardins and others. The flight to Kentucky started from the mouth of Redstone in Kentucky boats, which landed at Limestone (Maysville). This current was kept up during the decade of 1780-'90, and to some extent afterwards; but now it began to blend with another current which ran into the cheap and tempting plain of Ohio, a current which continued to flow with increasing force and breadth during the residue of that century, and for many years afterwards; and indeed until after a protracted struggle she was completely supplanted in the affections of our people by Illinois and Iowa.

These early removals to Kentucky brought to our county overpowering numbers of settlers from Eastern Pennsylvania and New Jersey, who availed themselves of the opportunity to buy out the improvements of the settlers upon easy terms. Of this class of new settlers were the Friends, or Quakers, who settled about Brownsville, and the Scotch-Irish Presbyterians generally. Many, however, of the Friends, especially those earliest here, came from Berkeley and Frederick counties in Virginia. Of such were the Beesons, who were here as early as 1766-'7. There were also Presbyterians here before 1770—among them Rev. James Finley, who took up the lands where his grandchildren, Robert, Ebenezer, and Eli now reside, as early as 1772, having bought out one Nace Thompson. The Presbyterian settlers located generally on Dunlap's creek, and between Redstone and the Yough—a few scattering in other places. The Rev. John McMillan, in his journal of his tour from the Valley of Virginia to Southwest Pennsylvania, in 1775, speaks of having lodged one night at "one Coburn's"—probably the place where the first Monongalia election was held;(o) then, ten miles distant, he came to and lodged at Col. Wilson's,(p) (now New Geneva,) and preached at "Mount Moriah."(q) Thence he went to John Armstrong's, on Muddy creek—thence to John McKibben's, on Dunlap's creek, (the old Judge Breading place, now

---

(o) See "Boundary Controversy"—Chapt. IX.

(p) See Memoir of Col. George Wilson among "Early Settlers," and "Boundary Controversy"—Chapters VII. and IX.

(q) This was, and is a Presbyterian church; and is where there is now a small frame meeting house, once used as a school house, originally part of the old Caldwell tract of land, now Lee Tate, adjoining the late James C. Ramsay's, in Springhill township, about two miles southeast of New Geneva. The lot, four acres, (including a spring) on which it stands, was conveyed to Col. George Wilson and John Swearingen, (father of Captain Van Swearingen,) as trustees of the church, by Joseph Caldwell, by deed, (of record in Book A.) dated July 1, 1773, and is, perhaps, the oldest church title in the county.

EARLY SETTLEMENTS.   101

George E. Hogg,) at both of which places he lodged and preached. Thence to Mr. Adams', about four miles, and preached at James Pickett's; thence, about five miles, to David Allen's. Mr. Adams was Robert Adams, Esq., a Presbyterian Elder, who lived on the Solomon Colley place, seven miles west of Uniontown, on the pike. David Allen's was where Robert Smith, Esq., now resides, in Franklin township. James Pickett's we cannot certainly locate. From David Allen's he went to Col. Edward Cook's, a well known place, on Speer's run, north of Cookstown, and thence to Pentecost's, in Elizabeth township, Allegheny county, now John Torrence's, and thence to Chartiers, where he settled.

And, as we have but little material for an Ecclesiastical History of Fayette, we may as well here insert what little we have.

The Baptists were early in the field in this county, as early as 1766--'8. They settled generally near Uniontown, on Georges creek and Redstone, the former having for their minister, perhaps as early as 1769, the Rev. Isaac Sutton,(r) who founded the church at Uniontown, called "Great Bethel," and the one near Merrittstown, called "Little Bethel." He settled about two miles south of Uniontown, where some of his descendants still reside. Among his people were the Brownfields, Gaddis, &c. Among the Redstone Baptists were the Linns, Colvins, &c., having for their minister the Rev. W. Stone. The Rev. John Corbly, of Muddy creek, or rather Whiteley creek, in now Greene county, whose wife and children (five) were killed and scalped by Indians when on their way to church, in 1782, was a son-in-law of old Andrew Linn, who settled the Linn's Mill tract—"Crab-tree Bottom," on Redstone, near Brownsville, at a very early day, that tract being the first official survey in the county, made August 22, 1769. The Redstone Association, like the Redstone Presbytery, is the oldest of its kind west of the Mountains.

The Methodists did not reach this county until some years after the Revolution—about the close of the last century.(s) They rapidly

---

(r) The Baptist historian, Benedict, gives this honor to Elder John Sutton, a brother of Isaac, and who had another brother, Moses, who was a preacher. They all, we believe, settled in the same vicinity. There was also a Rev. James Sutton, on Georges creek, who went about 1790—another brother, we presume. The Georges creek Baptist Church at Smithfield was founded in 1780, with 34 members.

(s) The oldest Methodist Ep. Church title in Fayette county that we can find is a deed from Isaac Meason to Thomas Moore, Jacob Murphy, Zach'h. Connell and Isaac Charles, Trustees, &c., for one acre, for a meeting house, dated May 26, 1790:—but where it is—in what township, or other locality, we do not

rose in numbers and influence,—their system of itineracy, or circuit riding, being admirably fitted to a new country.(t) They had preaching stations at Uniontown, Brownsville, Connellsville and elsewhere, at an early period of their progress. Among their earliest preachers and exhorters at Uniontown, and perhaps at other stations, were Messrs. Henry Tomlinson, William McClelland, John and Thomas Chaplin and Moses Hopwood. The Rev. William Brownfield began his clerical labors in that Church, but his deep rooted Calvinism soon led him to the Baptists, for whom he has long labored. The Rev. Thornton Fleming of excellent memory, was among their early preachers.

The Protestant Methodists arose about 1829,—the Cumberland Presbyterians in 1833, coming here from Tennessee and Kentucky, where they originated about 1810.

The Associate Reformed, or that branch of the Presbyterian family which adheres rigidly to Rouse's version of Psalmody, called by various names, have firmly occupied some ground in Fayette from its earliest settlement, but have not kept up with the progress of population. The locality of their denominational existence is now restricted to Dunbar and Tyrone townships, with a few members in contiguous localities. Among their people are, and have been, the Junks, Gilchrists, Byers, Parkhills, Pattersons, &c. The Rev. David Proudfoot was their ancient minister. Indeed, in early times all the Presbyterians used Rouse's version of the Psalms, many churches as late as 1825-'30. The introduction, about 1800, of the new, or Watt's Psalms and Hymns, created much excitement, and caused many secessions, especially at Laurel Hill, whence two Meeting Houses in close contiguity. These sturdy defenders of the ancient faith and practice are among our best citizens.

The Episcopal Church had numerous adherents among our earliest settlers, that being then the established Church of Virginia, from which they came. Their system being, however, the reverse of that of the Methodists in adaptedness to new settlements, and

---

know. It is in the northern part of the county somewhere. The title for the Meth. Ep. Church property, Uniontown, bears date August 6, 1791, from Jacob Beeson and wife to David Jennings, Jacob Murphy, Samuel Stephens, Jonathan Rowland and Peter Hook, Trustees, &c.

(t) "I believe the first Methodist Camp Meeting held in this part of Western Pennsylvania was in 1802, on Pike run, about two and a half miles from Brownsville, on the old Ginger Hill, or Pittsburgh Road, in Washington county. The first one in this county was in 1805, near Jennings' run, about two and a half miles west of Uniontown, on part of the old David Jennings and James Henthorn tracts, now owned by James Veech, Esq. It was the largest concourse of people I ever saw."　　　　　　　　　　　　　　　　　　　F. L.

EARLY SETTLEMENTS.   103

not having the missionary, or extension ingredient so well developed as had the Presbyterians, Baptists and some other sects, they were long postponed in obtaining fixed places of worship, or a regular administration of church ordinances. They have, however, long maintained churches at Brownsville and Connellsville; and, more recently, at Uniontown and elsewhere.

For a long period,—but how long, we cannot state, the Roman Catholics have had a chapel at Brownsville; and within a few years past they have erected one at Uniontown.

There are other religious sects among us, of whose history we know almost nothing. Among these are several which are confined almost exclusively to our German population, including the Lutherans, Tunkers, or Dunkards, Mennonites, &c., some of whom date from a very early day.(u) Besides these, in more recent times have arisen the Disciples, or Campbellites, the New Lights, Free Will Baptists, &c. We have no Unitarians, Universalists, Mormons, or Congregationalists.

We regret that our materials are so scanty as not to allow us to refer this important branch of our early history to a separate sketch. As the subject relates to a "Kingdom not of this world," its memorials are not so accessible as are those of the rise and progress of temporal affairs. Indeed, when we reflect upon the decisive but often unseen influence which religious faith and church discipline exert upon political movements and every day life, the dearth of materials for our ecclesiastical history is much to be regretted. The Rev. Doctor Smith, in his valuable work, "Old Redstone," has done a good work for the Presbyterian Church in Southwestern Pennsylvania; and we commend his example to the historians of other denominations.

As the author of "Old Redstone" has well said and shown, nearly all our early temples were in the country, away from the noise and revelry of the villages, rearing their humble roofs beneath

---

(u) We believe the first meeting house for Christian worship erected within the limits of Fayette county, was on or near the site of the present "German Meeting House," in German township. It was a small log-cabin building. Its founders were known by the name of German Calvanists, or Lutherans. This was as early as 1770. We believe it is the only Church in the county having a **glebe**, or tract of land, attached to it. The Germans had also at a very early day—say 1774, a meeting house on Captain Philip Rogers' land, now Alfred Stewart's, near the Morgantown Road, in Georges township. It was burnt by the woods being fired. Near its site is an ancient graveyard, indicated by a few moss-grown grave stones, "with shapeless sculpture decked." Capt. Rodgers is buried there.

the shade of the oak, on some flower-decked eminence, or in some quiet vale, beside some noiseless spring, or prattling rill;—fit localities at which to drink of the wells of the water of life, and to hymn the praises of the Redeemer in unison with the bird notes of the bushes and the deep diapason of the forest. Who, that can remember their attendance, in dry days or wet, in warm days or cold, upon these rural sanctuaries that does not deprecate the modern departure from those primitive habits; when, instead of people coming from the country to worship, or gossip, at edifices begirt with noise and stench, and made cheerless by cold receptions, the villagers rode or trudged joyously into the country, there to meet warm greetings, and to listen to the tidings of salvation wafted to their ears in a pure atmosphere, uncontaminated by the smell of a pig-sty, and unmixed with the cries of a dog-fight! There is poetry, as well as piety, yet, in a country church and a country parson.

We will not attempt a catalogue, or further description of these old country cathedrals. Many of them have mouldered down and disappeared; and the places of others have been supplied by edifices of more stately structure. While, as to all but a few, the forest trees which sheltered and adorned them, have been cut away; and, in too many instances, their worshipers have not had enough of the grace of taste to plant and protect a substitute. A treeless church is worse than an untombed grave.

And then, the old country schools, with their puncheon floors and benches, and long grease-paper-glazed windows, and "out"-paddles, and ferrules, and beech rods, and pedagogue dominies—where are they? All gone. Hallowed be their memory! They were plentifully scattered among our early settlements. There is scarcely a neighborhood in the cis-montane part of the county, where some survivor of the second generation cannot point you to the spot where his young ideas were taught to shoot and he to play. And if in those days the stream of knowledge was not so much diffused as now, yet perhaps the current was deeper, and its fertilizing influences more durable. Be it our aim still more to expand it, and to deepen and purify it.

Nor were the higher branches of education neglected by our ancestors. True, chartered Academies and Colleges and Union Schools, with all their paraphernalia of Trustees and Faculty and Superintendents, and Libraries and Apparatus, and Endowments, were unknown; but it was not less true, that in all that imparts dignity and strength and a love of further acquirements, to the hu-

EARLY SETTLEMENTS. 105

man intellect, the facilities then were as ample as now. Almost every country preacher was then a teacher of Latin and Mathematics—a branch of their calling was it for which they were often better qualified than many modern "professors." They seldom had a separate building for the purpose—their own humble cabins were the recitation halls, and contiguous groves the study rooms, where many a youth, truly ambitious of fame and usefulness, was wont

"Inter sylvas Academi querere verum."

We have before us a newspaper of 1794, wherein is an advertisement by Rev. James Dunlap, then the Presbyterian Pastor of Laurel Hill and Dunlap's Creek, afterwards President of Jefferson College, Pa., and William Littell, Esq., afterwards a lawyer and author of eminence in Kentucky, setting forth that they had opened a school in Franklin township,(v) where they teach "Elocution and the English language grammatically, together with the Latin, Greek and Hebrew languages, Geometry and Trigonometry, with their application to Mensuration, Surveying, Gauging, &c., likewise Geography and Civil History, Natural and Moral Philosophy, Logic and Rhetoric," and where "boarding, washing, &c., may be had at reputable houses in the neighborhood, at the low rate of ten pounds ($26.67) per annum." How long this nursery of Literature and Science continued we know not—probably until 1803, when Mr. Dunlap's accession to the College Presidency occurred. Who, or how many were its students we cannot tell. It was, however, for a while well sustained, and several of the clergy and other professional men who rose in this country and in the West in the close of the last century, there received their "learning."(w) Among them was the Rev. George Hill, father of Col. A. M. Hill of this county, who found his wife at one of the "reputable houses in the neighborhood" (John McClelland's) where he boarded.

Thus deeply did our forefathers lay the foundations of that prosperity which we now enjoy. Take them all in all, they were generally men and women of whom their posterity may be proud. Unlike most of the proud nations of Europe, ancient and modern,

---

(v) We believe this was on the old Tanner farm, formerly owned by Col. Wm. Swearingen, now Charles McGlaughlin, and in Dunbar township.
(w) After his Presidency at Cannonsburg, in 1811-'12, and when age and infirmity had somewhat impaired his mental, as well as bodily vigor, Dr. Dunlap taught a Latin and Mathematical school at New Geneva. Among his pupils there were Samuel Evans, James and Thomas W. Nicholson, Stephen Wood, and David Bradford, Jr., son of David Bradford, Esq., of Washington, Pa., of Whiskey Insurrection celebrity.

we have no need of a fabulous antiquity in which to bury the misdeeds of our progenitors. We may glory in the fullest and most authentic emblazonry of their conduct. Even those of us who do not boast a Fayette ancestry, will find many things in the character of our early settlers to command our admiration—many to attract our imitation; while in a few, their errors and aberrations stand out as beacons to warn us that with all their heroic excellencies they still were men.

It is not within our purpose, or our ability, to portray their character. It was that of original settlers every where—in many respects; but in others it was one peculiar to the men and women of that age and of this country. The first settlers came here not merely to better their condition, but to gratify their taste.(x) Many, in crossing the mountains, supposed they had passed the ultimate bound of that refined and conventional civilization, which to that class of men denominated pioneers, is too grievous to be borne. Rough they were, but strong. Patient of toil and privation, yet impatient of restraint. Poor in the wealth which engenders pride, but rich in expedients for substantial comfort. Fearless of danger, yet fearing their God. Extravagant in the noisy sports of the chase, the raising, the harvest and the husking, but frugal of all the means of quiet fireside enjoyment. Strong in their likes and dislikes, their attachments were inviolable, but their resentments dreadful. Yet, amid all this rudeness and horror of legal restraints, persons and property were generally more secure, and female chastity more sacred, than even now. And there were less of those petty trespasses which now annoy neighbors, and of those malicious tale tellings which now set neighborhoods in an uproar. The people of that day were governed less by law than by public opinion. Their capital—their stock in trade, as well as their personal security, depended much more upon the amount of esteem and confidence conferred upon them by their neighbors than upon their ability to drive a hard bargain, or make a show of superior wealth and equipage. They lived more directly under the sway of the original elements of the social compact—mutual aid and dependence. And, notwithstanding their heterogeneousness as to colonial paternity, religious sentiment and even language, there existed more unity, more **esprit du corps,** and less segregation into

---

(x) We have heard old settlers say, that, in early times, the common opinion was that this region of country, despite its rich soil and fine springs and water courses, could never come to much for want of iron and salt!

EARLY SETTLEMENTS. 107

classes and castes than now. What they lacked in refinement, was more than compensated by their abundant hospitality. The new comer, or the stranger was always welcomed to their home, and their assistance, for they had themselves been strangers in a strange land.(y) If to resent an injury, or an insult, was in them an ever present feeling, there was just as constantly absent from their breasts that cold selfishness which is too apt to seize upon men in more advanced society, and which generally chills and dries up the social virtues to their very fountains.

We have already referred to our early religious and educational engraftings, as evincing a healthy condition of our social beginnings. But there are other proofs, not less unequivocal. That petty litigation, which now crowds our Court-houses and Justices' offices, was then unknown. The "hundred dollar act" was not then enacted, nor any of its prototypes. Our county was seven years in existence before it had a resident lawyer. And when our courts of justice were held at Carlisle, or Bedford, or Hannastown, or even at old Beesontown, the sturdy yeomanry from Cheat and Georges creek, from the Monongahela and Redstone, and the Yough, who resorted to their sittings, went there more to exchange greetings and hear the news of the day, than to foment disputes, or testify against their neighbor's honesty or reputation. Assaults and batteries. unless highly aggravated, were settled at home, or in the field; petty thefts were punished by frowns, or banishment. Many a court passed without the grand jury having to find a single bill. And whoever will consult our early court records will learn that nearly all the actions brought and contested related in some way to the title or possession, or payment of lands; while **certioraris** and appeals from justices of the peace, actions for slander and on horse swaps, and "suits for settlement" and on express contracts, were comparatively unknown. The men of that day sought to be

---

(y)A remarkable instance of kindness to strangers occurred in what is now Luzerne township, on Coxe's run, at a very early day. A stranger, from the vicinity of Hagerstown, by the name of Applegate, had somehow got his leg badly broken in the woods, and in that condition was found by an old settler, who at once had him borne to his cabin, where every aid and comfort within reach was provided. But being late in the fall, and the stranger knowing that the remedy for his misfortune was time and patience, was very anxious to be again among his family and friends. There was then no carriage road across the mountains, nothing but a pack-horse path. To convey him home. eight of the neighbors agreed to carry him on a sort of hammock, swung on two poles like a bier. This they did, all the way to Hagerstown! Four of the men were Michael Cock, William Conwell, Thomas Davidson and Rezin Virgin. Tradition has failed to preserve the names of the other four "good Samaritans."

a law unto themselves, and were of too lofty a spirit to be actors in the low kennels of modern chicanery. Their word was their bond—its seal their honor —its penalty the fear of social degradation.

We have yet to sketch the trying times of the Boundary Controversy—the Revolutionary and Indian Wars and the Whiskey Insurrection;—events in our early history which are too prominent, and too full of interesting incident, to be crowded into any general narrative. For their prompt resistance to the foes of their lives and liberties, native and foreign, our early settlers ask not even the apology of fondness for adventure. And it must not be inferred because of the wild excitements into which they were thrown in 1774, and again in '94, that they were lawless and turbulent. Their resistance to doubtful rule and questionable taxation sprang less from criminal propensities than from their antecedents and present privations. Their very simplicity and hardy virtues made them an easy prey to interested partizans and designing demagogues. And, while thus wrought upon, like the placid ocean by the unseen wind, they were enacting the stormy resistance of those periods, they, when the appliances which aroused them were removed, yielded as submissivly and heartily to the gravitating influences of law and order, as if nothing had ever occurred to disturb them.(z)

(z)The Hon. William Findley in his "History of the Western Insurrection of 1794," devotes a chapter to exhibit this peculiarity of character among the early yeomanry of Southwestern Pennsylvania—ready and entire acquiescence after impassioned and well grounded, though unlawful resistance; in which respects they compare most favorably with the Connecticut claimants in our own State, the Massachusetts rebellion, and other similar troubles in our early national history.

CHAPTER VII.

MEMOIRS OF EARLY SETTLERS.

1.—The Browns—Wendell, Maunus, Thomas and Adam. 2.—Christopher Gist and Family—Thomas, Nathaniel, Richard, Anne and Mrs. Cromwell. 3.—Col. William Crawford. 4.—Col. James Paull. 5.—Col. George Wilson. 6.—Col. Alexander McClean. 7.—John Smilie. 8.—Gen. Ephraim Douglass. 9.—Albert Gallatin.—Appendix--List of Early (1772) Settlers in Fayette, and parts of Greene, Washington, Westmoreland and Allegheny; and the townships then existing—Spring Hill, Tyrone and Rostraver.

We arrange these, as nearly as we can, in the order in which the subjects of them became inhabitants of what is now Fayette county.

WENDELL BROWN AND SONS.

The most prominent facts, known to us, in the lives of these men have been already noticed—that they were the first white settlers within our limits, having come here as early as 1750-'51, when our county was an unbroken wilderness, and their only associates and neighbors the tawny sons of the forest. We suppose the West is full of such instances of self exile; but we cannot define the peculiarity of mental organization which leads to it.

They came from that hive of our early settlers—Virginia; but from what part of it, we are uninformed; and we believe that until their second advent—after the dangers from Indian hostility which attended and followed the old French war had subsided, they were unaccompanied by any females or children. These indispensable ingredients in the cup of domestic life would but have added bitterness to the anxieties which beset their forest abode.

When Washington's little army was at the Great Meadows, or Fort Necessity, the Browns packed provisions to him—corn and beef. And when he surrendered to the French and Indians, on the 4th of July, 1754, they retired, with the retreating colonial troops, across the mountains; whence they returned to their lands after the re-instatement of the English dominion by Forbes' army in 1758.

"I could repeat numerous Indian stories told by Abraham and Christopher Brown, sons of Manus and grandsons of Wendell Brown; but one or two must suffice.

"It is well known that while the Indians held undivided sway in this region they had one or more lead mines in our mountains, the localities of which they guarded with inviolable secrecy. The discovery of these by the Browns would have been an invaluable acquisition to their venatorial pursuits. Many efforts did they make to find them, and many sly attempts to follow the Indians in their resorts to the mines, but all in vain. And more than once did they narrowly escape detection and consequent death, by their eagerness to share the forbidden treasure.

"Abraham Brown used to relate of his uncle Thomas, that having offended the Indians by some tricks played upon them, (perhaps in contrivances to discover their lead mines and by repeatedly escaping from them when taken prisoner,) he once escaped being burnt only by the timely interposition of a friendly chief; but that eventually they caught him, when no such intercessor was nigh, and knocked out all his teeth with a piece of iron and a tomahawk. This was savage cruelty. Now, for savage honesty. In a season of scarcity, some Indians came to the Browns for provisions. The old man sold them eight rows of corn. He afterwards found they had taken just the eight rows, and not an ear more.

"I knew Adam Brown—'old Adam,' as he was called. He boasted of having been a king's lieutenant in his early days; having probably served with the Virginia provincials in the French and Indian wars. For his services he claimed to have had a Royal grant of land, of nine miles square, extending from near Mount Braddock along the face of Laurel Hill southward, and westward as far as New Salem. I have seen a large stone, standing a little Southwest of the residence of Daniel (or William) Moser, in Georges township, which the late John McClelland said was a corner of Adam's claim. The old lieutenant, it was said, induced many acquaintances to settle around him, on his grant,—the Downards, McCartys, Brownfields, Henthorns, Kindells, Scotts, Jenninges, Greens, McDonalds, Higginsons, &c.; and, out of abundant caution, he and his brother Maunus, and they, entered applications for their lands in the Pennsylvania Land-Office, on the 14th of June, 1769, and had them surveyed soon after. They seem to have been quiescent in the 'Boundary Controversy.' But it was said that early in 1775, Adam and some of his associates had employed an agent to go to London to perfect the Royal grant; when, upon the breaking out of the Revolution, which ended the King's power in this country, they gave up the effort, and in due time perfected their titles under Pennsylvania. From this and some other grounds, arose the current allegation that old Adam and sundry of his neighbors were unfriendly to the cause of American independence. We believe they were never guilty of any overt acts of Toryism. They are now all gone; and, with two or three exceptions, none of them have now any descendants in the county. The Maunus Brown branch of the family has always been considered free of the taint charged to 'old Adam,' and has been productive of good citizens."

CHRISTOPHER GIST AND FAMILY.

The ancestral head of the Gists in Fayette has been already noticed, as having come here as agent of the old Ohio Company, and settled on the Mount Braddock lands in 1753. The fact that the body of this Company was in Virginia, although its head was in London and a limb extended into Maryland, has led to the belief, generally adopted, that Christopher Gist came from Virginia. And it seems that, for a while at least, he was domiciled in that colony, although he was, we believe, a native of England. But when his agency for the Ohio Company commenced he had his abode away down in North Carolina, on the Yadkin, near the confines of Virginia. Returning home after his mission to the Ohio Indians, in 1751, he found his house burnt by the Southern savages, and his family driven up into Virginia, on the Roanoke. In this vicinity, it is probable, he resided until he removed to the Monongahela country, in 1753.

Christopher Gist was among the earliest adventurers into this region of country, and had probably been west of the mountains before his agency for the Ohio Company. Our first traces of his travels indicate a considerable knowledge of our mountain paths and passes, and of the Indian tribes who peopled the Ohio valley. The Ohio Company was formed in 1748, and began its preliminary operations in 1750, in which year we find Mr. Gist the bearer of a speech from the Governor of Virginia to the Ohio Indians. He was out again in 1751; when he visited the Indian tribes on the Muskingum, Scioto and Miami. He returned by the valley of the

Kentucky river to North Carolina. He thus became one of the earliest Anglo-Saxon explorers of what are now the rich States of Ohio and Kentucky; of which he said "nothing is wanted but cultivation to make this a most delightful country." He set out again in the spring of 1752, and attended an Indian treaty, or council, at Logstown, on the Ohio, some sixteen miles below Pittsburg. These missions were all on behalf of the Ohio Company, to conciliate the Indians and look out for good lands. In the latter part of 1753, he accompanied Washington, as his guide, from Wills' creek (Cumberland) to the French posts on the Allegheny. He was again with him in his military expedition of 1754, and was with Braddock in 1755. He had also been with Capt. Trent in the abortive effort of the Ohio Company to build their fort at the "Forks of the Ohio," in February, 1754.

The defeat of Braddock, in July, 1755, seems to have ended his agency for the Ohio Company, and he now turned his energies into other channels. Virginia kept up her efforts to repel the French and Indians until after the conquest by Forbes, in 1758, and Gist found ample employment in the service of that colony. In the fall of 1755, he raised a company of scouts in the frontiers of Virginia and Maryland; and thereafter he becomes known as Captain Gist. In 1756, he was sent Southwest to enlist a body of the Cherokee Indians into the English service, and succeeded. He thereupon, in 1757, became Deputy Indian Agent in the South, a service "for which," says Col. Washington, "I know of no person so well qualified. He has had extensive dealings with the Indians, is in great esteem among them, well acquainted with their manners and customs, indefatigable and patient; and as to his honesty, capacity and zeal, I dare venture to engage."

What part, if any, he took in Forbes' campaign, we do not know. Perhaps his Indian agency kept him employed elsewhere. He seems to have been well educated, and was a good surveyor. He was, moreover, a man of great natural shrewdness and energy—a "woodsman" of the highest order. We are left to conjecture, to assign a motive for fixing an abode in these then inhospitable wilds. Perhaps it was to establish a station for expeditions of the Ohio Company:—perhaps the beautiful body of land upon which he reared his cabin was a temptation too powerful to be overcome by the quiet and comforts of civilized society. Although he returned and resumed his possessions here after Forbes' conquest, we think he did not again permanently settle with his family until about 1765. He transferred his land claims to his son Thomas, and having settled him, and his son-in-law, Cromwell,(a) he soon afterwards returned to Virginia, or North Carolina, and there died, and was buried among his kindred. Doubtless, like the poet of "Sweet Auburn," the wish had never been lost, amid all his perilous wanderings,

"—————————— his long vexations past,
There to return—and die at home at last."

There are some incidents in the return of Washington and Gist from their embassy to the French in 1753-'54, which we must narrate in their own language, as found in their journals. The time is December—the scene, the unbroken wilderness of what is now Butler and Allegheny counties, North and West of the Allegheny river. Snow had fallen. It was becoming very cold. The horses were very weak and were giving out, scarcely able to carry the baggage. Washington determined to leave them in charge of Vanbraam and other "servitors," and hasten on with Gist, afoot.

Says Washington, "I took my necessary papers, pulled off my

(a) The following affidavit of William Stewart sheds light on several subjects and localities embraced in these sketches:—

"Fayette County, ss.

Before the subscriber, one of the Commonwealth's justices of the peace, for said county, personally appeared William Stewart, who being of lawful age, and duly sworn on the Holy Evangelists of Almighty God, saith:—That he was living in this country, near Stewart's Crossings, in the year 1753, and part of the year 1754, until he was obliged to remove hence on account of the French taking possession of this country,—that he was well acquainted with Captain Christopher Gist and family and also with Mr. William Cromwell. Captain Gist's son-in-law. He further saith that the land where Jonathan Hill now lives, and the land where John Murphy now lives, was settled by William Cromwell, as this deponent believes and always understood, as a tenant to the said Christopher Gist. The said Cromwell claimed a place called the "Beaver Dams," which is the place now owned by Philip Shute, and where he now lives; (part of Col. Evan's estate) and this deponent further saith that he always understood that the reason of said Cromwell's not settling on his own land (the Beaver Dams) was, that the Indians in this country at that time were very plenty, and the said Cromwell's wife was afraid, or did not choose to live so far from her father and mother, there being at that time but a very few families of white people settled in this country. And this deponent further saith * * * * that when this deponent's father, himself and brothers first came into this country, in the beginning of the year 1753, they attempted to take possession of the said Beaver Dams, and were warned off by some of said Christopher Gist's family, who informed them that the same belonged to Wm. Cromwell, the said Gist's son-in-law. And further deponent saith not.

WILLIAM STEWART."

Sworn and subscribed before me this 20th day of April, 1786.

James Finley.

clothes, and tied myself up in a watchcoat. Then, with gun in hand, and pack on my back, in which were my papers and provisions, I set out with Mr. Gist, fitted in the same manner, on Wednesday, the 26th (December). The day following, just after we had passed a place called Murderingtown, (in Butler county) we fell in with a party of French and Indians, who had laid in wait for us. One of them fired at Mr. Gist, or me, not fifteen steps off, but fortunately missed. We took this fellow into custody, and kept him until about nine o'clock at night, then let him go, and walked all the remaining part of the night, without making any stop, that we might get the start so far, as to be out of the reach of their pursuit the next day." Mr. Gist relates this occurrence thus:—We rose early in the morning, and set out about two o'clock, and got to Murderingtown, on the south-east fork of Beaver creek. Here we met an Indian, whom I thought I had seen at Joncaire's, at Venango, when on our journey up to the French Fort. This fellow called me by my Indian name and pretended to be glad to see me. I thought very ill of the fellow, but did not care to let the Major (Washington) know that I mistrusted him. But he soon mistrusted him as much as I did. The Indian said he could hear a gun from his cabin, and steered us more northwardly. We grew uneasy; and then he said two whoops might be heard from his cabin. We went two miles further. Then the Major said he would stay at the next water. We came to water, to a clear meadow. It was very light, and snow was on the ground. The Indian made a stop and turned about. The Major saw him point his gun towards us, and he fired. Said the Major, "are you shot?'—'No,' said I; upon which the Indian ran forward to a big standing white oak, and began loading his gun. But we were soon with him. I would have killed him, but the Major would not suffer me. We let him charge his gun. We found he put in a ball; then took care of him. Either the Major or I always stood by the guns. We made the Indian make a fire for us by a little run, as if we intended to sleep there. I said to the Major: 'As you will not have him killed, we must get him away, and then we must travel all night.' Upon which I said to the Indian, 'I suppose you were lost, and fired your gun.' He said he knew the way to his cabin, and it was but a little way. 'Well,' said I, 'do you go home, and as we are tired, we will follow your track in the morning; and here is a cake for you, and you must give us meat for it in the morning.' He was glad to get away. I followed him and listened, until he was fairly out of the way; and then we went about half a mile, when we made a fire, set our compass, fixed our course, and traveled all night. In the morning we were on the head of Pine creek."

"The next day," says Washington, "we continued traveling until quite dark, and got to the river (Allegheny) about two miles above Shannopin's town (two or three miles above Pittsburgh). We expected to have found the river frozen, but it was not, only about fifty yards from each shore. The ice was driving in vast quantities. There was no way to get over but on a raft, which we set about making, with but one poor hatchet, and finished just after sunset. This was a whole day's work. We next got it launched, then went on board of it, and set off. But before we were half way over, we were jammed in the ice in such a manner that we expected every moment our raft to sink and ourselves to perish. I put out my setting pole, to try to stop the raft that the ice might pass by; when the rapidity of the stream threw it with so much violence against the pole, that it jerked me out into ten feet of water; but I fortunately saved myself by catching hold of one of the raft logs. Notwithstanding all our efforts, we could not get to either shore, but were obliged, as we were near an island (Wainwright's) to quit our raft and make to it. The cold was so extremely severe that Mr. Gist had all his fingers, and some of his toes frozen; and the water was shut up so hard, that we found no difficulty in getting off the island on the ice the next morning, and went on to Frazer's."

Christopher Gist had three sons, Nathaniel, Thomas and Richard; and two daughters, Anne, never married, and Violet, wife of William Cromwell, whom her father settled on that part of his lands which is now owned by Isaac Wood. Cromwell afterwards ungratefully set up a claim to it in his own right, which he sold to one Samuel Lyon, with whom Thomas Gist had a protracted, but successful controversy for the title. Each of these sons, as well as the father, acquired inceptive titles to different parts of the Mount Braddock lands. All their rights were eventually united in Thomas Gist, who perfected the titles. He died in 1786, on the Mount Braddock estate, and there buried. By his last will, dated in 1772, he devised his estates to his only daughter, Elizabeth Johnson, who married Andrew McKown, and to his brothers and sisters and their children. These soon sold out to Isaac Meason, the elder,—many of them having before that time removed to Kentucky, where their descendants are still believed to reside. Anne, the maiden sister, resided with Thomas until his death, and became his administrator with the will annexed—as the executors named in the will, Gen. Mordecai Gist, of Baltimore, and George Dawson,(b) resided out of the State.

Thomas Gist was a man of some note. In 1770, while we were part of Cumberland county, he was commissioned a justice of the peace. His commission was, in 1771, renewed for Bedford county, and in 1773, for Westmoreland, where he presided in the October Sessions of the Courts of that year. Washington dined with him on the 25th November, 1770, when returning from his Western land tour of that year; whence, after dinner, he proceeded to Hogland's, at the Great Crossings. We judge that the dinner must have been served up at an early hour, and that but little time was spent "after the cloth was removed."

Of Richard Gist we know, certainly, nothing worthy of record. His celebrity, if he acquired any, was in Kentucky, whither he removed at an early period.(c)

Nathaniel Gist became the most conspicuous of the sons, at least in a military point of view. Obscurity rests alike upon his early and later career.(d) He seems to have been a subordinate

---

(b) General Gist is named in the will, which is dated in 1772, as "Mordecai Gist, merchant, of Baltimore." He afterwards becomes Brigadier General of the Maryland Line in the Revolution; and was probably a younger brother of Christopher Gist. He died at Charleston, S. C., in August, 1792. In 1771, he had a claim to some land "near the Big Meadows, on Braddock's road," taken up for him by Thomas Gist. So also had Joshua Gist.

George Dawson was the grandfather of the present George and John Dawson, Esq., of Fayette, and great-grandfather of Hon. John Littleton Dawson. He was really dead before 1786. But his son Nicholas, who in 1783, had removed into the Virginia "pan-handle" on the Ohio, just below the State line, was his executor, and was thereby supposed to be entitled to become executor of Gist. Hence the record reads as stated in the text. The Dawsons owned and resided on the lands in North Union township, recently the home of Col. Wm. Swearingen.

(c) See note (e).

(d) In a note to one of Col. Washington's letters in II. Sparks, 283, under date of May, 1758, we find the following story related, and as Christopher Gist at this time was designated as "Captain Gist," we presume Lieutenant Gist was his son Nathaniel:—"An Indian named Ucahula was sent from Fort Loudoun (Winchester) with a party of six soldiers and thirty Indians, under command of Lieutenant Gist. After great fatigues and sufferings, occasioned by the snows on the Allegheny mountains, they reached the Monongahela river, where Lieutenant Gist, by a fall from a precipice, was rendered unable to proceed, and the party separated. Ucahula, with two other Indians, descended the Monongahela (from the mouth of Redstone) in a bark canoe, till they came near Fort Du Quesne. Here they left their canoe, and concealed themselves on the margin of the river, till they had the opportunity of attacking two Frenchmen, who were fishing in a canoe, and whom they killed and scalped. These 'scalps' were brought to Fort Loudon by Ucahula."

officer on the Virginia and Maryland frontier in the French and Indian war. In January, 1777, he was, by General Washington, appointed colonel of one of the sixteeen new battalions ordered by Congress, and was sent into the Cherokee country, to add to his four companies of rangers, five hundred Indians. He failed in this, but held command of his battalion of rangers for some years, and was in the service at the close of the war. He commanded a detachment in the march of the American army from Englishtown, New Jersey, to King's Ferry, in July, 1778. Prior to this, in March, 1778, he was again sent southward, to enlist the Cherokees into the service of the struggling colonies, and seems to have had some success. Gen. Washington speaks of him as well acquainted with that powerful tribe of Indians and their allies. He had doubtless been with his father in his Indian agency, in that quarter, in 1756-'8; and, it seems, succeeded to the office after his father's death. We trace him, from 1786 to 1794, as General Gist, of Buckingham county, Virginia; within which period he was several times in Fayette county, on business with Judge Meason.(e)

It may be that we have not done full justice to Col. Nathaniel Gist's Revolutionary services, from our inability to discriminate between him and his Baltimore relative, who also bore the rank and designation of "Col. Gist" until January, 1779.

(e)From a letter of Benjamin Sharp, in II. American Pioneer, 237, dated Warren county, Missouri, March 3, 1843, we take the following; which gives some light upon the history of the Gists:—

"In the year 1776, he (Col. Nathaniel Gist) was the British Superintendent of the Southern Indians, and was then in the Cherokee nation. And when Col. Christian carried his expedition into the Indian country, he surrendered himself to him; and although the inhabitants were so exasperated at him that almost every one that mentioned his name would threaten his life, yet Christian conveyed him through the frontier settlements unmolested; and he went on to head-quarters to General Washington, where, I suppose, their former friendship was revived. He became a zealous Whig, and obtained, through the General's influence, as was supposed, a Colonel's commission in the Continental army, and served with reputation during the war. He afterwards settled in Kentucky, where he died not many years ago. I well recollect of the friends of Gen. Jackson boasting that a luxuriant young hickory had sprung out of his grave, in honor of old hickory face, the hero of New Orleans. One of his uncles, also a Col. Nathaniel Gist (Mordecai?) was uncle to my wife by marriage; and his younger brother (Query—the uncle's or the nephew's?) Richard Gist, lived a close neighbor to my father in 1780, and went on the expedition to King's Mountain, and fell there, within twenty-five or thirty steps of the British lines, of which I am yet a living witness."

COL. WILLIAM CRAWFORD.

Was a native of Virginia, and we believe of Berkeley county: He was a surveyor, and in that pursuit had early in life become acquainted with Washington, when on some of his surveying excursions into that the then frontier part of Virginia. Crawford was a Virginia captain in Forbes' army against the French and Indians at Fort Du Quesne, in 1758; and in that expedition behaved so well as to gain largely upon the confidence of Washington, who was ever afterwards his steadfast friend.(a) After that signal event, we lose sight of him until 1767, when he came into and settled in what is now Fayette county—then Bedford, or, as he supposed, West Augusta county, Virginia. He fixed his abode on Braddock's road, on the western bank of the Youghiogheny river, a little below New Haven. The place was then, and long afterwards, known as Stewart's Crossings. Here he continued to reside until his tragical death. We fix 1767 as the date of his settlement from two pieces of evidence. The one is an account of his against one James McKee, which his executors sued on in Fayette county court, in 1785, which account began in 1767. The other is a letter from Washington to him, dated Sept. 21, 1767,(b) requesting him to survey lands for him in this country. It has been said, however, that he did not remove his family until 1768, which is probable. His wife, Hannah, was a sister of John Vance, the father of Moses Vance, of Tyrone township. He had a brother, Valentine Crawford, who figured to some extent in these parts in the Boundary troubles.(c) Colonels John and Richard Stevenson were his half-brothers. Col. Crawford had, we believe, but one son, John, and two daughters, Ophelia, wife of William McCormick, and Sarah, who married Major Wm. Harrison, and, after his death, became the wife of Major Uriah Springer. She left issue by both marriages. Mrs. McCormick also left children. But it is said that few of these descendants of Col. Crawford inherit his energies, either physical

---

(e) He accompanied Washington on his land tour, down the Ohio to Kenhawa, in 1770.

(b) See this letter in full in the sketch entitled: "Washington in Fayette."

(c) Valentine Crawford, styled Colonel, owned land in Bullskin township, which, about 1784, was sold by the Sheriff of Westmoreland county to Col. Isaac Meason. He was dead in 1785, and John Minter was his administrator. In 1773 he resided in Frederick county, Maryland. The land of John Gaddis, Esq., now his son, Jacob Gaddis, above 'Sock,' was held originally by George Paull, Jr., in the right of Valentine Crawford

or mental. The reader will remember that Major Harrison, William Crawford, Jr., (son of Valentine, we presume,) and Major William Rosse, another nephew of Col. Crawford, lost their lives in Crawford's campaign, while John, the son, escaped. He, a few years afterwards, sold his land to Col. Isaac Meason, and settled near the mouth of Brush Creek, on the Ohio river, where he died.

It appears from the account above referred to, and other evidence, that when Capt. Crawford first came into this region, he, as well as Valentine, was engaged in the Indian trade, a pursuit very common to our early settlers. He also exercised, to a limited extent, his vocation of surveyor, and in that capacity made numerous unofficial surveys for Washington and his brothers, Samuel and John Augustine, and his relative, Lund Washington, as well as for others,—even before the lands were bought from the Indians. The object was to acquire Virginia rights. The captain also took up several valuable tracts for himself, in the vicinity of Stewart's Crossings, but none of them, we believe, in his own name. The home tract, at the Crossings, is in the name of his son John,—others are in the names of Benjamin Harrison,(d) Wm. Harrison, Battle Harrison, Lawrence Harrison, Jr., &c. He owned other lands by purchase from the original settlers.

Upon the erection of Bedford county, in 1771, Capt. Crawford was appointed a justice of the peace. His appointment was renewed after the erection of Westmoreland, in 1773. He was Presiding Justice of the Courts of that county, when his commissions were revoked in January, 1775, for the reason noticed in our sketch of the "Boundary Controversy,"—he having become a very active and somewhat indiscreet Virginia partizan against the Penn Government. After Virginia had, in 1776, undertaken to parcel out the disputed territory into counties, and establish land offices within it, Capt. Crawford was appointed the land officer, or surveyor of Yohogania county, which office he held during the Revolution and until Virginia surrendered her pretentions, in 1779-'80.

Crawford was fitted by nature to be a soldier and a leader. Ambitious, cool and brave, he possessed that peculiar courage and

---

(d)The ancestor of this Harrison family was Lawrence Harrison, who owned the tract of land adjoining the Crawford lands, and which is now owned by Daniel Rogers and James Blackstone, and perhaps others. His daughter, Catharine, was the wife of Hon. Isaac Meason, the elder of Mount Braddock.

skill which is adapted to Indian or border warfare. His ardent love of adventure and fight, got the better of his prudence and Pennsylvania loyalty in the controversy with Virginia. In 1774, while a sworn peace officer of Pennsylvania, he, contrary to the Penn policy, led two bodies of troops down the Ohio, in Dunmore's war, and, for a while, commanded at Wheeling. He, however, had no fighting to do.

We find him taking part, as a good American patriot, in the first Revolutionary meeting held at Fort Pitt, in May 1775, along with Smith, Wilson and others, to whom, as firm adherents to Pennsylvania in the recent conflict, he had been actively opposed.

Soon after this he seems to have entered the military service of Virginia. In February, 1776, he is appointed Lieutenant Colonel of the Fifth Regiment of the forces of that colony; and in September following we find him with his regiment at Williamsburg, the ancient capital of the Old Dominion. In October, 1776, he became Colonel of the Seventh Virginia Regiment. In February, 1777, Congress appropriated $20,000, "to be paid to Col. William Crawford for raising and equipping his regiment, which is part of the Virginia new levies." In a letter from the Colonel to Gen. Washington, dated at Williamsburg, in September 1776, he expresses his apprehension of Indian troubles about Fort Pitt, and says if they arise he will be sent there. This expedition was not realized until November, 1777, when Congress "Resolved that Gen. Washington be requested to send Col. Wm. Crawford to Pittsburgh to take command, under Brig. Gen. Hand, of the Continental troops and militia in the Western Department." He seems then to have been with Gen. Washington at his headquarters at Whitemarsh, near Philadelphia; and Congress being in session at York, Pa., the colonel repaired thither to receive his instructions, and soon after departed for the scene of his command. How long he held it, and what he did, are involved in obscurity. The only trace we find is, that in 1778, he built a fort on the Allegheny, some sixteen miles above Pittsburgh, called Fort Crawford; and Mr. Sparks, in a note to II. Sparks' Washington, 346 says he took command of the regiment in May 1778. It is probable that the regiment referred to was one of the two which Congress, early in that year, ordered to be raised on the frontiers of Virginia and Pennsylvania for their defense; and that the regiment of "Virginia new levies," to which the $20,000 had been appropriated, was assigned to some other officer.

The danger from Indian aggression having subsided or being

COL. WILLIAM CRAWFORD.

otherwise provided against, it seems that Col. Crawford, in 1779, returned home and resumed his duties as land officer of Virginia for Yohogania county, in which the sittings of the Virginia Commissioners at Coxe's Fort and Redstone Old Fort, in the latter part of that year and beginning of 1780, gave him ample employment. We believe he never again engaged in military service until he went into the ill-fated campaign of 1782, which cost him his life.

As a distinct military enterprise, Crawford's Campaign belongs to another sketch,(e) to which we refer the reader. Our purpose here is limited to its fatal personal relations to its renowned commander.

Whether from a presentiment of his untimely end, or from the dictates of that prudence which Washington evinced in like circumstances, Col. Crawford, before setting out in the perilous march, made his last will,(f) and disposed of his estate among his children. And on the 14th of May, 1782, three or four days before leaving home, he and wife, for the consideration of natural love and affection, and five shillings, conveyed to his son-in-law, who accompanied him, Major William Harrison, sixty-eight acres of land on the Yough river, adjoining where said Harrison then lived. The deed is acknowledged the same day before Providence Mountz, Esq., and appended to it is a curious memorandum, in imitation of the old English feudal feoffment,—that on the day of the date thereof, full and peaceable possession of said land being taken and had by said Crawford, the same was by him, then and there, in due form, by turf and twig, delivered to said Harrison, and the five shillings thereupon paid:—Test: Providence Mountz and P. Mountz, Jr. Col. Crawford, however, left his private affairs in a very unsettled condition, as he passed through the excitements and vicissitudes of the later years of his life; the necessary result of which was, that his estate, soon after his death, was swept away from his family by a flood of claims, some of which, doubtless, had no just foundation. His widow was sustained for many years by a pension.

In another sketch, already referred to, the reader may acquaint himself with the most prominent incidents of the march and of the disastrous encounter of the 5th of June, 1782, on the plains of

---

(e) See "Revolutionary and Indian wars,"—Chap. X.
(f) His will, recorded in Westmoreland county, bears date May 16, 1782.

Sandusky, where Col. Crawford "fought his last battle,"—and we believe his first one also.

The Colonel headed the retreat of the main body of his discomfited band. To assure himself whether or not his son and other relatives were safe, he stopped and went back, or let the army pass him, to make inquiry. Not finding them, he left the line of retreat to make further search—but in vain. And now, so rapidly had the army moved, and so jaded was his horse, that he was unable to overtake it. This separation from his command cost him his life, as a sacrifice to parental solicitude.

He soon fell in company with Dr. Knight, the surgeon of the regiment, and two others, and guided by the stars they traveled all night in varied directions to elude the pursuit of the enemy. On the next day they were joined by four others, of whom were Capt. John Biggs and Lieut. Ashley, the latter badly wounded. These eight now held together, and on the second night of the flight ventured to encamp. The next day they came to the path by which the army had advanced; and a council was held as to whether it would be safer to pursue it, or to continue their course through the woods. The Colonel's opinion decided them to keep the open path. A line of march was formed, with Crawford and Knight in front, Biggs and Ashley in the centre, on horseback, while the other footmen brought up the rear. "Scarcely had they proceeded a mile when several Indians sprung up within twenty yards of the path, presented their guns, and in good English ordered them to stop. Knight sprung behind a tree, and leveled his gun at one of them. Crawford ordered him not to fire, and the Doctor reluctantly obeyed. The Indians ran up to Col. Crawford in a friendly manner, shook his hand and asked him how he did. Biggs and Ashley halted, while the men in the rear took to their heels and escaped. Col. Crawford ordered Capt. Biggs to come up and surrender, but the Captain instead of doing so, took aim at an Indian, fired, and then he and Ashley put spurs to their horses, and for the present escaped. They were both overtaken and killed the next day.

"On the morning of the 10th of June, Col. Crawford, Dr. Knight and nine other prisoners, were conducted by seventeen Indians to the old Sandusky town, about thirty-three miles distant. They were all blacked by Pipe, a Delaware chief, who led the captors, and the other nine were marched ahead of Crawford and Knight. Four of the prisoners were tomahawked and scalped on the way at different places, and when the other five arrived at the town, the boys and squaws fell upon them and tomahawked them in a moment."

We now approach the "last scene of all, which ends this strange, eventful history," and we borrow the eloquent description of it by Captain McClung.(g)

"As soon as the Colonel arrived they surrounded him, stripped him naked and compelled him to sit on the ground near a large fire, around which were about thirty warriors, and more than double that number of squaws and boys. They then fell upon him and beat him severely with their fists and sticks. In a few minutes a large stake was fixed in the ground and piles of hickory poles, about twelve feet long, were spread around it. Col. Crawford's hands were then tied behind his back; a strong rope was produced, one end of which was fastened to the ligature between his wrists, and the other tied to the bottom of the stake. The rope was long enough to permit him to walk around the stake several times and then return. Fire was then applied to the hickory poles, which lay in piles at the distance of several yards from the stake.

"The Colonel observing these terrible preparations, called to the noted Simon Girty, who sat on horseback at a few yards distance from the fire, and asked if the Indians were going to burn him. Girty very cooly replied in the affirmative. The Colonel heard this with firmness, merely observing that he would try and bear it with fortitude. When the hickory poles had been burnt asunder in the middle, Captain Pipe arose and addressed the crowd in a tone of great energy, and with animated gestures, pointing frequently to the Colonel, who regarded him with an appearance of unruffled composure. As soon as he had finished, a loud whoop burst from the assembled throng, and they all at once rushed upon the unfortunate victim. For several seconds the crowd and confusion were so great that Knight could not see what they were doing; but in a short time they had sufficiently dispersed to give him a view of the Colonel. His ears had been cut off, and the blood was streaming down each side of his face. A terrible scene of torture now commenced. The warriors shot charges of powder into his naked body, commencing with the calves of his legs, and continuing to his neck. The boys snatched the burning hickory

---

(g)See Patterson's "History of the Back-Woods."

poles and applied them to his flesh. As fast as he ran around the stake to avoid one party of tormentors, he was promptly met at every turn by others, with burning poles and red-hot irons and rifles loaded with powder only; so that in a few minutes nearly one hundred charges of powder had been shot into his body, which had become black and blistered in a dreadful degree. The squaws would take up quantities of coals and hot ashes and throw them upon his body, so that in a few minutes he had nothing but fire to walk upon.

"In this extremity of his agony the unhappy Colonel called aloud upon Girty, in tones that rang through Knight's brain with maddening effect—'Girty! Girty! shoot me through the heart! Quick! Quick! Don't refuse me!' 'Don't you see I have no gun, Colonel," replied the monster, bursting into a loud laugh; and then turning to an Indian beside him, he muttered some brutal jest upon the naked and miserable appearance of the prisoner.(h)

"The terrible scene had now lasted more than two hours, and Crawford had become much exhausted. He walked slowly around the stake, spoke in a low tone, and earnestly besought God to look with compassion upon him and to pardon his sins. His nerves had lost much of their sensibility, and he no longer shrank from the fire brands, with which they incessantly touched him. At length he sunk, in a fainting fit, upon his face and lay motionless. Instantly an Indian sprung upon his back, knelt lightly upon one knee, made a circular incision with his knife upon the crown of his head, and, clapping the knife between his teeth, tore off the scalp with both hands. Scarcely had this been done, when a withered hag approached with a board full of burning embers, and poured them upon the crown of his head, now laid bare to the bone. The Colonel groaned deeply, rose and again walked slowly around the stake!—But why continue a description so horrible? Nature at length could endure no more, and at a late hour in the

---

(h)Girty's conduct in this savage scene is placed in a very different light by Mr. McCutchen's statement, appended to our subsequent sketch of Crawford's campaign, in "Revolutionary and Indian wars," which see. A few years before this tragedy, Crawford and Girty were acting in unison in their resistance of Pennsylvania rule, in the Boundary Controversy. It is said that Girty was a frequent guest at Capt. Crawford's hospitable cabin, and aspired to a Captaincy in the Revolutionary war, but was disappointed, and thereupon turned Tory. He had before been made an Indian Chief of the Senecas. Another story is that he blamed Crawford for his failure to receive a command in the American forces. And there is yet another silly tale that he aspired to the hand of one of Crawford's daughters, and was denied.

night he was released by death from the hands of his tormentors."(i)

It is believed that Major Harrison, Major Rosse and Ensign Wm. Crawford, Jr., being officers and known to some of the Indians, met a like fiery end, at other places. What a gorge of infernal revelry did the Crawford family afford to the infuriated savages. Of the five, John, the son, only escaped, to mourn their untimely end with his widowed mother and sister. For awhile the wild grass of the prairie refused to grow upon their unurned ashes; but over their undug graves often since hath "the peaceful harvest smiled."

"Dr. Knight was doomed to be burnt at a Shawnese town about forty miles distant from Sandusky, and was committed to the care of a young Indian to be taken there. The first day they traveled about twenty-five miles and encamped for the night. In the morning, the gnats being very troublesome, the Doctor requested the Indian to untie him that he might help him to make a fire to keep them off. With this request the Indian complied. While the Indian was on his knees and elbows blowing the fire, the Doctor caught up the end of a stick which had been burned in two, with which he struck the Indian on the head, so as to knock him forward into the fire. Rising up instantly, he ran off with great rapidity, howling most piteously. Knight seized the Indian's rifle and pursued him, but drawing back the cock too violently he broke the mainspring, and relinquished the pursuit. The Doctor then took to the woods, and after many perils by land and water, reached Fort McIntosh (Beaver) on the twenty-second day, nearly famished. During his journey he subsisted on young birds, roots and berries." He recruited a little strength and clothing at the fort, and then came home. He owed his life—and we the tale of Crawford's tortures—to the simple credulity of his young Indian bailiff.(j)

(i)The widow of Col. Crawford used to relate in addition to what is here stated, that the Indians stuck his body full of dry, sharp sticks, until he looked like a porcupine, and after he was tied to the stake they first set fire to these sticks, and laughed to see how they blazed and crackled around his naked body.

(j)Dr. John Knight was a man of small size, for that age of stalwart men. He resided in Bullskin township—was a son-in-law of Col. Richard Stevenson and brother-in-law of Presley Carr Lane. He removed to Shelbyville, Ky., with Mr. Lane, whose son John married the Doctor's daughter. The same John Lane was Marshal of Kentucky under President Polk.

COL. JAMES PAULL.

This brave and magnanimous old settler, who was long spared to us as a noble specimen of the men of the heroic age, was born in Frederick, now Berkeley county, Virginia, on the 17th September, 1760. He died on the 9th July, 1841, aged nearly eighty-one years. He was the son of George Paull, who removed with his family into what is now Fayette county, in 1768, and settled in the Gist neighborhood, in what is now Dunbar township, on the land where his son, the subject of this notice, ever afterwards resided, and on part of which his son, Joseph Paull, now resides. He became the owner there of two or three contiguous tracts of land, and of several other tracts elsewhere in the county.

Col. Paull early in life evinced qualities of heart and soul calculated to render him conspicuous; added to which was a physical constitution of the hardiest kind. Throughout his long life, his bravery and patriotism, like his generosity, knew no limits. He loved enterprise and adventure as he loved his friends, and shunned no service or dangers to which they called him. He came to manhood just when such men were needed.

His military services(a) began ere he was eighteen years old. About the first of August, 1778, he was drafted to serve a month's duty in guarding the Continental stores at Fort Burd (Brownsville) —an easy service, which consisted in fishing and swimming all day, and taking turns to stand sentry at night. Robert McGlaughlin, to whom we have elsewhere referred, was his commanding officer.

About the first of May, 1781, (having, in the meantime, gone frequently on occasional brief tours of service to the Washington and Westmoreland frontiers) he, with a commission as First Lieutenant, signed by Thomas Jefferson, Governor of Virginia, was ordered by Col. George Rogers Clarke, to recruit in Westmoreland (or Augusta) county, for the projected campaign of that year against Detroit, then held by the British and Tories. His captain was Benjamin Whaley, father of Captain James Whaley, now of Uniontown, and an officer of distinction in the war of 1812. A company was raised, who, taking boat at Elizabethtown, on the

---

(a) For most of these, down to the end of the Revolution, in 1783, we rely upon Colonel Paull's own statement, when he applied for a pension under the act of June, 1832. His other services we gather from other reliable sources.

Monongahela, floated down to the mouth of Chartiers, where they halted for reenforcements. At Pittsburgh they were joined by Capt. Isaac Craig's artillery. They soon proceeded, with other troops to the falls of the Ohio, now Louisville, from which the expedition known as Clark's Campaign was to start. He was attached to the regiment commanded by Col. Crockett; and among the other officers were Col. Hardin, Col. Morgan and Major Lowder, of Virginia, the last of whom deserted at Blennerhassett's Island. They arrived at the falls in August, and went into garrison. The requisite forces for the expedition having failed to assemble, it was abandoned. And now the trouble was to get home. He returned with about one hundred others, through the wilderness of Kentucky and Virginia, to Morgantown, where the Colonel—Zachariah (or Zachwell) Morgan, resided. His return was a labor of more than two months, amid dangers seen and unseen, and privations innumerable. Paull arrived home in December.

Early in the ensuing April (1782) he was again drafted for a month's frontier duty at the mouth of Turtle Creek (Myers') some nine miles above Pittsburg, which he served as a private, under Captain Joseph Beckett, of the forks of the Yough settlement.

No sooner was this brief and inglorious month of service ended, than, determined to encounter the perils of Indian warfare, he volunteered as a private in Crawford's Campaign of June, 1782— the most prominent incidents and horrors of which are elsewhere detailed in' these sketches. His captain was John Biggs, Lieutenant Edward Stewart, Ensign William Crawford, Jr., nephew of the Colonel—all of whom fell a prey to the tortures or butcheries of the savages. Paull was in the engagement of the 5th of June, on the Sandusky prairie. In the retreat, or flight, he went in a squad with five or six others. They were soon surprised, and all, save Paull, were killed, or made prisoners. At the Mingo encampment, Paull had the misfortune to burn one of his feet severely, and was lame throughout the march and retreat. He lost his horse in attempting to pass the swamp near the battle ground. When surprised in the flight he was very lame, and barefoot. The man at his side, on whom he was leaning for assistance, was shot down. Paull instantly fled from the path into the woods—an Indian after him. He quickly came to a steep, bluff bank of a creek, down which he instinctively leaped, gun in hand. His pursuer declined the leap, and with a yell gave up the pursuit. In the descent he hurt his lame foot badly; but having bound it up with part of the ragged nether extremity of his pantaloons, he wandered on; and by betaking himself to fallen trees and crossing his trail occasionally, he escaped further molestation. For two days, like Doctor Knight, he subsisted on roots, bark, leaves, berries and young birds—very fresh fare, the Colonel used to say, but wholesome. He had saved his gun and some ammunition, but he was afraid to discharge it, lest its report might be heard by the Indians, and then all would be over with him. He was very lame, and had become very weak. Having taken some rest, he rose with the dawn and resumed his wanderings. Being very hungry, and seeing a deer cross his path, he shot it. But he had lost his knife, and the only device he could adopt by which to open and remove part of the skin and get at some of the flesh, was to cut it with his gun flint. This he did, and having got a good piece of the round out, he went on, eating it raw as he traveled. At length he came to the Ohio, near Wheeling.(b) The river was too high and he too feeble to swim it. He therefore constructed a raft, with drift logs and grapevine, launched it, and thus got out of the Indian country. Having landed on the southern shore, he caught an old horse which he found wandering about the river hills, and bestrode him. After a little equestrian recreation, he got into a path which led him to a settler's cabin. Here he was hospitably received and for some days entertained. And after regaining some strength and clothes, the settler kindly sent a boy and horse to help him home.

In 1784 or '85 he commanded a company of scouts or rangers, on a tour to Ryerson's station, on the western frontier of, now Greene county.

In 1790 he served with honor, and in the most dangerous position as a Major of Pennsylvania Militia in Gen. Harmar's Campaign against the Indians at the head of the Maumee, as elsewhere related in a subsequent sketch, but we are unable to give any further particulars of this important service. History and tradition both accord to Major Paull, in this perilous march and series of encounters, the character of a brave and good officer, although most of the troops belonging to his command have been sadly traduced.

With Harman's Campaign he, we believe, ended his soldiering, except that in after life he was elected colonel of a regiment on

---

(b)It is related that Paull struck the Ohio opposite Wheeling Island early in the morning, in a fog so dense as to prevent his seeing the Island. He discovered which way the current ran, and wandered up the river to the mouth of Short creek, where he made his raft and crossed.

the peace establishment. Having married, he settled down to the pursuits of domestic and agricultural life, in which he was eminently successful. He raised a large and highly respected family—seven sons, James, George,(c) John, Archibald, Thomas, William and Joseph, and one daughter, Martha, wife of William Walker. He had some concern in the iron manufacture, and was occasionally, in middle life a down-the-river trader. But he was a lover of home, its quiet cares and enjoyments. He was never ambitious of office. The only one he ever held, or sought, in civil life, was that of Sheriff of the county, which he filled from 1793 to '96, with credit and success. This gave him something to do with the "Whiskey Boys," and he had to hang John McFall for the murder of John Chadwick.(d)

We have said that Col. Paull was generous and devoted to his friends. Of this we could give many illustrations. One must suffice. Having become heavily bound for a friend, he had to sell some cherished land in the West to enable him to pay the liability. At length it was paid. Thereupon a more cautions friend remarked to him, "I suppose, Colonel, you are now cured of endorsing." "No," he replied quickly, "I will endorse for my friends when I please."

Such was Col. James Paull, a man of heroic and generous impulses, of integrity and truth; which he evinced by many deeds and few words.

(b)George Paull was Colonel of the 27th Regiment U. S. Infantry (Ohio troops) in the war of 1812, and served bravely under Gen. Harrison in the Northwest army.

(d)This was the only case of capital punishment ever executed in Fayette county. The killing was on the 10th November, 1794. Chadwick kept the old White Horse tavern where James Hughes now lives, about a mile northeast of Brownfieldtown. McFall was drunk, and his first purpose was to kill one Martin Myers, a constable, but Chadwick interfering, and having shut the door on him, he fell on him and beat him with a club, from which he died two days afterwards. McFall, after conviction, broke jail and escaped, and was on his way to Lancaster to get a pardon, when he was apprehended at Hagerstown. He was hung on land of Gen. Douglass, in the woods between the old Zadok Springer mansion and Wm. Crawford's, about a mile north of the court house. The place is yet known as the "gallows field." Col. Paull did not hang him himself, but employed one Edward Bell as executioner—father of the late Edward Bell. See the case reported in Addison's Reports, 255.

COL. GEORGE WILSON.

Our materials for a memoir of this ancient worthy are very scanty, being little more than what appears elsewhere in these sketches. He was a Virginian, from the town or vicinity of Staunton, Augusta county, in which he owned property; also in Romney, Hampshire county. He had evidently been a military officer of the King, in that colony, doubtless in the French war. The proof of this is, that in the inventory of his goods and chattels appraised and filed in our Register's office, are a scarlet coat, breeches and vest, valued at £15, besides an American Revolutionary "Regimental coat," valued at £40, and plush breeches and vest at £15. Another proof is in one of his own letters to Major Luke Collins, copied in part in our "Boundary Controversy," wherein he says—"we had the happiness of joining in sentiment in the Colony of Virginia, and as I may say, even wading through blood in supporting the cause of our country, heart in hand." And in his previous letter to Arthur St. Clair, referred to in the same sketch, he says, "I have in my little time in life taken the oath of allegiance to his Majesty seven times."

He seems to have come into this country as early as 1769, and settled at the Mouth of Georges Creek, becoming the owner of the lands on both sides of it for a considerable distance up that stream, as well as other adjacent lands, including Elk Hills, recently the home of J. W. Nicholson, Esq., now owned by Michael Franks, and several other tracts in this county. It is said he first came into this region at the head of a party to reclaim some white prisoners from the Indians, in which he succeeded; and being pleased with the country about the mouths of Cheat and Georges creek, soon afterwards returned and took up his residence.

Col. Wilson figured conspicuously as an active and influential Pennsylvanian in the Boundary Controversy, as is apparent from our sketch of that important dispute. This is the more remarkable, as he was by nativity, interest and family associations, a Virginian. When Westmoreland county was erected, in 1773, he was appointed by the Penn Assembly one of the trustees for selecting a county seat; and in the same year he was appointed a Justice of the Peace.

When the eighth Pennsylvania Regiment of the Line was formed at Kittanning, in the fall of 1776, he was appointed by Congress, upon the recommendation of the Pennsylvania convention, its

Lieut. Colonel—his son John being one of its Captains. He did not live to distinguish himself in battle; but died in Quibbletown, N. J., near Amboy, early in April, 1777, from pleurisy, brought on by exposure and overmarching, and was buried there. On the 10th of September, 1776, before going into the service, he made his last will, disposing of his estates—lands, lots, negroes, &c., with great precision. He had three sons, John, William George,(a) and Samuel; and six daughters, Agnes Humphreys, Elizabeth Kincade,(b) Jane, Mary Ann, Sarah and Phebe. Jane was thrice married—first to a Mr. Bullitt, then to the father of Hon. Wm. G. Hawkins, formerly State Senator from Greene and Washington, now of Allegheny county; and lastly to Hon. John Minor, long an Associate Judge of Greene county, thereby becoming the mother of L. L. Minor, Esq., of that county, and of Mrs. John Crawford, of Greensboro. To her he gave the land now in Nicholson township, recently owned by John and Samuel Ache. We cannot trace the other descendants of the old Colonel.

COL. ALEXANDER M'CLEAN.

This veteran Surveyor, and Register and Recorder of Fayette county, came into this region of country in 1769, as an Assistant Surveyor to his brothers Archibald and Moses, the regular Deputies for this part of the Province. The opening of the Land Office, on the 4th of April, 1769, for the acquisition of lands in the "New Purchase," gave employment to a great number of surveyors. Being unmarried, he seems, for severals years, to have changed his residence to accommodate his employment. His earliest local habitation in the West was perhaps in Stony Creek Glades, in Somerset, then Cumberland county. In 1772 we find him assessed as a Single Freeman, in Tyrone township, then Bedford county. He was married in 1775, in the Glades, near Stoystown, to Sarah Holmes, and in the Spring of 1776, removed to the vicinity of Uniontown. In

---

(a) Elected Justice of the Peace for Springhill in 1789. He was the founder of New Geneva, by the name of Wilson's Port.

(b) Wife of Samuel Kincade, who settled just at the junction of Cheat and Monongahela, north side, in Springhill. This land, with half the ferry rights, was devised to him by his father-in-law. This Samuel Kincade narrowly escaped being killed while with a party of Militia, on Ten Mile Creek, when marching to Wheeling in Dunmore's war in 1774. Captain McClure commanded the party, and Kincade was Lieutenant. They were attacked by four Indians of Logan's party, and the Captain killed and Kincade wounded. Gen St. Clair said "it would have been no great matter if he had been killed."

the Spring of 1779 he moved into the town, and there continued to reside until his death, on the 7th of January, 1834, aged a little over eighty-eight years, having been born on the 20th November, 1746.

He was a native of York county, Pennsylvania, being the youngest of seven brothers, of whom Moses and Archibald were perhaps the eldest, and who, besides being the first Deputy Surveyors in this part of Pennsylvania, were men of distinction—especially the latter, in old mother York and her daughter Adams. James and Samuel M'Clean, who settled very early near the base of Laurel Hill, in N. Union township, were also brothers. James was the only one of the seven who was not a surveyor. Archibald, Moses, Samuel and Alexander were with Mason and Dixon in running the celebrated line between Pennsylvania and Maryland and Virginia, in 1766-'7, Alexander being then only about twenty-two years old. Archibald had had a good deal to do in running the lines between Maryland and Delaware, and between Maryland and Pennsylvania, before Mason and Dixon were employed, and Alexander accompanied him. Such were the schools and instructors he enjoyed in acquiring the art of surveying.

Although Col. M'Clean was, with other Assistants, busily employed in executing orders of survey in this part of the Province, from the summer of 1769, yet the earliest survey executed by him as a deputy, that we can find, within the limits of Fayette county, was in 1772. Prior to that year the returns are all signed by Archibald and Moses; who also, within that year and afterwards, signed returns as deputies. It is probable, however, that Alexander was a regular Deputy Surveyor at an earlier period, but operated in what is now the Somerset county part of the New Purchase. We find him making surveys at Turkey Foot in 1769.

In 1776 he was one of the Westmoreland members of the Assembly—the first after the revolt. In September of that year he was one of the Justices of the Peace for that county, appointed by the Revolutionary State Convention. He was also a member of the Assembly for the year 1782-'3; the same by which Fayette county was erected. Indeed he was elected for its accomplishment; an effort at the previous session having failed by reason of the opposition from the Northern parts of Westmoreland. The reason assigned was if the new county was erected, the old one could not support itself—the common argument in such cases. On this occasion it was attempted to be sustained by the fact that the territory proposed to be dissevered was the only part of the county exempt

COL. ALEXANDER M'CLEAN.   133

from Indian depredations—to which fact, rendered more impressive by the burning of Hannastown, in July, 1782, Fayette county owes its early erection. Long prior to this—in 1778, Col. M'Clean had urged Henry Beeson to lay out Uniontown, with a view to a county seat; which he did, and the Colonel surveyed it for him, providing a lot for the county buildings at the elbow, adjacent to which, on the east, he bought a lot, to which he removed in 1779, and where he died.

The State Land Office being in effect closed from 1776 to 1784, no Deputy Surveyors were needed. For a while, therefore, his occupation was gone. In the meantime he took to "soldiering," then the great business of the country. We believe the Colonel was never a soldier of the Line, but served occasionally in the frontier ranges. He was also in M'Intoch's campaign of 1780; but in what capacity, or how he got there, we are at some loss to know. Pennsylvania sent no men into that campaign—Virginia did; though many of them were from this, the disputed territory. Of such were those we have named in our notice of that expedition. (a) When one of them, Col. Robert Beall, of Bullskin, a zealous Virginia partizan, was appointed County Lieutenant, in 1784, great indignation was evinced by the old Pennsylvania adherents. Col. M'Clean was called upon to write to the Sup. Ex. Council on the subject. In writing to President Dickinson, on the 16th of July, 1784, he says: "With those very people who are said to have had so little share in the burthen of the war, I have shared the fatigues of the most difficult campaign that has been carried on in this country, and was a witness to both their sufferings and fortitude. Many of them have been in the Continental service, and Col. Beall in particular, during a great part of the war." This, we believe, refers to M'Intosh's campaign. If so, then the Colonel served under the Virginia standard; although in the Boundary Controversy he was a decided Pennsylvanian. Of this there is a clear proof in his correspondence concerning running the Temporary Boundary and the New State project, some of which will be found in our sketch of those events.(b) In going with "Virginians" into McIntosh's campaign, he went as a soldier and patriot, not as a partizan.(c)

(a)See Chap. X.—"Revolutionary and Indian Wars."
(b)See Chap. IX.—"Boundary Controversy."
(c)In July, 1781, he wrote a letter to his brother Archibald, of York, informing him of the high-handed measures adopted by Gen. Clark and the Virginia

In 1782, Col. M'Clean was appointed a Sub-Lieutenant for the county of Westmoreland, in the room of Col. Edward Cook, promoted to be Lieutenant upon the death of Col. Lochry. To this appointment he owed his rank of Colonel.

In 1781, Col. M'Clean was appointed by the Sup. Ex. Council of Pennsylvania as the artist, in conjunction with a similar appointee from Virginia, to run the temporary boundary lines which had been agreed upon in 1779. A vexatious succession of disappointments and difficulties delayed the execution of this task until the winter of 1782-'3, when he performed it, in connection with Joseph Neville, of Virginia, an eminent surveyor, who was afterwards a member of Congress from that State. They run out our Southern boundary from where Mason and Dixon stopped, at the Indian war path' on Dunkard creek, in Greene, and the Western line, to the Ohio river.(d) Although the Council had at first offered only twenty shillings per day, "and found," yet they afterwards resolved that "taking into consideration the trouble Mr. M'Clean has had in running said line, and the accuracy (?) with which the same hath been done, he be allowed thirty-five shillings per day:"—being $4.67 —a daily pay to which he ever afterwards adhered in his charges as a surveyor.

---

party, in reference to recruits for his projected campaign of that year. The letter was sent to the Sup. Ex. Council, and we gather its import from his brother's account of it; who, in writing to the Council from Yorktown, August 13th, 1781, says: "I have received no letter from him since, but hath certain accounts from an inhabitant in those parts, who left my brother's house about ten days ago, that Alexander is drafted to go with Colonel Clark, and that he was actually gone to Fort Pitt on the day before the person left home who informed me. * * I am well assured he must have went with great reluctance on any Virginia expedition." This turned out to be a mistake—at least Alexander did not go, for we find him in Uniontown on the 13th September, ready to go out to survey the Temporary line with Virginia.

(d) These surveyors, it seems, run the Southern line a little too far, perhaps a mile or more. This was no fault of theirs; for they were instructed to begin where Mason and Dixon stopped in 1767, "at the crossing of Dunkard creek," and extend the line twenty-three miles. The true distance required to accomplish the five degrees of longitude from the Delaware river, (266 miles, 24 chains, 80 links,) was a little less than twenty-two miles. So the astronomical surveyors of 1784 determined. It is said also that Messrs. M'Clean and Neville deflected their due North line a little too much to the East, at its Southern end; for they seem to have struck the Ohio at the right place. Among the consequences of the error first stated was, that some Philadelphia gentlemen—the Cooks, and perhaps others, who wished to appropriate some western lands between the dates of the two runnings, had their warrants laid, in now Greene county, abutting upon the temporary line; and when the line came to be finally run in 1784, parts of their surveys were excinded and thrown into Virginia, without any title to rest upon. We think Pennsylvania should have refunded them the cost—which perhaps they would rather have yet than the lands.

Upon the erection of Fayette county in September, 1783, Col. M'Clain sought the appointment of Prothonotary and Clerk of the Courts. Gen. Douglass was the successful applicant. The Colonel was, however, on the 31st of October, 1783, appointed by the Council to be Presiding Justice of the Fayette Court of Common Pleas and Orphans' Court. In that capacity he presided in those Courts at their first sittings in December, 1783, and until April, 1789, when Col. Cook succeeded him for a brief period. He was also on the 6th of December, 1783, appointed to the offices of Register and Recorder of the county of Fayette—offices which he filled uninterruptedly until his death, in 1834, amid all the political vicissitudes of that long period. He was an expert and elegant pensman, and could crowd more words, distinctly written into a line, than most modern writers will put in three.

In March, 1784, he was one of three Justices of the Peace, elected in February, commissioned for Union township,(e) to serve for seven years, under the old Constitution of 1776. He does not appear ever to have done much business in that office, beyond that of presiding in the Courts when at home. He had too many offices.

When the Land Office was re-opened in 1784, under the Commonwealth, there was a perfect avalanche of warrants to be executed in this country. Col. M'Clean was thereupon appointed Deputy Surveyor for a district embracing all of Fayette county, the township of Rostraver in Westmoreland, which then included what, after 1788, became Elizabeth in Allegheny, and the townships of Turkey-foot, Milford, and that part of Quemahoning lying southward of the great road to Fort Pitt, in Bedford county, afterwards Somerset. His commission was renewed for the same district on the 12th of January, 1790. How long he continued to serve so large a territory we do not know. It was, however, contracted to Fayette county alone, for which he held the appointment until 1825, when he declined its renewal. He had numerous assistants, among them Levi Stephens and William Hart. He, also, in the earlier years of his service, executed numerous surveys beyond his district limits, in what are now Allegheny, Greene, Washington and Westmoreland counties.

Besides his official duties at home, he performed numerous extra

---

(e) See postscript of February 6th to Gen. Douglass' letter of February 2, 1784, appended to memoir of him, postea;—and "Outlines of Civil and Political History"—Chapter XVI.

duties as surveyor, abroad. In 1773, he was one of the commissioners, appointed by the act erecting Westmoreland, to run the line which separated it from Bedford. He performed the same office for Fayette in 1784, after its severance from Westmoreland, and, in conjunction with Gabriel Blakeney and John Baddolet, for Greene in 1796, when it was dismembered from Washington.

After the purchase from the Indians of Northwestern Pennsylvania, by the second treaty of Fort Stanwix, he was, in 1783, appointed to survey District No. 1 of the Depreciation lands, north and west of the Allegheny and Ohio rivers, on our Western boundary. The fulfillment of this appointment required him to determine where that boundary was; and from his instructions, now before us, dated in August 1784, we infer that, somehow, he had in the previous winter, ascertained that line for some distance north of the Ohio. The district was a parallelogram of twelve miles wide between the Ohio river and the latitude of the mouth of Mogulbuctetim (Redbank). He was at the same time appointed to survey the reserved tracts of 3000 acres each, opposite Pittsburgh, and at the mouth of Big Beaver, which he did in this and the next year.

In the Spring of 1786, Col. M'Clean, in connection with Col. Andrew Porter,(f) were appointed by Pennsylvania, to run, by astronomical observations, &c., and mark, the Western boundary of the State, from the Ohio to Lake Erie. They began in June, and, it seems, some fifty miles north of the Ohio, near where the line strikes the Shenango—near Sharon, and finished the work on the 4th of October. It is probable, however, that they afterwards retraced and marked by a "vista" and stones, the Southern part of the line to the Ohio: for Col. M'Clean writes from Uniontown, October 10th, 1784, that "having visited my family after my return from Lake Erie, I now proceed to finish the line of division between the certificate (Depreciation) and donation lands, and lay out the residue of the lots in District No. 1;" meaning, we presume, those abutting on the Western boundary, which he could not do until it was authoritatively fixed.

While the State was pursuing the project of making a "good wagon road" from Shippensburg to Fort Pitt, Col. M'Clean was, in November, 1789, appointed one of the commissioners to make

---

(f) Father of Ex-Governor David R. Porter, who had been commissary to the Boundary Commissioners in 1784, and who afterwards assisted in running our Northern Boundary with New York.

the location from Bedford to Pittsburg. He began it at Bedford, in December, and, as the other two commisioners failed to attend, he went through it himself.(g)

Besides all these, Col. M'Clean, in middle life, executed numerous other special official duties of smaller moment, but requiring skill and fidelity. He was also, in 1783, together with the Rev. James Sutton, appointed a trustee of Dickinson College, Carlisle, by the Act of Assembly which founded that venerable institution— an office which he for a while filled more **dejure** than **de facto**.

Col. M'Clean was a quiet, unobtrusive man, devoted to the duties of his offices, and caring for little else than to discharge them with diligence, accuracy and fidelity. He held office longer—from 1772 to 1834—than any other man who has ever resided in Western Pennsylvania; and it is not probable that in this respect he will ever have a successor, so unyielding is the rotatory tendency of modern "progress." As Register, Recorder and Surveyor, for more than half a century, he had been conversant with all the estates, titles and land of the county, with all their vacancies, defects and modes of settlement; yet with all these opportunities of acquiring wealth, he died in comparative poverty—a sad monument to his integrity. He wrote more deeds and wills at seven and sixpence each, ($1) and dispensed more gratuitous council in ordinary legal affairs, than, at reasonable fees, would enrich a modern scrivener or counselor.

He left a numerous family of sons and daughters, most of whom, with their descendants, are now dispersed in the Western States. A few yet remain in Uniontown and vicinity. The late Thomas Hadden, Esq., long a favorite attorney and justice of Uniontown, was a son-in-law.

(g)For the benefit of our geometrical readers we annex the method adopted by the Colonel of determining the direct course from Bedford to Pittsburgh:— "In order to gain the true situation of this place (Bedford) I went to the 158th mile post, standing about 10 perches west of the road from Bedford to Fort Cumberland; from thence by a series of courses, traversed the valley of Cumberland to this place, and find it to be 19 miles 290 perches north of Mason & Dixon's Line, and 10 miles 86 perches east of the above mile post. And my memory aiding me in the situation of Pittsburgh, I proceeded to calculation to find a course to Pittsburgh; and estimate it to stand 25,685 perches west, and 9,830 perches north of this place, being north 69 deg. 27 min. west, 27,432 perches equal to 85 miles, 232 perches; which course will, I think, lead me at least into the neighborhood of Pittsburgh."

JOHN SMILIE.

Our labors would be unpardonably incomplete without a memoir, meager though it be, of this ancient political favorite of the people of Fayette, to whom they steadfastly and almost uninterruptedly adhered, from even before their separate county existence to his death—a period of nearly thirty years.

Mr. Smilie was a native of Ireland, and came to America when a young man, shortly before the outbreak of the Revolution, but in what year we cannot ascertain. He settled in Lancaster county, Pa., and at once espoused the cause of American liberty. He rapidly acquired the confidence of his co-patriots, and soon became a leader in the resistance which they resolved and executed against the tyrannies of the King and Parliament.

Being one of the Committee of Safety of Lancaster county, we find him, in June, 1776, a member of the Provincial Conference of County Committees of Pennsylvania at Philadelphia, which declared formally the sundering of the ties which hitherto bound the colony to the parent power, by resolving "to form a new Government for this Province, upon the authority of the people only." This conference called and provided for the Convention which formed our first State Constitution—that of 1776.

In 1778, and again in 1779, he was elected one of the Representatives of Lancaster county in the Assembly, of which he was an active and useful member.

Having married Miss Janet Porter, a daughter, we believe, of Col. Thomas Porter, a distinguished citizen of Lancaster county, he was induced, in 1780, to seek a home in the West for his rising family. In that, or the subsequent year, he removed to Fayette, then Westmoreland county; and after looking round for a while, eventually bought an improvement from old Joseph Huston, on the north side of the Yough river, about five miles below Connellsville, where he settled and where he henceforth resided until his death. He perfected his title to the tract—about 400 acres, in 1786. It was held by the family until recently, and is now owned by Stewart Strickler, George Dawson, and others. The Pittsburgh and Connellsville Rail Road passes through it.

Mr. Smilie's energies and good sense soon gave him prominence in his new abode. In the fall election of 1783, he was chosen, along with the celebrated William Findley, to represent Westmoreland in the Council of Censors—an anomalous revisory body provided for by the Constitution of 1776. It was to consist of two members from each city and county, to be chosen in 1783, and every seventh year thereafter, and to preserve its existence for one year if necessary. It was a kind of Grand Jury for the State. Its duties were to inquire and present—whether the Constitution had been kept inviolate; whether all officers did their duty and no more; whether taxes were justly laid, collected and expended. It could pass censures, order impeachments and advise the repeal of laws; and, by a vote of two-thirds, call a convention to alter the Constitution, to meet two years thereafter. The first Council—the only one ever chosen, sat in Philadelphia from November, 1783, to January 21st, 1784 and again from June 1st to September 25th, 1784. They were rather discordant, and fruitless of any other good than affording convincing proofs to the people of the defectiveness of that old and hastily framed Constitution. Indeed, to do this was one of the principal purposes for which the Council was provided; but they accomplished it in a very different manner from what was originally intended.

At the first session of the Council, the friends of change, or reform, were in the ascendency, but in the summer session of 1784, by the accession of Judge George Bryan, of Philadelphia, the reputed father of the Constitution of '76, and other new or substituted members, the conservative party prevailed. Mr. Smilie acted uniformly with the latter, opposing most pertinaciously the proposed amendments of the Constitution. By that old instrument, the Legislative power was vested exclusively in one body—the Assembly, without check or veto. The Executive power reposed in a Supreme Executive Council of one member from each county; and the judicial tenure, from the Chief Justice of the Supreme Court down to Justices of the Peace, was for terms of seven years—the Judges being chosen by the Assembly, and the Justices by the freeholders of the townships—all commissioned by the Ex. Council. The powers of these separate branches of the Government were illy defined, and confusedly interlocked. It was proposed to make a radical change—to add to another branch to the Legislature, denominated a Legislative Council, similar to the Senate—to abolish the Sup. Ex. Council, and vest the Executive power in a Governor; and to make the judicial tenure during good behavior. Mr. Smilie opposed all these changes, uniting with the minority at the first session in denouncing the Governor and Senate feature because "it tended to introduce among the citizens new and aristocratic ranks, with a chief magistrate at their head, vested with powers which exceed those which fall to the ordinary lot of kings." In this he acted with his colleague, Mr. Findley, and with Messrs. Edgar and M'Dowell of Washington, and others of the then Democratic, or weak government opinions, and in opposition to the views of Fred. Aug. Muhlenburg, Generals Wayne and St. Clair, and others, members of the Council. In these respects, however, Mr. Smilie's opinions underwent a thorough change in a few years; for, in the convention of 1789, which framed the State Constitution of 1790, he cooperated decidedly with the dominant party in favor of a Governor, with the veto power as it now is, two legislative branches, and a judicial tenure during life, or good behavior, although in the last he stood opposed to his distinguished colleague, Albert Gallatin, with whom he generally acted.

In 1784, Mr. Smilie became the first elected member of Assembly from Fayette. He was re-elected in 1785.

In 1786 he was elected for the term of three years, the second Fayette member of the Supreme Executive Council—John Wood, of Uniontown, having been chosen in 1784 for two years, and Isaac Meason, the elder, having been, in 1783, elected for three years from Westmoreland and Fayette combined, though actually dissevered at the time of the election.

Mr. Smilie's career in these State bodies,(a) although not marked

---

(a) We notice one movement of Mr. Smilie, in the Supreme Executive Council, to which we confess our dislike. General St. Clair, after having been the champion of Pennsylvania in the contest for the dominion of her Western territory, against Virginia; and after having, with acknowledged honor, skill and bravery, borne the rank and perils of Major General through almost the whole of the Revolutionary war, thereby entitling himself, if not to the friendly regard, at least to the gratitude and liberality of every true Pennsylvanian, had become so poor as to be obliged to earn the sustenance of himself and family, in 1786-'7, by the labors of a licensed Auctioneer in the city of Philadelphia, then by no means the lucrative business that it has since become. He was at the same time a member, elected by the Assembly of Pennsylvania, of the Confederation Congress, of which he was, in February, '87, elected President. The unkind movement of Mr. Smilie is thus recorded in the Minutes of the Supreme Ex. Council, April 13th, 1787:—"Motion by Mr. Smilie—'That Arthur St. Clair, Esq., be removed from his present office of Auctioneer for the city of Philadelphia, and that Council proceed to the appointment of a person in his stead.' A postponement of this motion (generally) was moved by Mr. Muhlenburg and negatived. Mr. Redick, (of Washington Co.) then moved the postponement of it for the purpose of taking up the following, viz: 'Whereas the Hon. Arthur St. Clair, Auctioneer for the city of Philadelphia, hath lately been advanced to a high station by the United States, in Congress assembled, and as it is the opinion of this Board that his office of Auctioneer is incompatible with his present dignified station, therefore, Resolved: That the said Arthur St. Clair be no longer continued in said office; and that an Auctioneer be appointed to fill the vacancy." This motion prevailed, and he was removed. The "incompatible, dignified station" could be

by any brilliant prominence, was characterized by great diligence, integrity and usefulness, and by unabated devotedness to the wants, private and public, of his constituents. These were the traits of character which gave him such a strong and enduring hold upon their confidence and suffrages.

In 1789, Mr. Smilie was, with Albert Gallatin, chosen to represent Fayette in the State Convention which framed the Constitution of 1790. This body sat at Philadelphia, from November 24th 1789, to February 26th, 1790, and again, from August 9th to September 2d, 1790. It was a very grave and able body, having in it the embodiment of the learning and wisdom, lay and legal, of the Commonwealth. Among its members were Judge Wilson and William Lewis, Esq., of Philadelphia—the afterwards Governors Mifflin, M'Kean, Snyder and Heister, and Judge Charles Smith. Judge Addison, James Ross, John Hoge and David Redick were the Washington county members. Westmoreland was represented by William Findley and William Todd. Allegheny sent General John Gibson. Thomas Mifflin was President of the Convention, and William Findley was chairman of the committee which reported the original draft of the new Constitution, associated therein with Judges Wilson, Addison and Smith, and with Messrs. James Ross, William Lewis, and others. Who prepared the draft is unrevealed.

Although the call of this Convention had been long resisted in the Council of Censors and in the Assembly, and was finally

---

nothing else than the Presidency of Congress, of which he had been for nearly two years a member; for he was not appointed Governor of the North-west Territory until the succeeding October. Mr. Redick's preamble was a friendly act, to give a plausible cloaking to a "forgeone conclusion;" but the incompatibility was neither constitutional, legal, or perceptible. To how many ungenerous cruelties was that brave old soldier subjected during his long and eventful life! The only apology for this one was that the General was in arrears to the State in the payment of his auction duties. But the Treasury neither lost, nor was in danger of losing, anything. Mr. Smilie seems to have allowed his antagonism to the politics of Gen. St. Clair (who was a decided Washingtonian Federalist) to interfere with his habitude of justness and liberality. For when, in 1811, the General, in the extremity of want, asked Congress to remunerate him for monies advanced, while in the Revolutionary service, Mr. Smilie resisted it, although his friend Findley, of Westmoreland, nobly advocated it. We think it would have been more commendable in Mr. Smilie to have done likewise, and to have said, as did Gen. Ogle, of the Somerset district, in 1817, when the same subject was before Congress,—"As to the case of the aged St. Clair, Mr. Ogle said, that was a subject which ought not to be mentioned in this house in the face of day—the treatment of that man ought to be spoken of here only in the night! For his part, if there was a statute as strong as brass, or as solid as the pillars of the Capitol, he would blow it to powder to do justice to a soldier of the Revolution."

opposed in the latter body by a large minority, among whom were our then county members, John Gilchrist and Theophilus Phillips, yet in the Convention, on all the leading features of change, already indicated, the vote was nearly unanimous, on some of them entirely so. The vote on the change of judicial tenure from terms of seven years, &c., to during good behavior, was fifty-six to eight; for two Legislative branches, fifty-six to five; for a Governor, unanimous; and for the veto power, sixty to four. The Constitution finally passed the Convention with but one dissenting voice—George Roberts, of Philadelphia. It stood the tests and trials of nearly half a century; and it is yet to be determined whether modern innovations upon some of its leading provisions are really improvements.

The "Debates" of this Convention are not reported. But its journal shows that Mr. Smilie acted with the majority on all important questions, generally coinciding with his colleague, though occasionally, as on the judicial tenure, differing with him. His radical change of views since he was in the Council of Censors, in 1783, has been already noticed. We regard his course in this particular, not as evincing a weakness, or a wish to surrender his judgment to the popular current, but as a manifestation of candor and good sense. The defects of the Constitution of '76, which had worked well enough during the simplicity and harmony of the Revolutionary era, became very palpable after 1783, amid the growths of selfish interests and political partizanry. Mr. Smilie, as well as other sages, saw these defects becoming more and more striking and dangerous, and hence most commendably relaxed his former equally commendable adherence to the maxim that "governments, long established, should not be changed for light and transient causes."

In 1790, Mr. Smilie and John Hoge, of Washington, were elected the first State Senators from the District composed of Fayette and Washington counties. The term for which he was elected was four years; but having, in 1792, been elected to the third Congress of the United States, which was to meet in December, 1793, he resigned the last year of the Senatorial term, and the late Judge James Finley was elected in his stead.

In 1792, Mr. Smilie was one of a general ticket for thirteen members elected, from Pennsylvania, for the third Congress, under the new Federal Constitution of 1789;—Thomas Scott, of Washington, having been our member, on a general ticket for eight members elected to the first Congress, and William Findley, of

JOHN SMILIE.

Westmoreland, our member, elected in 1791, to the second Congress, for the District composed of Fayette and Westmoreland. For the fourth and fifth Congresses, elected in 1794 and '96, Mr. Smilie gave way to his friend Findley, who represented the same District. (b) In 1798 and 1800 Mr. Findley reciprocated the friendly "non-intervention," and Mr. Smilie resumed the representation of the District. In 1801 Fayette and Greene were made the 9th District, from which Mr. Smilie was successively returned in 1802-'4-'6-'8-'10-'12. He died at the city of Washington, while attending the second session of the twelfth Congress, on the 29th December, 1812, and was, on the 31st, interred, with the customary honors, in the Congressional Cemetery, where his remains yet repose, designated by one of the uniform monuments which Congress erects to deceased members, even though their bodies be removed.

There are but few additional memorials of Mr. Smilie's long Congressional career which require notice. Reports of the proceedings and speeches in Congress, during that period, were far from being as copious as they have since become; and very little can be gathered of the sayings and doings of the members from the journals. These exhibit Mr. Smilie as generally acting with the anti-federal, or republican party, of which he was at all times a consistent member and leader. In the sessions of the third Con-

---

(b)Mr. Findley, after the severence of Fayette and Westmoreland in the arrangement of Congressional Districts, continued to represent the Westmoreland District from 1803 to 1817, when he retired. He became the patriarchal member of the House. He died at his residence, near Youngstown, in April, 1821. He was an Irishman, and we believe by occupation, originally, a weaver. He had been a captain of the Pennsylvania Line in the American Revolution, and settled in Westmoreland at an early day. He was a man of vigorous and active intellect, and a good debater. These endowments gave him great prominence in all the deliberative bodies of which he was a member. He was moreover a very decided partizan, of the Republican or Anti-Federal school, and mingled with his political tenets and deportment considerable ultraism and acrimony. But his ability, uprightness and consistency held him firmly in the confidence of his party and friends, who, during his political career, were constantly in the ascendant in his District. His complicity with the "Whiskey Insurrection" induced him, soon after its suppression, to write its history. The book bears the impress of haste and passion; its leading purposes seeming to be to attack Gen. Hamilton and defend himself. Yet the work is valuable as the version of a conspicuous cotemporary and actor.

Most modern compilers of political history and statistics confound him with the William Findlay of Franklin county, who, from 1817 to 1820, was Governor of Pennsylvania, and from 1821 to 1827, a Senator in Congress. They were very different men. Gov. Findlay, we believe, was never a member of the lower House of Congress.

In Garland's Life of John Randolph, Findley is represented to have been habitually intemperate while in Congress. The statement has some support from tradition.

gress—in 1793,'4-'5, the first of which he was a member, party affiliations were repressed by the almost venerated fame and wisdom of President Washington. Towards the close of his Presidency, however, the party antagonisms, which had been gradually growing ever since the formation of the Constitution,—nay, since the close of the Revolution, became fully developed. And perhaps no event contributed more aliment to their growth than the "Whiskey Insurrection" of 1793-'4 in Southwestern Pennsylvania, and the financial policy of Secretary Hamilton, which was, apparently, its immediate provocative.

Mr. Smilie was not in Congress when the Excise laws were passed, nor during the fervors of the "rebellion." His opposition to the policy of those laws is, however, well attested. But he was against unlawful resistance. As a private citizen at home, he took no very prominent part in the troubles of 1792-'3-'4.(c) His friend and compeer, William Findley makes but little mention of him in his history of those events. Indeed he is known to have pursued a conservative and conciliatory course—sympathizing with the resistants, yet doing nothing offensive to the Government, though strongly suspected. Mr. Findley says that great efforts were made by "the Secretary" (Hamilton) to implicate him, as a worthy victim, but unsuccessfully. Doubtless he followed the current of popular opposition, but kept in the middle of the stream, exposing himself neither to submergence by resistance, nor to danger by collision with the headlands and shore bushes. Notwithstanding this, his influences were peaceful and commendable. Indeed, amid the turgid popular phrenzy which then prevailed, it may well be doubted whether a cautious compliance was not the only medium through which its fury could be abated. And although his son Robert, in the thoughtless folly of youth, was a participant—whether willful or constrained is uncertain—in the first attack on B. Wells' house, yet, having been arrested and carried to Philadelphia for trial, he escaped conviction, by the weakness of the evidence against him and by a doubt cast upon his guiltiness by some proof of an alibi—in Kentucky. Doubtless his father's good name and influence were strong ingredients in his impunity.

When Mr. Smilie returned to the second session of the third

(c)The verity of this statement is perhaps not impuned by Mr. Smilie's participation in the Pittsburgh meeting of August 21, 1792, copied in our sketch of the "Whiskey Insurrection," and noticed in our memoir of Albert Gallatin. He was one of its members; but rather an acquiescent than an active one.

Congress, in November, 1794, the recent insurrection and its suppression were, of course, prominent topics of Congressional discussion. In his annual message, or address,(d) to Congress at the opening of the session, President Washington dwelt at considerable length upon the rise, progress and recent suppression of the revolt, which he in very plain terms attributed to the malign influence of "certain self-created societies," In the responsive address which in those times Congress was wont to frame and send to the President, it was proposed to say to him that, "In tracing the origin and progress of the insurrection, we entertain no doubt that certain combinations of men, careless of consequences, &c., have had all the agency you ascribe to them in fomenting this daring outrage, &c., it was moved to amend this clause by inserting between the words certain and combination, the words "self-created societies and." This was carried by the federal or administrative party, 47 to 45. To engraft upon this amendment an "exclusion of the conclusion" that these societies were, as charged by Washington and Hamilton and their friends, diffused all over the country, it was moved further to amend by adding after the words combination of men, the words "in the four western counties of Pennsylvania and parts adjacent." For this amendment the whole anti-federal party voted, including Messrs, Findley and Smilie:—thus fastening the odious combinations upon the backs of their own constituents— Mr. Scott, of Washington, voting the other way. And so determined were they upon an exclusive appropriation of these unlawful "combinations" for the four counties, that in the very next vote they refused even to admit that they were "countenanced by self-created societies elsewhere." We cite this as an early illustration of the excesses and absurdities into which partyism leads its votaries— not more frequently then than now, many of us even sanctioning, if not enacting, vagaries of partizanry which posterity will be as ready to smile at, or condemn, as we are to wonder at those of our precursors in the race of politics.

When Mr. Smilie resumed his membership of Congress in December, 1799, he found the administration or federal party still maintaining a firm, but fast-fading ascendency in the national

---

(d) Presidents Washington and Adams always read their annual messages to Congress, orally and in person—the House going into the Senate Chamber to hear them. Mr. Jefferson discontinued the practice. A reason assigned was that he was not a fluent reader or speaker.

councils. In the next year, with the election of Mr. Jefferson, it passed into a minority, from which it never recovered.

Mr. Smilie's integrity, firmness and long legislative experience began now to give him a prominence in the councils and labors of Congress. In the sesson which began in November, 1800, we find him, for the first time, on any important committee. He was then placed on the Committee of Ways and Means—generally regarded as the leading committee of the House. He kept his position on this committee in the sessions which began in December, 1801 and 1802. He was displaced in 1803,. but resumed his place in October, 1807, and continued to be appointed on that committee during every successive session, until 1812.

In November, 1812, Henry Clay being Speaker of the House, Mr. Smilie was appointed Chairman of the Select Committee on Foreign Relations, being at that critical juncture—the first year of the war with Great Britain—the most important committee in Congress. Besides the tribute to his merit, implied in the well known discernment and zeal for the war possessed by the eminent Speaker who appointed him, he was additionally honored by having, as his associates on the Committee, men of such masterly minds as Calhoun, Grundy, Macon, Nelson, (of Va.) and Desha, (of Ky.,) with whom were Goldsmith, (of Md.,) Harper, (of N. H.,) and Seaver, (of Mass.) It is well known that Mr. Clay had great respect for, and influence with Mr. Smilie, which he manifested by once or twice visiting him at his residence.

In connection. with this elevated position in the "War Committee," we may notice the singular fact that during the preceeding session of Congress, that of 1811-'12, in which the administration of Mr. Madison and its friends were vigorously preparing for the bloody issue which even then seemed inevitable, with either France or England, or both, Mr. Smilie is very frequently—generally indeed, found voting with the New England Federalists, against nearly all the leading war measures which were proposed. This shows, at least, his independence of party rule. However, in the next session—his last—he came in patriotically and zealously to the support and prosecution of the war. Whether this change of front, and his chairmanship had any of the relations of cause and effect in them, is a question not for us to solve. It cannot be supposed that Mr. Clay would assign him to that important station without being well assured of his cordial co-operation in the justice and purposes of the war. Indeed in a speech by Mr. Smilie in the secret sessions of the House, in April, 1812, he fully acknowledges the recentness of his entire accession to the war party:—"The embargo," says Mr. S., "is intended as a war measure. He would assure his colleague that it was so intended by the Executive and the Committee of Foreign Relations. And being now up, he would observe that at the beginning of the session (he might have said also at the last session) he was not so warm for war as many were, but he was for commercial restrictions. He was not for the 25,000 men; (increase of the army) but as the House have determined otherwise, he would now go to war. If we now recede we shall be a reproach among all nations."

It is a well known trait in the history of the early supremacy in Congress of the Republican, or old Democratic party, that they resisted all the efforts of New England and the seaboard to strengthen and extend the Navy. And it was not until, by its brilliant victories in the early part of the war of 1812, it had conquered favor and popularity with the people, that it came to be a cherished child of power and patronage. In the ancient hostility to this glory-covered protector of our coasts and commerce, Mr. Smilie acted with undeviating fidelity to his party policy. Had he lived a year longer, his characteristic candor, and readiness to change upon good and sufficient reasons, would doubtless have brought him to its support.

In May, 1812, Mr. Smilie took a prominent part in the Congressional caucuses by which Mr. Madison was unanimously renominated as the Republican candidate for President, and Elbridge Gerry, (of Mass.,) for Vice President; and was appointed on the Committee of Correspondence and Arrangement to inform them of their nomination, and to secure their election. He did not, however, live to witness their inauguration.

Such is an outline and review of the public life of a man, who if not so gifted as to be great, was so well constituted in temper and intellect as to possess the confidence, if not the control, of the voters of the corner counties for a longer period than has fallen, or perhaps ever will fall, to the lot of any other man. The part cast for him in the drama of life was not that of Wolsey or King Henry, nor yet that of Brutus or Anthony, but more resembled, in the favor which followed fidelity, that of the good Earl of Westmoreland,

"———————— a summer bird,
Which ever in the haunch of winter sings
The lifting up of day."

The private character of Mr. Smilie was most estimable and exemplary. In dress and address he was dignified and decorous, sufficiently familiar to be affable, yet not so much so as to be degrading. He did not seek popularity, by the low arts and plottings to which demagogues of more talent ofttimes resort, but made his approaches to the citadel of public favor and distinction by doing all the duties of a good citizen, and by fearlessly and faithfully representing his constituents in all that he believed to be for their true interests, yet so as therein not to thwart their determined will. In four out of nine times that he was elected to Congress, he had no opponent; and in the other five, the opposition, though respectable, was not formidable.

Mr. Smilie was moreover "the highest style of man, a Christian;" having lived and died in the faith and membership of the Tyrone Presbyterian Church, of which, if not an elder, he was perhaps a founder and a liberal supporter. In this respect his life gave clear evidence that the highway to political honors is not necessarily divergent from "wisdom's path,"—a parallelism much oftener found in the good old times than in these days of railroad routes to popular favor, which must needs traverse low ground,

"——— through many a dark and weary vale,
Rocks, caves, lakes, fens, bogs, dens and shades of death."

Mr. Smilie had one son and two daughters. Robert, the son, died a few years ago, leaving a numerous family of sons and daughters, nearly all of whom have removed to the West. Mary, one of the daughters, was the wife of Joseph Huston, a well known old ironmaster of Fayette. They had but two children, daughters—Jane, wife of Isaiah Marshall, who removed to Iowa, and Sarah, now the wife of George Dawson, Esq. Jane, the other daughter, was the wife of Captain William Craig—their only child is John S. Craig, of N. Union township.

GEN. EPHRAIM DOUGLAS

GEN. EPHRAIM DOUGLASS.

We are at a loss to locate, with certainty, the nativity of this patriarchal officer of Fayette. By some he is made to be a native of Scotland, which his father undoubtedly was—by others, of Maryland, in the vicinity of Hagerstown, and by others of Carlisle, or its adjacents, in Cumberland county, Pennsylvania. The last is, we think, the most probable. All his early associations in business and friends cluster around Carlisle, while we find nothing among his books or papers which point to Maryland, or indicate that he was a foreigner.

His father was named Adam Douglass. He had one brother,(a) Joseph, and one sister, the wife of —— Collins, who left three sons. This is all we know of his family relations. He died on his farm, about two miles north-east of Uniontown, on the 17th July, 1833, in the eighty-fourth year of his age. We believe he never was married, yet he adopted, as his own, the children of one Mary Lyon, and made ample provision for her and them out of his estates. Ephraim, the son, died in Uniontown in April, 1839. Sarah, who was the wife of Daniel Keller, a well known old ironmaster of Fayette, was a daughter. The other daughter was Eliza, wife of Allen King, now, we believe, residents of Clark county, Ohio. These all have a numerous offspring.

Our first traces of the eventful early life of Gen. Douglass begin at Pittsburgh in the Spring of 1769, whither he seems to have come in the preceding year, leaving his father, mother and brother at Carlisle, until 1774, when they seem to have joined him at Pittsburgh. Ephraim was then not over nineteen years old; yet, having a good English education, steady habits and unusual energy, diligence and skill, he appears at once to have enjoyed the confidence and patronage of the fort officers, and of many of the most eminent Indian traders and settlers in and around that old frontier post, among whom we may name William and Richard Butler, Devereaux Smith, Daniel and William Elliott, Alexander Ross, Samuel

---

(a) Joseph Douglass seems to have been a kind of attache of his brother during the latter period of his operations at Pittsburgh, and the early years of his official tenures at Uniontown, chiefly as clerk and partner in a store. He was appointed State Excise Collector in December, 1786, a very unproductive office. About 1790 he removed to Greensburg, where he died in January, 1792, unmarried. He too, had been a Revolutionary soldier. See further as to Joseph's history in 2 Yeates' Reports, 46.

Sample, John Ormsby and George Croghan, the Deputy Indian Agent. Although without any apparent direct connection with the fort, he lived, with others, in a "mess."

For the first two or three years of his residence at Pittsburgh, young Douglass appears to have been engaged in almost every kind of work—clerk, scrivener, carpenter, (his chief business,) cabinet maker, lumberman, blacksmith, gunsmith, stone mason, shop keeper, &c., &c. We could not better illustrate his universal genius and multiform employments than by a few extracts from his books of accounts—but we cannot afford the space. They show him to have been a handicraftsman such as is rarely met with; and are an early display of that remarkable system, neatness and precision which characterized his long official career in Fayette county;—and then so young was he. He surely never could have learned all the arts he practiced—they must have come to him by intuition. He was equally at home from making and glazing sash for Mr. Samuel Sample's bar-room window to making new Billy pins for his fiddle;—was as ready at "a day's writing and drinking" for Mr. Wm. Christy, or copying bills and accounts for Mr. Butler, as in tearing down and rebuilding Mr. Spear's cellar wall,—and was as prompt at cleaning Col. Croghan's **coteau de chase** as at shoeing his horse,(b) or "laying a grubbing hoe" for John Ormsby. He had for sale all sorts of things, from a pint of rum, or a walnut board, to a canoe load of wood, or a bushel of lime. He made axes, jackplanes, keys, mill irons, grain cradles, fish darts and counter drawers; and repaired everything from "the rum store" lock to a gun lock—from a looking glass to a tea table. Nothing came amiss to him that required skill and the use of tools. And were it not for the indubitable evidence that he was doing all this on his own account, we would be led to believe that he was general superintendent of all the work shops in Pittsburgh. And we do believe he was then the only mechanic there, except Peter Roletter, the tailor, and Barney Vertner, the turner.

In 1771 he began to engage in the Indian trade,(c) then, and for

---

(b) He had a journeyman horse-shoer, George Phelps, of whom are these entries:—"George Phelps, Dr: To driving a set of shoes wrong for Col. Croghan, for which he would not pay—3s."—the key to which, is the following: "From the 20th July gave George Phelps a pint of rum a day, as he would not work without it, and I must have the work done."

(c) The General used to tell a somewhat remarkable occurrence that happened to him in one of his early hunting excursions. He was ascending the Allegheny in a canoe, with a companion, when, upon striking the current of French Creek, which was high, his canoe was upset, and guns, powder, peltry

many years before and after, the great business of Pittsburgh. It consisted in selling shirts, leggings, beads, powder, lead, wampum, tomahawks, tobacco, and other unmentionables to the Indians, for peltry of all sorts—bear, beaver, elk, fox, raccoon, cat, deer, &c., &c., rated, not by money, but by bucks—as, "By five deer skins, three bucks." These, when dried, &c., were sent to Philadelphia on pack-horses and sold by the pound, the pack-horse train bringing back goods for the traders. Douglass engaged in this at first on his own account, but from 1772 to 1774 he operated as partner with Devereaux Smith, Esq., famous in the "Boundary controversy." They were extensive dealers, having establishments not only at Pittsburgh, but at Kuskuskia, on Beaver river, near the mouth of the Mahoning, and elsewhere in the Indian country. Gen. James O'Hara was in their employ. The Messrs. Gratz and Thos. Ashton were their factors at Philadelphia. The business become overdone in 1773, and the Indian troubles in 1774, and the Revolution in 1776 put an end to it. Douglass seems to have, however, made money at the business. He took no part in the Boundary war—his aim being to keep on fair terms with, and extract profit from, both parties. He was always too much of a business man to be much of a partizan.

The firm of Smith & Douglass continued in business until 1776, when Richard Butler came into the firm for a short period. But when the West became fully roused to the cause of Independence, and a fort was, in 1776, being built at Kittanning, they established a store there. In September of that year, the 8th Pennsylvania Regiment rendezvoused and was organized at that place. Aeneas Mackay, Colonel; George Wilson, Lieutenant Colonel; Richard Butler, Major, &c.; and Ephraim Douglass, Quarter Master. We have his official book of receipts, and the Company's (of Smith, Butler & Douglass) books of accounts at that post. The Regiment marched to Amboy, New Jersey, in January, 1777, and Quarter

---

and hunters were precipitated into ten feet water. Douglass clung to the canoe, which he took ashore and tied. Then, by diving and feeling about, he recovered his gun and ammunition; but his companion, who failed to regain his, left him and returned home. Douglass, after regaining his peltry, which had floated off, made a fire, and constructed a bark-shelter from the rain, and bivouacked for the night. In the morning he was so stiff as to be unable to move. He remained in this condition for several days, almost without food. He concluded he must die, and getting a piece of bark, he scratched upon it this auto obituary:—"I have lived doubtful, but not dissolute—I die undetermined, but not unresigned—E. Douglass." He, however, soon got better, dried his powder, shot some game for food, and made a successful hunt.

Master Douglass with it—the Company sending the residue of their goods and liquors back to Pittsburgh, in care of Joseph Douglass, who sold for a while and then boxed up the remnants for better times.

Soon after joining the main American army near New York, Major Douglass became an Aid de Camp to Major General Lincoln, of Massaschusetts, and was serving in that capacity with a small body of troops, under the General's command, at Boundbrook, New Jersey, on the Rariton, when, on the 13th of April, 1777, Lord Cornwallis made an ascent upon them from Brunswick, and took sundry prisoners, among whom was the Major. He was carried to New York, then held by the enemy, where he underwent great rigors and privations. How long he was held in captivity we do not know. Gen. Washington wrote to Gen. Lincoln on the 25th of October, 1777, that he would try to get him exchanged for some of the captives of Gen. Burgoyne's army, as soon as his turn came. But the odds, especially in officers, were then greatly against us—the British having five prisoners to our one of theirs. This, and the difficulties as to the treatment of prisoners which about this time arose between the contending armies, no doubt postponed the Major's release for a considerable time longer. He says himself that he did not rejoin the army until November 4, 1780. And it is probable that he had not been long released. During his captivity his health, especially his eyes, suffered severely. And it is said that from sleeping in a North British officer's bed he contracted a certain cutaneous disease, to cure which he resorted to remedies and expedients —mercury and bathing—which well nigh cost him his life. While a prisoner he received from our Commissaries of Prisoners sundry sums of money for subsistence, in all £266, and soon afterwards $2,000 more, continental money.

In August, 1781, we find Major Douglass again at Pittsburgh, recruiting his health, and settling up his old Indian trade business. In the fall of that year, or in the succeeding winter, he undertook a special secret mission for the Government into the Indian country, for which precise purposes we do not know. Its hazardous character may be best inferred from part of a letter to him from his friend General Jas. Irvine, dated Philadelphia, July 10, 1782, wherein he says: "I had heard of your magnanimous enterprise in penetrating alone into the Indian country—that you had been absent and not heard from for some months—that the time fixed for your return was elapsed, and that your friends about Pittsburgh had given you up as lost." He returned in May. From the first of September, 1782, to the last of April, 1783, he served as Intendant of Prisoners at Philadelphia, the duties and emoluments of which we cannot determine, but presume it related to the care of British prisoners of war.

On the first of May, 1783, Congress resolved upon another embassy to the Indians of the North-west, to inform them that peace had been agreed on and hostilities ceased with Great Britain—that the forts within the limits of the United States held by British troops would soon be evacuated—that the United States wished to enter into friendly treaties with them, and that unless they acceded to these friendly offers and ceased their hostilities, Congress would take measures to compel them thereto.

The Secretary of War immediately selected Major Douglass for this delicate and dangerous mission. He set out from Fort Pitt on the 7th of June, with horses and attendants, passing through the hostile wilderness of the North-west to Sandusky, where he was detained several days; thence to Detroit, thence to Niagara, Upper Canada; and thence to Oswego, on Lake Ontario; all of which posts were then held by British Garrisons. In this tour he met with his old Pittsburgh acquaintances, Elliott and M'Kee, now tory employees of the British, and with the celebrated Indian Chiefs, Captains Pipe and Brant. The British commandants would not permit him to make to the Indians a public exposition of the objects of his mission.(d) They, however, as well as the Indians, treated him with great civility and respect. Brant wanted him to visit him at his Mohawk castle, but the British officers forbid.

(d) In a letter from General Douglass, dated at Uniontown, in February, 1784, to the President of Council, he communicates some valuable information about Indian affairs which had come to his knowledge since he left the Canadian country. Its substance is, that Sir John Johnson, the British Indian Agent, had assembled the western Indians at Sandusky, and after a lavish distribution of presents, had told them that, although the King, whom they had served, had made peace with the Colonies and granted them his lands, yet he had not given them the Indians' lands—that the Ohio river was to be the boundary in this quarter, over which they should "not allow the Americans to pass and return in safety;" and that as the war was now ended, "he would, as was usual at the end of a war, take the tomahawk out of their hands, though he would not remove it out of sight, or far from them, but lay it carefully down by their side, that they might have it convenient to use in defense of their rights and property if they were invaded or molested by the Americans." Such incitements as this greatly conduced to keep up the Indian annoyances in the North-west, costing us much blood and treasure during many years, and until Wayne's great victory of 1794.

While at Detroit there was a Grand Council of eleven Indian tribes. They seemed glad to hear of peace and, says the Major in his report, "gave evident marks of satisfaction at seeing me among them, (an old acquaintance.) They carried their civilities so far, that all day, when at home, my lodging was surrounded with crowds, and the streets lined with them to attend my going abroad."(e) He returned in August, and immediately repaired to Princeton, New Jersey, where Congress was sitting, and prepared an extended report of the incidents and results of his mission. For this service, Congress voted him five hundred dollars.

Upon his return from this expedition, he found the Legislature about to erect the new county of Fayette, and, waiting its accomplishment, he applied for and was, on the 6th of October, 1783, ten days after the Act passed, appointed by the Supreme Executive Council, Prothonotary and Clerk of the Courts. His competitors were Dorsey Pentecost, recently Clerk of Yohogania county Courts under the Virginia usurpation, Alexander McClain, and Joseph M'Cleery. He entered at once upon the duties of his new offices, being here at the first Court, held on the fourth Tuesday in December following; offices which he held uninterruptedly until December, 1808, when he resigned.

In 1784 he was appointed County Treasurer, which office he filled until January, 1800. The duties of this office during those fifteen years were exceedingly onerous and responsible. Besides the county levies during all the period, a State tax of greater amount had, yearly until 1790, to be collected and remitted, to meet the State's quotas to support the Federal Government and pay the war debts. For, until the new Federal Constitution of 1789 became effective, Congress assessed certain sums of revenue to be furnished by each State, and the State apportioned the sum among its counties. This had to be paid in gold or silver, or in certain Government certificates. And the great scarcity of money in this country made the burden of its payment very grievous, and its collection exceedingly difficult and unpleasant. Nevertheless Fayette was

---

(e) By long intercourse with the Indians he had learned their language and manners so well as, with the aid of their dress, which he could assume, to make a very good "counterfeit presentment" of a Chief. It was on this, or the former mission, that he undertook in that character to speak in Council. He played the part so well that when he sat down an old Chief rose and anxiously inquired—"What Chief is that who has spoken?—I don't remember to have ever before heard his voice in Council!"

generally prompt to pay her quota.(f) In writing to the State Treasurer, February 6, 1786, Gen. Douglass says: "John Smilie, Esq., will deliver you a sum of money agreeable to the enclosed inventory. And trifling as this sum may appear, it was with great difficulty that we collected so much. How the tax for the present year will be raised, God only knows." And to show as well the amount of our yearly State tax in those days, when our population was only about 8,000, as the kind of funds sent to pay it, we copy the following letter from Gen. Douglass to the State Treasurer, dated

Uniontown, 20th August, 1787.

"Sir:—I have the honor to remit you by Col. Phillips the following orders and bills of credit:

	£.	s.	d.
Col. Andrew Porter's order and receipt thereon for	87	0	0
Your order in favor of Andrew Linn for	17	1	3
Do. " John M'Farland for	33	8	8
Do. " Robert Brownfield for	3	7	1
Amounting to	140	17	0

		£	s.	d.
1	20s. bill	1	0	0
25	10s. "	12	10	0
12	5s. "	3	0	0
1	9d. "	0	0	9
		16	10	9

	£	s.	d.
Will make	157	7	9
Which, with what I sent by J. Smilie, Esq.,	231	19	3
Will amount to half our quota for this year,	£389	7	0

(f)Comptroller General's Office,
September 9, 1786.

"Sir:
The honorable situation in which the county of Fayette is placed by the punctual discharge of her taxes, reflects high credit upon the officers employed in the laying, collecting and paying the same, as well as upon the county at large. May you long continue, and I hope you will long continue in the same laudable situation. Your example will have a good influence upon others, so that you not only do your duty yourselves, but in some degree procure the same to be done by others. The bearer is riding the State for money, but from you we ask none. You have anticipated our demand, and I know will continue to send it down as fast as you receive it.
I am, with respect, Sir,
Your most ob't. very humble serv't.
JOHN NICHOLSON.

"Ephraim Douglass, Esq.
Treasurer Fayette County."

"I trust there will be no difficulty about the order of Col. Porter.(g) His public as well as private character, and the necessities of the Commissioners at the time, I hope will excuse me for advancing the money without your order.

"I have the honor to be, most respectfully,
"Sir, your very obedient servant,
"EPHRAIM DOUGLASS.
"David Rittenhouse, Esq."

Besides the moneys he had to collect and remit as County Treasurer, he had also, as Clerk of the Courts, to collect and remit tavern license fees, fines and forfeitures, and fees on marriage licenses. Concerning the latter, he writes, in January, 1785, that having "ten marriage licenses, their number will not be likely to diminish so long as there is no penalty for marrying before almost any body without a license." He writes again in August that "there are yet nine marriage licenses on hand, and very little demand for them."

We could illustrate these now forgotten difficulties to a much greater extent by letters and extracts from the papers of Gen. Douglass now before us, but having some of another class to copy, we must hasten on.

Gen. Douglass brought out to Uniontown, shortly after he came here, a small stock of goods, the proceeds of some of his peltries, which were packed over the mountains from Shippensburg, at five dollars per hundred weight. He never, we believe, renewed the stock, but soon began investing his surplus funds in town lots and lands.

Besides his other offices, he was, in 1785, appointed to survey part of District No. 3 of Depreciation Lands, north of the Allegheny river, which he seems to have executed chiefly by the aid of one Robert Stevenson. We find, however, among Gen. Douglass' papers a beautiful copy of the map of the lands in his own handwriting. It is of a part of the district chiefly in Allegheny county, being three miles wide and over thirty miles long, embracing two hundred and eighteen tracts. For this service he got £763, of which he paid Mr. Stevenson above half the sum.

General Douglass held also, about 1785, the appointment of Agent for the sale of confiscated estates of Tories in Fayette. We

---

(g)Father of Ex-Governor David R. Porter, who had recently been engaged as a Commissioner to run and mark our Western and Northern boundaries.

GEN. EPHRAIM DOUGLASS. 157

are glad to say that he had but one case, and he a non-resident. That was to sell the lands of Dr. Anthony Yeldall, of Philadelphia, who owned the Mendenhall Dam tract, now owned by William Wood and David Poundstone. The General sold, it we believe, to one James M'Donald. Yeldall was supposed to own another tract on the high hill west of McClellandtown, held in the name of Edward Green, now owned, we believe, by John Wilson, Esq., and Messrs. Parshall and Renshaw, and the Agent sold it to, perhaps, Michael Cock; but Green afterwards recovered it, as really his property and not Yeldall's.

In April, 1793, Governor Mifflin commissioned Douglass to be Brigadier General of the county of Fayette, and tradition yet preserves the memory of his splendid erect appearance on his charger in the field, and the rigid exactness of his commands. He took pride in appearances, and for many years drove the only landau or four wheeled carriage in the county.

Gen. Douglass was a man of high stature and most imposing appearance, remarkably neat and exact in gait and dress, with long queue and powdered hair.(h) He was a peer among the great and high minded judges and attorneys of his day—Addison, Ross, Smith, Brackenridge, Meason, Galbraith, Hadden, Lyon, Kennedy, &c.; enjoying their society and confidence. He had a repulsive sternness and awe-inspiring demeanor which repelled undue familiarity and rendered him unpopular with the masses. His temper was very irritable, and he was subject to impetuous rage. He was conscious of these frailties, and assigned them as a reason why he never married. Yet he was a man of great liberality, generous and kind to the poor, and especially to a friend in need. It is said that in a season when a great scarcity of grain was threatened, he providently bought up large quantities at fair prices, which, when the expected wants of his neighbors came upon them, he sold at cost, or lent to be repaid in kind and quantity after the next harvest. But the most striking proof of his generosity is the following, which we find among his papers. To understand its force the reader must remember that at its date Gen. St. Clair had become old, broken in spirit, and very poor, eking out a subsistence for

---

(h)He was, moreover, when in his prime, a man of great athletic vigor and endurance. It is related of him, that having been taken prisoner by the Indians, in the winter, he enticed his keepers to the river to try their skill with him in skating. After amusing them for a while by letting them excel him, he at length put spurs to his skates and away he went with such rapidity and continuance as to defy pursuit, and thus escaped.

himself and an afflicted family by keeping a poor old log tavern by the way side, on Chestnut Ridge mountain, in Westmoreland:

"Uniontown, 13th February, 1809.
"Received of General Ephraim Douglass, one hundred dollars, which I promise to repay him on demand, or at furthest by the sixth day of June next. Signed,
"AR. ST. CLAIR."

Underneath which, in Gen. Douglass' handwriting, is:—

"Never to be demanded. To save the feelings of an old friend I accepted this receipt, after refusing to take an obligation.
Signed, "E. DOUGLASS."

A nobler monument is this scrap of paper than was ever reared in brass or marble. Who would not rather wear the rank which its inscription gives, than be the possessor of all the titles, with all the cold domains, of the Emperor of all the Russias!

"The rank is but the guinea's stamp,
The man's the gold, for a' that."

We will close this memoir, already perhaps too extended, with some extracts from his early correspondence, copies of which he carefully preserved.

GEN. DOUGLASS' LETTERS.

To John Dickinson, Esq., President of Supreme Executive Council:
"Uniontown, 2d February, 1784.
"Sir:— * * * *
"The courts were opened for this county on the 23d of December last. The gathering of people was pretty numerous; and I was not alone in fearing that we should have had frequent proofs of that turbulence of spirit with which they have been so generally and perhaps too justly stigmatized. But I now feel great satisfaction in doing them the justice to say that they behaved, to a man, with decency and good order. Our Grand Jury was really respectable—equal at least to many I have seen in courts of long standing. Little business was done other than dividing the county into townships, a return of which is under cover.

* * * * "The instructions of Council respecting the opposition to assessment in Menallen township, I laid before the Justices as directed, but they have not yet come to any resolution thereon. Some of them, I find, are of opinion that the reviving it at this

distant time might be attended with more vexatious consequences than the suffering it to be forgotten will probably produce. For this reason, and in consideration of their since peaceable demeanor, I should incline to be of opinion with the others, that for the present, until the authority of the court becomes, by degrees and habitude of obedience, more firmly established in the general acquiescence of the people of the county, and a jail and other objects of popular terror be erected, to impress on their minds an idea of the punishment annexed to a breach of the laws, lenient measures might produce as good effects as the most rigorous ones that justice could adopt, were not the wisdom and directions of Council opposed to this opinion. To these reasons for declining the prosecution of the offenders, if their identity could be made appear, (which I think very doubtful,) might be added others that I am distressed to be obliged to take notice of. The tax not having been assessed till after the division of the county, the authority of the Commissioners of Westmoreland county then became justly questionable; and the total want of Commissioners in this county, to levy a tax of any kind, either for the State or to answer the exigencies of the county; and the consequent inability of the Trustees to perform the duties assigned them by the Legislature, may all be subjects of consideration in this case. For, from an unhappy misconception of the law for dividing Westmoreland, the county of Fayette has not an officer of any kind, except such as were continued, or created by the Act, or by the appointment of Council. Denied the power of a separate election for a member of Council and Representative in Assembly till the general election of the present year, they unfortunately concluded that this inability extended to all the other elective officers of the county, and in consequence of this belief, voted for them in connection with Westmoreland. The remedy of this evil is, I fear, not easily pointed out; but if there be a possible one, it is to be found in the wisdom of Council, to which I now beg leave, as I shall in all other difficulties, to make my humble appeal.(i)

"The Trustees have appointed next Monday to meet on, and begin the partition line between this county and Westmoreland; on this condition, which Col. M'Clean, who is to be the executive person, has generously agreed to, to pay the expense at some future

---

(1)The trouble here referred to occurred in October, 1783, just after Fayette county was erected. It grew to a more desperate resistance in the spring of 1784. See Letters of May 29th and July 11th, 1784, postea, and notes.

time, when it shall be in their power to call upon the Commissioners for the money. Necessity has suggested to us the expedient of building a temporary jail by subscription, which is now on foot.

* * * * *   ☞"February 6th—in continuance.

"Want of an earlier conveyance gives me the opportunity of enclosing to Council the return of an election held there this day for Justices of the Peace for this township; and I trust the importance of the choice of officers to the county will excuse me to that honorable body for offering my remarks on this occasion.

"Col. M'Clean, though not the first on the return, needs no panegyric of mine; he has the honor to be known to Council. James Finley is a man of a good understanding, good character, and well situate to accommodate that part of the township most remote from the town. Henry Beeson is the proprietor of the town, a man of much modesty, good sense and great benevolence of heart; and one whose liberality of property for public uses justly entitles him to particular attention from the county, however far it may be a consideration with Council. Jonathan Rowland is also a good man, with a good share of understanding, and a better English education than either of the two last mentioned, but unfortunately of a profession rather too much opposed to the suppression of vice and immorality—he keeps a tavern. John Gaddis is a man whom I do not personally know—one who has, at a former election in the then township of Menallen, been returned to Council, but never commissioned, for what reason I know not. His popularity is with those who have been most conspicuous in opposition to the laws of this Commonwealth. Moses Sutton is remarkable for nothing but aspiring obscurity, and a great facility at chanting a psalm, or stammering a prayer.(j)

"Duty thus far directs me to give Council an impartial description of the men who are to be the future officers of this county, but both duty and respect forbid my saying more, or presuming to express a wish of my own; for I have no predilection in favor of, or personal prejudice against either of them.

"I have the honor to be, &c.,
"EPHRAIM DOUGLASS."

(j)Father of the late Samuel Sutton, and, we believe, a Baptist preacher. M'Clean, Finley and Gaddis were commissioned.

To John Nicholson, Comptroller General:
"Uniontown, 16th April, 1784.
"Sir:— * * * * *
"And now, Sir, I will, for the last time, trouble you with the mention of an affair which has already created some trouble to us both. My opinion, when founded on principle, I can never sacrifice to any other gentleman, but I am less wedded to my interest. The efforts I have already made to accommodate the dispute between us have convinced me that you are not less tenacious of yours. I have neither leisure, opportunity nor inclination to undergo the drudgery and expense of a tedious lawsuit, whereby this matter might be settled in time; nor am I of that importunacy of disposition to trouble the Legislature, after having once troubled the Supreme Executive power of the State, with an application on this subject; though I should not doubt of a determination in my favor. To avoid therefore both the one and the other, and to satisfy you, I have sent you my certificate, in the confidence that I shall now be allowed to enjoy the satisfaction I shall derive from the recollection of having served and suffered, forfeited my interest and ruined my constitution, without any other reward: for rather than accept of less than I believe myself entitled to, I would wish to have nothing.(k)
"I have the honor to be, &c.
"EPHRAIM DOUGLASS."

To John Armstrong, Jr., Esq., Secretary of State:
"Uniontown, 29th May, 1784.
"Sir:— * * * * *
"There is so seldom a direct conveyance of a letter from this place to Philadelphia, that I expect every communication I can make will be anticipated by some other person; but lest my silence might be attributed to inattention, I will give you, in this official letter, a short sketch of the affairs of this county.
"The County Commissioners are so much counteracted by the rabble of this county, that it appears hardly probable the taxes will ever be collected in the present mode. In the township of Menallen

---

(k)This difficulty related to the adjustment of Gen. Douglass' pay as a Revolutionary officer, while he was a prisoner of war. It was, we believe, finally settled according to his views.

in particular, which includes this place, agreeable to its limits in the duplicate, the terror of undertaking the duty of Collector has determined several to refuse it, under the severe penalty annexed. Two only have accepted, and these have both been robbed by some ruffians unknown, and in the night, of their duplicates.(1) The inhabitants of the other townships have not gone to such lengths, but complain so much of the hardship and the want of money that I fear very little is to be hoped from them.

"On the other hand, the banditti from (m) Bucks county, or some others equally bad, or both, have established themselves in some part of this county not certainly known, but thought to be in the deserted part of Washington county; whence they make frequent incursions into the settlements under cover of the night, terrify the

---

(1) These two were the Collectors for Menallen and Springhill. The tax was that which had been levied by the Westmoreland Commissioners. Who the Menallen Collector was, and what the facts of his case, we have not been able to ascertain. The Springhill Collector was Philip Jenkins. He was robbed at his own house, about nine o'clock at night, on the 2d of June, 1784, of his duplicate, about £25 in money, a pocket bottle, a razor and some soap. He testified to this being done by three men unknown to him, dressed in hunting shirts, with their faces striped, one of them very tall, with a long neck, each armed with a pistol and club. He and family, with some neighbors, among them James Bell, were sitting up with a sick child. Two of the robbers spoke Dutch. They cursed, abused and beat him badly. Their avowed purpose was to prevent tax gathering.

These cases were communicated by the Commissioners of Westmoreland to the Supreme Executive Council of the State, who thereupon, on the 29th June, 1784, issued a proclamation, offering a reward of £50 for the apprehension and convicition of each offender. We believe none of them were ever arrested or prosecuted.

(m) These were the Doanes, Abraham, Levi, Moses, Joseph, and his three sons, Aaron, Joseph and Mahlon, with whom were associated other persons, by the names of Vickers, Paul Woodard, &c., Tories and Refugees in the Revolution. They had robbed the Treasurer and several Collectors and citizens of Bucks county, in 1782, and had fled to the West. They were outlawed by the Legislature, and rewards offered for their apprehension. Two of the Vickers, two or three Doanes, and some others, were arrested, convicted and hung. Two Doanes were committed to Bedford county jail in 1783—Mahlon and Joseph having been caught in Maryland. Their fate is unrevealed.

The "deserted part of Washington county" was the Ten Mile country. 'Tis said these banditti had a den on the Monongahela river, in Luzerne township, between Davidson's lower ferry and Rice's Landing. Several years afterwards, one Myers and Pratt, supposed to be connections of this gang, were convicted of horse stealing in Fayette.

The gang was an extensive one, all over the State and in adjacent parts of Maryland, Virginia, and the North-west. They stole horses, negroes, and other property, and were exceedingly bold and successful, having many accomplices in the country. We will not name the three referred to by Gen. Douglass, as they were never tried. Abraham Doane had been arrested in Washington county and committed. A mob rescued him. He was again, with Thomas Richason and two women, pursued towards Detroit by an armed party, in June, 1784, and the four again committed to the Washington county jail. Abraham and Levi were hung at Philadelphia, in 1788.

defenseless inhabitants, sometimes treat them unmercifully, and rob them of their property, and then retire to their lurking places. What seems to confirm the belief of its being the Doanes, or some of their companions, is drawn from the circumstances attending the detection and confinement of one of the gang at Washington county in the beginning of this spring. After this wretch had been rescued from the guard there, he, with others of his companions, came to the house of the person who was the principal in taking him, robbed him of his horse and other property; and cautioned him against meddling with any of them hereafter; and this, added to the frequency of their robberies in that county, favors the belief of their residence there. This county, however, has also suffered by them, though they came in the character of thieves and not robbers here. And yet nothing has hitherto been attempted to punish them, or bring them to justice; partly, perhaps, because there are not yet a sufficient number provoked by their losses, but principally from the improbability of succeeding in the attempt. For, though they cannot be pointed out with certainty, or prosecuted to conviction, there must be too many in this county who aid and abet them, and who would readily notify them of any preparation making against them. And, from the representation of their number, which is said to have been twenty-eight at the forcing of the jail in Washington, nothing can be undertaken against them, without such preparation as must make it generally known.

* * * * * * * * * *

"I have the honor to be, &c.,
"EPHRAIM DOUGLASS."

To the President of the Supreme Executive Council.
"Uniontown, July 11th, 1784.
"Sir:— * * * * *
"Taking it for certain that Council have been informed of the capture of some of the robbers who have lately pursued the same practices here for which they fled hither, I shall not trouble them with the particulars of that transaction. Every thing in our power has been done to discover their connections in this quarter, without a certainty of having succeeded. Several have been apprehended on suspicion, and three of them, from a greater concurrence of circumstances, have, by the advice of the Attorney for the State, been recognized to the next Court of Oyer and Terminer for this county. The others have been suffered to return home without security,

they being either innocent, or too cautious to admit anything to appear against them, though much suspected by many.

"I can make no other communications of importance enough to merit the attention of Council, unless what relates to the taxes of this county; and even that not with sufficient accuracy. Some small sums have been collected in some of the townships. One of the collectors was robbed of what he had gathered, by the same banditti, it is thought, who committed the other robberies in the country. Some attempts have been made to raise money by the sale of goods taken by the collectors for taxes, but no one would bid for them. Thus the laws are eluded without open opposition.

"I have the honor to be, &c.,
"EPHRAIM DOUGLASS."

To His Excellency, Thomas Mifflin, Governor, &c.
"Uniontown, 24th April, 1791.

"Sir:—A heart susceptible of gratitude, or a mind subject to the impressions of vanity, cannot fail to be greatly delighted with your Excellency's condescending invitation to all your subordinate officers to a candid correspondence with the first gentleman in the State. I feel myself so greatly elated with the prospect, that I shall only restrain myself by the fear of becoming troublesome. I have, however, to lament and pray that your Excellency will admit it in excuse that my local situation is such as absolutely to deny me the frequent communications which duty and inclination would prompt me to make. Placed almost on the southern verge of the State, and at the distance of more than thirty miles from the post road to Pittsburgh.(n) I cannot avail myself of that conveyance. As an evidence of this, it was not until yesterday I was honored with your Excellency's circular letter of the 24th of December last, which, I trust, will remove the imputation I may have incurred of neglecting the injunctions of that letter. Other channels of communication with the city, or interior parts of the State, we can be

---

(n) There was no post-office in Fayette county until after the Whiskey Insurrection, (1794). The "post-road" referred to was from Philadelphia, and from Virginia by way of Bedford, to Pittsburgh; which was established (twice a month each way) in 1786—the contractors, or carriers, taking the postages for their pay. For many years Pittsburgh was the only post-office west of the mountains. We have seen a Pittsburgh Gazette of 1792, containing a list of advertised letters, among which were for men in Kentucky, and in Fayette county. The Gazette was distributed over the west by private carriers. See "Chapter (XV) of Micellanies."

said to have none certain, but the periodical meeting of the legislature. A precarious one, indeed, we have by people occasionaly going to the land office; and these are the only chances of writing from this place. The great road from Fort Cumberland, on the river Potomac to the Monongahela, at Redstone old Fort, passes through the centre of the county and county town. And by this road almost all our little trade is conducted to Hagerstown, Winchester, and Martinsburg, (if not intercepted at Cumberland and Old Town,) in the neighboring states. The consideration of attracting the trade of one of the best cultivated tracts of country westward of the mountains, ought, perhaps, (I say it with diffidence) to have suggested the policy of bringing the State road more to the southward than where it is now laid out. That to Cumberland is bad, almost in the extreme, and had we a good one through Pennsylvania to the back towns, I think there is little doubt of our preferring it. * * * *

"I have the honor to be, &c.,
"EPHRAIM DOUGLASS."

To His Excellency, Governor Mifflin.
"Uniontown, 6th August, 1791.

"Sir:—In obedience to your Excellency's commands, I have filled up the blanks of the schedule as directed, with the names of such persons as, from my own knowledge of their characters, or from the information of the principal gentlemen of the county, I think most likely to fill the office of Justices of the Peace with credit to government and to themselves, and satisfaction to their neighbors. I have placed them in that order in which my judgment places them, with respect to their abilities, without prepossession or prejudice.
* * * *
"The Act for erecting the county of Washington limits that county by the west side of the Monongahela river; and this county is limited 'beginning at Monongahela river where Mason and & Dixon's line crosses the same; thence down the river to the mouth of Speer's run, &c.' Now by these two acts, it would appear that the river still belonged to Westmoreland county, and that neither of the other counties have any jurisdiction on it. Cases may easily be supposed where this might eventually happen to be a very great evil, though no such a case has hitherto come within my knowledge or observation. * * * *

"I have the honor to be, &c.,
"EPHRAIM DOUGLASS."

ALBERT GALLATIN.

Last, but not least, of the ancient worthies who adorn the annals of Fayette, is Albert Gallatin: last to come upon the stage of action, last to leave it. Two centuries of his country's history inherit, in unequal shares, his character and services; Fayette county claims jurisdiction of their distribution. So ample is the inheritance, that, in the narrow limits allowed us here, we can attempt nothing more than a schedule of the most prominent items which compose it, with perhaps an occasional effort to examine and estimate those which come more directly within the scope and purpose of our labors.

Mr. Gallatin was born at Geneva, in the Republic of Switzerland, January 29th, 1761, and was allied, on the part of both his parents, to some of the most worthy families of that renowned country, including that of the celebrated Necker, and his daughter, Madame de Stael. His ancestor, John Gallatin, Secretary to the Duke of Savoy, emigrated to Geneva early in the 16th century; and having embraced the Reformation, was one of the city magistrates when it became an independent Republic.

Becoming an orphan in infancy, he was educated under the maternal care of a most excellent lady, who was a relative and intimate friend of his mother. His patrimony, though not large, was adequate to his thorough education and suitable outfit for the voyage of life. Had it been greater, he might have dissipated his energies upon some tranquil bay, or dashed them against the rocks of folly and vice: had it been less, he might have been forced to hug the shores of obscurity, or strand upon some ignoble island, for lack of canvas to stem the current.

Nor was he less fortunate in the era of his birth, and in the locality of his youthful education. Nowhere in the Old World could he have been so well fitted for the career he was destined to run in the New. The fruits of the Reformation had ripened in the city where its blossoms first bloomed. Geneva had become not more famous for the Institutes of Calvin than for her institutions of learning. At an early age he entered the University of Geneva, and graduated in 1779. His after-life attests the fidelity of his instructors, and his diligence and assiduity as a student. Then and there were acquired and disciplined those characteristic elements of his subsequent eminence—accuracy, thoroughness, reliance upon the power of truth and confidence in his ability to wield it.

Hon. Albert Gallatin

These were his fulcrum and lever, by which he moved others and sustained himself. That they were always rightly used is a question we are not now considering; but that they gave origin and success to all his great efforts as politician, statesman, orator, financier, diplomatist, philosopher, and scholar, is a solution so adequate to account for his eminence in all these departments as to call for no other.

Emerging from the retirement and restraints of study at the impulsive age of eighteen, young Gallatin saw the Old World aghast at the revolt of the American colonies, and at once felt the throb of sympathy which pervaded the enlightened mind of continental Europe. France, whose language he spoke, whose literature and history he knew, and between whose people and his own there was also a community of origin and jealousy of England, had just then come to the timely aid of the trans-Atlantic "rebels." The conjuncture of circumstances was attractive—the prospect of success cheering—the call to youthful heroism loud and charming— the field of prospective wealth and fame rich and expansive. To keep him back, he had within his acceptance the offer of honorable military rank in the service of one of the German sovereigns. This he declined. Unrestrained by any parental control, though against the will of his patroness and relatives, he resolved to seek the shores of struggling liberty, and to peril his fame and fortune, and perhaps his life, in the conflicts and consequences of the contest. To this high resolve he was perhaps stimulated by young Bache, whom his grandfather, Dr. Franklin, had sent to Geneva to enjoy the superior educational facilities of that city, and by others of his comrades and friends. An eminent Frenchman, La Rochefoucald D'Enville, then resident near Geneva, wrote to Dr. Franklin, May 22nd, 1780, asking his "kind attention for two young men whom the love of glory and of liberty draws to America. One of them is named Gallatin. He is nineteen years old, well informed for his age, of an excellent character thus far, with much natural talent. The name of the other is Serre. They have concealed their project from their relatives, and therefore we cannot tell where they will land. It is supposed, however, that they are going to Philadelphia, or to the Continental army." The fugitives landed at Boston, July 14th, 1780, doubtless from a French vessel which had sailed under convoy of the French fleet under Admiral De Ternay, which in that month landed the Count de Rochambeau and an army of 5,500 men at Newport, R. I., to aid us in our then waning efforts for independence.

Soon after his arrival, our young adventurer proceeded to Maine, and resided for some time at Passamaquoddy and at Machias, where he served as a volunteer under Col. John Allen, commander of the fort. He also contributed to the support of the garrison by advances out of his private funds. He seems, however, soon to have discovered that the tented field and "all the current of a heady fight" were not congenial with his temper and habits. And as the war seemed ended by the capture of Cornwallis, in October, 1781, Mr. Gallatin, in the spring of 1782, accepted the post of Instructor in the French language in Harvard University, to which he was chosen through the friendly intervention of the celebrated Dr. Cooper.

In the winter of 1783-'84, Mr. G. was engaged at Richmond, Virginia, in negotiating for payment by that state, of a claim upon it for funds advanced during the Revolution, by a European house. This brought him into contact with the public men of that proud commonwealth, and contributed much to the growth, if not to the germination, of an ambition for political life. During this sojourn in Richmond, he had his lodgings at the house of the widow of a French gentleman, Madame Allegre, with whose daughter, an accomplished lady, he became enamored. The daughter was more charmed with the interesting stranger than was the mother. The latter seriously objected to the marriage, because, whilst she had nothing else to say against him, "he was such a fool!" But while he was pursuing these two very dissimilar negotiations—pecuniary and matrimonial, he had occasion frequently to call upon Patrick Henry, then the governor of the Old Dominion, upon the subject of his mission, when the conversation would sometimes digress to general topics. The impression made upon the Governor by the brilliant and intelligent observations of Mr. G. was so favorable that he pronounced him one of the most extraordinary men he had ever seen, and predicted his future eminence. So differently was he viewed by the mother and the orator. Mr. G. conducted both his suits to successful terminations. The mother yielded, and Mademoiselle Allegre soon afterwards became Mrs. Gallatin.

Mr. Gallatin was advised by Gov. Henry to settle in Western Virginia; and, desirous of making the small residuum of ready money he had saved, go as far as possible, he, during 1784, purchased for a low price a large quantity of wild land in Monongalia county. He formed "one grand project" of settling his new domain with a colony of emigrants from continental Europe, and came out to survey the land, and make requisite preliminary arrangements. In the midst of this labor, the Indian aggressions upon the frontiers of Virginia, and of Pennsylvania west of the Monongahela, became so alarming and fatal to the white inhabitants, that the hopeful colony founder sought a temporary refuge just beyond the lines of danger, in Springhill township, Fayette county, Pennsylvania. The Indian troubles continued, the colony bubble burst, and Mr. G.'s temporary residence became ere long his permanent home. The name of Albert Gallatin first appears upon the assessment rolls of Springhill township, for the year 1787. In May, 1786, he bought from Nicholas Blake his settlement right for the "Friendship Hill" tract, upon which he so long resided. He was naturalized in Virginia, in 1785. It is probable, therefore, that for some two years prior to the fall of 1786, his residence was somewhat migratory, at and between Springhill and Morgantown, Virginia—inclination drawing him to the former, and business to the latter. During his sojourn at Morgantown, or while business continued to call him there, he made the acquaintance, among others, of Francis T. Brooke, Esq., then a young resident attorney of that place, and afterwards an eminent Judge of the Virginia Court of Appeals, between whom and himself a friendly correspondence and regard subsisted during life.

Notwithstanding his foreign manners and language, Mr. G. rose rapidly in the estimation of the primitive people among whom he had cast his lot. His first displays of political ability were by opposing the adoption of the constitution of the United States. In this he acted in concert with a great many Southern leaders of the Republican faith, of whom was his friend Patrick Henry. To other objections, Mr. G. added that of his opposition to the intervention of electors in choosing a President and Vice President. But after its adoption by the States he gave to it a cordial and steady support.

Mr. Gallatin made his debut in political life as a delegate from Fayette, associated with John Smilie, in the Pennsylvania convention which framed the constitution of 1790, to which he was chosen in October, 1789. Although but twenty-nine years of age, he soon acquired in that learned and grave body the rank of one of its best debaters, and defenders of his party, or peculiar opinions. He took ultra Republican—in modern parlance, Democratic grounds, was opposed to the judicial tenure for life, or during good behavior, and was for universal suffrage by all free males over the age of twenty-one, white and colored, limited only by a longer residence than is now required. It is said that the pertinacious advocacy of negro suffrage by him and some others, was the reason why the word white was not prefixed to that of freemen in defining the elective franchise—an omission which, as is well known, gave to free negroes in Pennsylvania for about forty years, in many places, the rights of voters. A current tradition is, that to the weightier reasons which were urged by Mr. G., he playfully added that the word white might operate rather forbiddingly upon men of swarthy visage like himself.

Simultaneously with the organization of the State Government under that Constitution, in December, 1790—for it was not submitted to the people for ratification—Mr. Gallatin was returned, with James (Judge) Finley, to the Assembly from Fayette, to which he was successively elected every year until 1794, except in 1793. In the Legislature he displayed the same readiness in debate which distinguished him in the convention; but his ultraism was somewhat abated. To his high order of talent in this particular—oftentimes the evidence of more show than substance, he superadded the possession of great financial skill, and a capacity for untiring labor and indefatigable research. In all his early legislative labors, he exhibited not only unusual ability and practical capabilities, but great coolness, candor and sincerity. These high qualifications for statesmanship led to his election by the legislature, in the session of 1792-'3, to the Senate of the United States, although a majority of the members were in political opposition to him, and he had himself expressed a doubt of his eligibility. We do not know who, or how many rivals he had. But when we consider that he was a foreigner of but some twelve years residence in America, and of only about half that short period in Pennsylvania, away west on its southern verge, that he was without family, influence, or long cemented political associations, and that he spoke our language with difficulty, we cannot but wonder at so signal a compliment to his character and talents. It must, however, be remembered that at this period there was in the United States, and no where more than in Pennsylvania, a very strong current of popular sympathy with French Republicanism; and the fact that Mr. G. was considered a Frenchman, and confessedly one of superior ability, naturally tended to concentrate upon him the favor so lavishly bestowed upon those who spoke his language, and fraternized in the tenets and partialities of his political school.

Mr. Gallatin took his seat as a Senator in Congress, in December, 1793. The question of his eligibility was at once raised against him, and referred to a committee, who reported adversely. The position taken was that he was constitutionally disqualified, because not nine years a citizen of the United States. Under the old Articles of Confederation between the States or Colonies, no provision existed for the naturalization of foreigners—each State doing that in its own way. They provided, however, that "the free inhabitants of each State shall be entitled to all privileges and immunities of citizens in the several States." The new Federal Constitution of 1789 conferred those privileges only upon citizens of each State, and in the same sense required a Senator to have been nine years a citizen. It was urged in support of his qualification, that having been more than nine years an inhabitant, the substitution of the word citizen should not have a disqualifying retroactive operation. This argument was somewhat unfairly, but effectively met by evidence that Mr. G. had in 1785—not nine years ago, acquired the rights of citizenship under the naturalization laws of Virginia—a resort imposed upon him to enable him to hold lands in that State. The result was that in February, 1794, he was ousted by a strict party vote of fourteen to twelve, and the legislature elected James Ross, of Pittsburgh, in his stead.

During this stay in the East—his first wife having been dead some two or three years, Mr. Gallatin married Hannah, a daughter of Commodore James Nicholson, of New York, the senior captain of the American Navy. This auspicious and happy matrimonial alliance, contracted in October, 1793, continued until near the close of his own long life—he surviving her only about three months.(a) In the mean time his friends in Europe, having heard of

---

(a)Mrs. Gallatin died in the city of New York, in the spring of 1849, in her eighty-third year. She was a most estimable woman, a wife worthy of her illustrious huband. After her marriage, she was his constant companion in all his subsequent public life, at home and abroad; relieving him from many of the ordinary cares and anxieties of life by her prudence and management, and sustaining and stimulating him by her consolations and council. He habitually consulted her not only in private affairs, but in all his public movements.

As the wife of a leading member of Congress, a cabinet minister, and Representative of the United States at the two principal courts of Europe, she of course participated largely and almost uninterruptedly, during a period of more than the third of a century, in the most elegant and illustrious society, at home and abroad. But while her urbanity and courtesy were manifested towards every one within her intercourse, she never would by her compliance or example, sanction any rule of high life which conflicted with the "higher law," by which she professed to be governed as a christian. Such was the respect which this course of conduct inspired, even at Paris, and from a French Princess, that when, at one of the greatest fetes known in the circle of Royal entertainments—that given to celebrate the birth of the heir presumptive, and which, as custom required, was given on the Sabbath, the Duchess D'Angouleme inquired of the American minister for his lady, Mr. Gallatin answered, "she is not here, because it is Sunday;" the Duchess at once as-his fame and fortunes, sent him—perhaps the residue of his patrimonial estate—a thousand guineas, which he received through the agency of Robert Morris, the financier of the Revolution. Thereupon and therewith he returned to Fayette county, in May, 1794, after an absence from it of eighteen months.

Having thus replenished his exchequer, he, in 1794-'95, bought from John and William George Wilson, the sons and devisees of Col. George Wilson, the land at the mouth of and on both sides of Georges creek, including the site of New Geneva, a village which had been for years before founded by William George Wilson, Esq., under the name of "Wilson's Port," but which Mr. Gallatin somewhat enlarged and changed, calling it after the name of his native city. About the same period he conceived and effected the establishment of the New Geneva glass works, which were started in 1796—the first west of the Allegheny mountains.(b) Attendant upon this enterprise, Mr. Gallatin, in 1795, formed an extensive trading co-partnership with Messrs. James W. Nicholson, his brother-in-law, late of New York, Louis Bourdelon, and Charles Anthony Cazenove, late of Geneva, (Switzerland,) then of New York, and John Badolet, of Washington county, Pa.,(c) under the name of A. Gallatin & Co., to continue for three years, with a capital of $20,000, subject to be increased. The business was to consist of buying and selling goods and lands, &c. The Wilson lands, several lots in Greensboro, over the river, and twenty-two acres adjoining that village, were purchased by Mr. Gallatin, and held in trust for this partnership. How long it

---

sented to her absence and said, "Mrs. Gallatin does right—she teaches us our duty."

As a set-off to this, we find the following among the "Foreign Items," in Niles' Register, September 20, 1817:—"There are several rumors that the Royal family of France has not treated Mr. Gallatin and his lady with the respect due their station at court. It is said that the Duchess of Angouleme addressed a few words to Mrs. Gallatin in French, who replied, 'I do not speak French, Princess,' on which the Princess said, 'I do not speak English,' and turned her back on Mrs. Gallatin." Besides Mrs. Gallatin, three others of the daughters of Commodore Nicholson became the wives of members of Congress:—one, of William Few, a Representative and Senator from Georgia; another, of John Montgomery, a Representative from Maryland, and the other, of Joshua Seney, also a Representative from Maryland, the father of Joshua Seney, Esq., formerly of Uniontown, Pa., afterwards of Tiffin, Ohio.

(b)See Chap. XIII.—"Our Early Manufactures."

(c)Afterwards a prominent man in Greene county, of which he and John Flenniken, (father of R. P. Flenniken, Esq., of Uniontown, Pennsylvania,) were the first Associate Judges.

continued, and what became of it, we do not know. It was the origin of the long and valued residence of James W. Nicholson and family in that vicinity; and in connection with the glass works, and while New Geneva was the head of navigation and trade in the Monongahela, it did no doubt a thriving business. But men and trade are subject to great mutations. This co-partnership must not, however, be confounded with that of the old Glass Works Company, which was a separate concern, although the two were connected to some extent. And, we believe, Mr. Gallatin's growing political fortunes induced him, early in their career, to withdraw from both.

We now come to a part of Mr. Gallatin's political life which is the most difficult to comprehend and exhibit:—we mean his conduct in the series of events denominated the "Whiskey Insurrection." This is not the place to narrate those events—they are reserved for another sketch. Mr. Gallatin was so prominent an actor, especially in the closing scenes, that, assuming the reader to be familiar with them, we will not incumber our present purpose with any tedious repetitions.

Caution, sagacity, and a love of popular favor were largely developed ingredients in Mr. Gallatin's mental construction; and he was so happily constituted as to be able effectually to exert any one of them without over-reaching, or impairing the force of the others. Of this, no part of his eventful public life affords clearer evidence than the safety and success with which he trod the perilous paths of this Vesuvian epoch.

Regarding the insurrectionary movements as extending over a period of about three years—from September, 1791, to October, 1794, Mr. Gallatin's course of conduct therein is divisible into two parts, each of which is distinct, and very different from the other. The line of separation is in the eighteen months—from November, 1792, to May, 1794, during which he was absent from Western Pennsylvania. Within this period of absence, events of absorbing interest to him occurred:—his election to the Senate of the United States, the contest for his seat therein and his ejection therefrom,— his courtship and marriage of Miss Nicholson, and his negotiations in Europe and efforts in this county for the establishment of his New Geneva Glass Works. The anxieties and kind and hopeful feelings attendant upon this cluster of great and good things, favored by his protracted absence from the infected district, would naturally tend to sever him from the plots and counterplots of the incipient rebellion, and soften down his insurgent animosities, supposing him to have been heretofore within their embrace and influence. That he was so—that he was really an instigator of the resistance in its early stages, is a conclusion, from the evidence, which is irresistable. In assigning to him this positon, so variant from that which has been generally ascribed to him, we indulge in no desire to detract from the merit of his pacific exertions in the later stages of the strife, nor to pluck one leaf from the laurels which grow upon his grave. The effort to do so, would be as vain as ungenerous; for, in the light in which we view his conduct, there was no criminality in his early purposes, nor dishonor in the change they underwent.

It is needless to say that Mr. Gallatin's mental habitudes and party affiliations were such as to lead him into the path of resistance. Implicit obedience to oppressive legislation was not among the canons of his political faith. And he had not that acquiescence in the cabinet counsels of Washington which would impel him to their defense against the antagonisms of his political associates. Besides, his own popularity had not become so impregnable as to defy the assaults of those who stood ready to raze its rising greatness. Hence he allowed himself to become identified with the early manifestations of popular resistance, and relied upon his caution and sagacity to save him from any perilous consequences that might ensue, but which were not perhaps then contemplated.

It is a creditable fact that no overt acts of resistance to the excise law or its officers, were ever committed in the immediate neighborhood of Mr. Gallatin's residence and personal influence. This, however, was owing more to the absence of irritating causes than to any prevalence of the spirit of submission among the people. And doubtless he diffused around him enough of his caution and conservatism to prevent any outburst, which might have involved him in danger or disgrace. But in Greene, then the "upper end" of Washington county, and in contiguous parts of Western Virginia, there were found unmistakable traces of his influence, upon leading men, calculated to foment resistance to the law and its officers, and to involve them, as eventually happened to some of them, in the privations and perils of governmental prosecutions:—results for which they censured him the more because he escaped upon the merits of his subsequent services in favor of "law and order."

The most clear and decisive evidence of Mr. Gallatin's leadership in the early movements of the resistants is his participation in the "meeting of sundry inhabitants of the western counties of

Pennsylvania, at Pittsburgh, August 21, 1792,"—the proceedings of which are given at large in another place in these sketches.(d) He was the Secretary of that meeting, and no doubt, conspicuous in its deliberations. Its resolves were unanimous, and they are certainly very reprehensible, treading closely upon the confines of treasonable resistance. Moreover, the officers of the law had already been resisted and maltreated, and Mr. Gallatin should have seen that the promulgation of the last resolution was giving sanction and incentive to such outrages. And it is no palliation that it was but the echo of a proscriptive and incendiary edict previously fulminated by a meeting at Washington. So much the worse. The first perpetration of a mischievous act may be excused, while its repetition should be severely censured.(e) It is worthy of notice that all the apologists of Mr. Gallatin's conduct in the "Insurrection," omit any mention of this meeting, or case over it very lightly.(f) Better have seized it boldly and condemned it, as he did himself. Although it mars somewhat the symmetry of his character, it detracts nothing from its greatness.

We do not find that Mr. Gallatin took part in any other meeting or proceeding connected with the disorder of the times, until after his return to the West in the spring of 1794. Having been chosen

---

(d) See Chap. XI.—"Whiskey Insurrection."

(e) The censure here bestowed accords with Mr. Gallatin's own condemnation of his conduct in that transaction, as we find it expressed in his published Speech before the House of Representatives of the Pennsylvania Legislature, in December, 1794, upon the question of declaring the elections of members from the "four western counties," in October, '94, unconstitutional and void, by reason of the insurrection; in which speech—an able and valuable document—he takes occasion to review the principal causes and events of that extraordinary excitement.

"I wish not," says he, "to exculpate myself, where I feel I have been to blame. The sentiments thus expressed were not illegal or criminal; yet I will freely asknowledge that they were violent, intemperate and reprehensible. For by attempting to render the office contemptible, they tended to diminish that respect for the execution of the laws which is essential to the maintenance of a free government. But whilst I feel regret at the remembrance, though no hesitation in this open confession of that, my only political sin, let me add that the blame ought to fall where it is deserved. That meeting was not one of delegates of the people, but of individuals voluntarily assembled. It was not a combination of the people," &c.

(f) Findley's "History, &c." Rev. Dr. Carnahan's Lecture, &c. The former covers it over and displaces it so adroitly as to give it neither prominence nor distinctness in his narrative; while the latter, who evidently has made Findley the basis of his observations, omits any notice of it, and is thereby foiled into the error of saying that Mr. Gallatin attended no meeting "growing out of the insurrection," prior to the delegate meeting at Parkinson's Ferry, on the 14th August, 1794.

to the Senate of the United States, he was not a candidate for reelection to the State Legislature, in October, 1793. Other pursuits, of honor, happiness and profit now engaged his attention; and perhaps he purposely prolonged his absence from the scene of tumult, until he saw that his presence was necessary to save his friends from the ruin to which they were rushing.

When he returned to Fayette, in May, 1794, he found the fires of rebellion just beginning to blaze, and with commendable alacrity enhanced doubtless by the consciouseness that he had himself helped to scatter the coal which kindled it, he betook himself to its extinguishment. He kept away from the tumultuous assemblages at Mingo creek meeting-house, Braddock's Field, and elsewhere, in Washington and Allegheny counties. He, perhaps, thought it best to let the fire spend its fury in those regions, and set himself to prevent its spread into his own vicinage. In this he was nearly successful. Had he returned to the scene a little sooner he might perhaps have been entirely so.

The spectacle had now become so alarming as to appall the stoutest hearts. In the language of an eminent cotemporary writer,(g) "Men of property and intelligence who had contributed to kindle the flame under the common error of being able to regulate its heat, now trembled at the extent of the conflagration. It had passed the limits assigned to it, and was no longer subject to their control."

Fortunately our new Federal Government, in this the first trial of its strength, had at its head a man who had been accustomed to contemplate and surmount all sorts of dangers. He confronted this one with his usual moderation and firmness; and, in the means employed, afforded ample verge and encouragement for the subsidiary efforts of all well disposed men who were dwellers upon eminences in the scene of strife. Of such was Mr. Gallatin. And it is no disparagement of his illustrious compeers—Ross, Brackenridge, Edgar, Findley and Smilie, some of whom, like himself, had stood god-fathers to, if not begotten, the infant monster, to assign to him a more bold, untiring, discreet and successful activity in its subjugation than was exerted by any other. He attacked the wild and warlike schemes of Bradford and his followers, in front and rear, covertly and openly, privately and publicly, in committees and before the masses, and always with success. But in doing all

---

(g)Marshall's Washington, Vol. II., 346.

this he had often to encounter the most trying emergencies, and bring into exercise all his powers; at one time affecting compliance—scudding before the gale; at another evading the issue tendered, and drawing his adversary off upon some more assailable ground; now, coaxing and persuading—anon, defying and intimidating; gaining all the while upon the entrenchments of the foe, and upon the confidence of the multitude.

The severest test which his aims and abilities underwent was at the Parkinson's Ferry meeting, of August 14th, '94. Among other displays of argument and evasion made at that juncture having ventured to intimate his disapproval of the burning of Kirkpatrick's barn—"What," said a fiery fellow in the crowd, "do you blame us for that?" Gallatin was embarrassed for a moment and paused. His success depended upon his reply. "If you had burned Kirkpatrick in it you would have done something, but the barn had done no harm." "Aye, aye," said his interrogator, "that's true enough." The threatened tumult subsided.

His resort to the secret ballot, at the subsequent meeting of the Committee at Brownsville, is a signal illustration of his coolness and sagacity. Nor was there throughout the whole of his brilliant forensic career a finer instance of his confidence in the force of truth, when not countervailed by extraneous influences. He saw, through the mists of terror and distraction, which the unthinking populace had thrown around the Committee, that they really wished to accept the proffered amnesty, and thus end the strife; but that they feared the taunts of their neighbors, and the opprobrium implied in any act of submission to a government they had so often defied. The secret ballot—the only pure medium of popular suffrage, enabled them to give a true declaration of their convictions, without an open defiance of the dangers which attended it. It was the potent alchemy which transformed confusion into order, and fiery frowns into peaceful smiles. It ended the strife—except as to the retributions which ensued.

It is thus seen that Mr. Gallatin passed through all the stages and phases of this insurrectionary excitement, from an active participant to an active opponent; yet so as therein never to endanger his own safety or forfeit his favor with the people. An inferior man would have overleaped himself and fallen, if not on the other side, at least so low as never to recover. Even the shrewd and versatile Brackenridge lost for a while his strong hold upon the popular confidence, not because he was not true to his political associates, or lacked in wise and masterly conformity to the circumstances which surrounded him, but because he was sometimes too blunt in his feigned attacks, and too sharp in his real ones—too frank when he should have been more reserved—too bold when he should have been more cautious. We will presently see how differently the people judged the conduct of these two eminent actors in this most anomalous of all the instances of political upheaval and subsidence.

It is well known that Washington county (which then included Greene,) and the southern part of Allegheny county, were denominated, and rightly, too, "the seat of the rebellion." There its master spirits rose, and there they fell. In the latter county, in the town of Pittsburgh, Mr. Brackenridge resided—Hugh Henry Brackenridge, an eminent and learned lawyer, author of "Modern Chivalry," and afterwards a Judge of the Supreme Court of the State. Mr. Gallatin resided fifty miles apart from him, in the southwest corner of Fayette. Both were distinguished leaders in the republican or democratic school of politics. Both had fought the fire of the insurrection in its fiercest form, and yet both had, by their seeming compliances with its exactions, won for themselves the honor—for so the "majority" regarded it, of being traduced by the officers and advocates of the government.

In October, 1794, Mr. Gallatin was one of the republican candidates for the Assembly from Fayette—Mr. Brackenridge was the candidate of the same party for Congress, from the rebellious district. There were three other candidates already in the field —Thomas Scott and Daniel Hamilton, of Washington, and John Woods, of Pittsburgh; but he had the lead, and was confident of election. But his wily policy in the insurrection had given great offense even to many of his own political friends. They wanted to shake him off. To effect this, a few persons got together at Canonsburg, a few days before the election, and determined to run Mr. Gallatin against the field—even though he did not reside in the district, and, it is said, without consulting him. The result was that he was elected over all competitors—one account says by a large, others say by a small majority; probably by only a plurality. It is also said that this was accomplished by its having been given out that Mr. Brackenridge (who came in "second best") had declined. It is certain, however, that but a small vote was polled— in some of the election districts none at all. Mr. G. was, on the same day, elected to the Assembly of the State from Fayette. But, upon the assembling of the legislature, in December, both branches vacated the elections of members that year from the counties of

Allegheny, Fayette, Washington and Westmoreland, on account of the insurrection—declaring them "unconstitutional and void." New elections were held in February, 1795, and every one of the ejected members returned again, except Senator John Moore, of Westmoreland, who declined being a candidate, and Presley Carr Lane, of Fayette, was elected in his stead. On this occasion Mr. Gallatin made and published a long and able speech before the House, in defense of his seat. The speech may be regarded as his history of the insurrection; and as such we will have further use for it in another sketch.

As the Congress to which Mr. Gallatin was elected did not meet until December, 1795, he was enabled to serve under both elections. He was successively reelected to Congress in the years 1796, 1798 and 1800, from the same district—Allegheny, Washington and Greene, the latter county having been erected in 1796.

"There is a tide in the affairs of men, which, taken at the flood, leads on to fortune," and Mr. Gallatin had now taken it in that stage. With the commanding talents for public life which he possessed, his success was now secure. His Congressional career covered a period of intense party excitement, embracing the whole of the Presidential term of the elder Adams, and the two last years of his illustrious predecessor. He rose almost at once to one of the highest seats of the opposition benches, and held it bravely and uninterruptedly. In those days great and grave questions were the subjects of discussion, subjects of first impression—new, vital, and exciting. Of these were the systems of finance which sprung out of the national debt, the assumption of the war debts of the States, the tariff, the funding system, a national bank, and all the innumerable collateral questions which attended upon these great ones, like the moons and belts of Saturn. Added to these were others of a more angry character, such as the alien and sedition laws, and all that series of plagues blown upon both our foreign and domestic relations from the shores of revolutionary France. In all these great questions Mr. G. bore a conspicuous and influential part, battling side by side with Madison, Giles, Livingston, Macon, Varnum and Randolph, against Hamilton, Ames, Otos, Sitgreaves, Bayard and Marshall. There were giants in those days, and these were of them.

There is one vote given by Mr. G. at the opening of the last session in General Washington's administration, which we would rather he had evaded or reversed. In the responsive address by the House to the President's annual message, they proposed to say to him that, "For our country's sake, for the sake of republican liberty, it is our earnest wish that your example may be the guide of your successors; and thus, after being the ornament and safeguard of the present age, become the patrimony of our descendants." It was moved to strike this out, and Mr. G. was one of the twenty-four who voted for doing so. In this, however, he had the company of Wm. B. Giles, Edward Livingston, and Andrew Jackson, with other stars of lesser light. The motion failed, and then Mr. G. voted for the address, although his associates named held out against it to the last. We exhibit this ultraism of party rancor more in regret than in resentment, and are even glad to record that Mr. G. did not cling to it with the tenacity of others who have risen to higher fame.

Although a firm partisan of the popular school, Mr. G. did not, on many great occasions, allow his party affiliations to drag him down into factious opposition. Especially was this the case as to the measures sought to be adopted by the administration of John Adams, in 1797-'8, having in view a war with republican France, for spoilations on our commerce—one of which measures resulted in again calling Washington to the head of the army, with the rank of Lieutenant General, or, rather—General. In this patriotic manliness he deserted the lead of such party zealots as Findley and Giles and Livingston, and his course is the more commendable as it was against the popular leanings towards a nation to whom he was allied by the treble ties of lineage, language and party allegiance.

Up to the period of Mr. Gallatin's advent to Congress, there existed no standing Committee of Ways and Means, that favorite legislative palladium against the financial schemes of the executive. And it is said that Mr. G. was largely instrumental in its creation. Thereupon he became one of its members, and continued to be during every successive session while in Congress.

The reported congressional debates of that period, meagre though they be, concur with tradition and cotemporary writers in representing Mr. Gallatin as a fluent debater, always cool, always ready, dignified, direct, candid and convincing. In all great conflicts, he was the champion of his party, its Achilles in attack, its Hector in defense, and its Nestor in council. Mr. Gallatin was particularly at home on financial questions. In this, he had the advantage of all his compeers, Giles being too lazy, Livingston too discursive, Nicholas too impetuous, Randolph too erratic, and Madison too judicial. But Gallatin's mind was of that exact, systematic construction which fitted him for such subjects. He had, moreover, strong powers of analysis and concentration, united to unfaltering endurance of labor;—traits of character which grew stronger with age, and went with him to the grave.

Mr. Jefferson, who presided in the Senate during Mr. Adams' Presidency, became an early admirer and devoted friend of Mr. Gallatin. Their relations were always intimate and confiding. Indeed, during some stages of the great struggle of 1797-1800, ending in his elevation to the Presidency, he considered Mr. Gallatin his most steadfast coadjutor and defender, standing by him in Congress when others of more vaunt but less valor forsook him and fled. So he wrote to a friend, in the retrospect of after years; and John Randolph said of him, in 1824, that he had done as much as any other man to achieve the revolution of 1800, and had got as little for it.(h) In this, we think, John run out his devotedness too far. Mr. Gallatin got all he ever asked, perhaps all he ever wished.

In 1797, the Legislature of Pennsylvania passed an Act to procure twenty thousand stand of arms for the use of the State. This, and the then imminent danger of war with France, greatly stimulated the establishment of gun factories, or armories, public and private throughout the country. Among others, Mr. Gallatin embarked in the business; and in company with Melchor Baker,(i) a practical gunsmith, in 1799, or 1800, established an extensive manufactory of muskets, broad-swords, &c., in what is now Nicholson township, on land now owned by Philip Kefover. For a while they gave employment to between fifty and one hundred workmen. In the State Treasury accounts for 1800, we find two payments in that year to Albert Gallatin of $2666.66 each, "on

---

(h)"I once, Sir, had the honor of being under the federal regime in what was called the reign of terror. I then enjoyed the liberty of speech—I had a right to protest against the acts of the men in power. The present Secretary of the Treasury (Mr. Gallatin) was attempted to be stopped in debate on the rule which required no man to speak more than once to any question. That great man—for great let me call him, laughted in derision at the attempt."—John Randolph's Indignation Speech in Congress, May 26, 1812, on not being allowed to speak against declaring War, until the House would decide to consider his Resolution.

(i)One of the unfortunate Col. Lochrey's men in the expedition to join in Clark's Campaign of 1781. See note to Cap. XVI.—"Outline of Civil and Political History," &c. After the suspension of the gun factory, Mr. Baker removed to Clarksburg, Virginia.

account of his contract to supply the State with two thousand stand of arms." The partnership had also, about the same time, a contract with the national government, whose further patronage of the factory was eminently desirable. But, upon the election of Mr. Jefferson to the Presidency, in February, 1801, it became a foregone conclusion that Mr. Gallatin must go into the cabinet as head of the Treasury Department. He determined to accept the office. But, before he could do so, it became necessary, in his estimation, to sever himself from all governmental contracts, subsisting or in prospect; and from all interest therein, direct or indirect, fixed or contingent. He recognized the human frailty which makes "lead us not into temptation" a most wise and necessary petition in the best of all prayers. He therefore deferred his acceptance of the secretaryship until he could become discharged from the existing contract, and, by settling with his partner, and withdrawing from the business, relieve his own official conduct from suspicion and Mr. Baker from the disability to enter into future contracts, which his further connection with him would impose. Mr. Gallatin accordingly came home, dissolved the co-partnership, and sold out his interest in it and its contracts to Mr. Baker. The settlement required an amicable reference, in which, it is said, Mr. Gallatin behaved with great liberality towards his less wealthy partner. Mr. Baker carried on the business for some years afterwards—how long, we do not certainly know. In 1804, we find the State paying him $1333.33 for supplying arms. But, the national armories at Springfield and Harper's Ferry becoming too strong for private competition, the old Fayette Gun Factory was abandoned.

Having thus disencumbered himself of this gun contract business, Mr. Gallatin was, on the 14th of May, 1801, appointed by Mr. Jefferson to be Secretary of the Treasury, which, but for that disability, would have been conferred upon him ten weeks earlier. In assigning him to this exalted place, the new republican President was not embarrassed by the conflicting claims of any competitor. He gave it to Mr. Gallatin in accordance with his own wishes and in compliance with the unanimous call of his political friends. No other man was thought of by him, or named by them. Mr. Gallatin had well earned this exalted cabinet place by his efficient political services and eminent financial abilities. He continued to hold it during the entire residue of Mr. Jefferson's two Presidential terms, the whole of the first term of Mr. Madison, and until

February, 1814, in the second,(j)—the longest cabinet tenure ever enjoyed by one man since the foundation of the government. Except the Secretaries of State, Madison and Monroe, his ministerial associates were not men of superior talent, or great eminence. The truth is, that in those days the heads of the departments of State and Treasury, with the President, constituted "the government,"—the other two departments, of War and the Navy, being regarded as of secondary importance, to be filled by second-rate men.(k)

Having accompanied Mr. Gallatin somewhat leisurely into the field of his greatest fame, in which nearly one-third of his public life was spent, we must not rush over it without some attempt to trace the leading features of his financial policy. Fortunately these are so prominent as to require no nice exercise of skill in the limner.

We have said that the place and plan of Mr. Gallatin's youthful education were eminently adapted to his future career. "Just as the twig is bent, the tree's inclined," is an adage of profound truth. Nearly all the peculiarities of human character and effort find their solution in the influences and habits of early life. Among the Genevans, great stress and stringency were given to

---

(j) Although Mr. Gallatin went to Europe, as a negotiator for peace, in April, 1813, he continued to hold the secretaryship until, February, 1814. If we discount these ten months from his term, then Gideon Granger, as Postmaster General from November, 1801, to March, 1814, exceeded him by about five months.

(k) We mean no undue disparagement of the worthy men who filled these offices under the four first Presidents. Except, perhaps, during a part of the war of 1812-'15, they were fully adequate to the duties of their departments, and discharged them well. Until more recently, the head of the Post-office Department, and the Attorney General, were not considered cabinet officers. These were sometimes eminent and able men—Pickering, Granger, Meigs; and Edward Randolph, Parsons, Rodney, Pinkney, &c. Without intending any invidious comparison with more ancient or modern cabinets, we may point to those of Mr. Monroe and J. Q. Adams as combinations of pre-eminent abilities: —John Quincy Adams, Secretary of State, W. H. Crawford, Secretary of the Treasury, John C. Calhoun, Secretary of War, and Smith Thompson, Secretary of the Navy, under Mr. Monroe; and Henry Clay, Secretary of State, Richard Rush, Secretary of the Treasury, James Barbour, Secretary of War, and Samuel L. Southard, Secretary of the Navy, under Mr. Adams; and John McLean, Postmaster General, and William Wirt, Attorney General under both. Mr. Monroe's administration was so signally exempt from party contentions as to acquire the designation of "the era of good feeling." Mr. Adams sought to prolong it, but failed, owing to the peculiar circumstances of his election, and the unbounded popularity of his competitor—Gen. Jackson; who, having gilded the lustre of his country's arms, was destined to impress himself upon its polity and history.

the maxim that debt was dangerous, and disability to pay disgraceful. They built upon this the somewhat unjust corollary, that the children of a bankrupt were disqualified for any public trust so long as their father's debts were unpaid. The policy thus inculcated, was a ruling ingredient in the youthful prejudices of Mr. Gallatin, and controlled his after life, private and public. He abhorred debts of all sorts, and exacted their just and full payment from individuals and governments. He knew how to be generous; but generosity and defalcation were not kindred terms in his vocabulary. Least of all could he tolerate repudiation by a debtor having power to enforce it against a needy or helpless creditor. To illustrate this trait of his character, requires us to go back a little upon his public pathway.

The requirements and revulsions of our Revolution had brought upon the States and the Confederacy a mass of debt, at home and abroad. Its evidences were in every form, from "contracts" with the King of France and the States General of the Netherlands, down to a sixpenny "certificate of loan." The foreign debts gave no trouble, except—to provide for their payment. But the domestic indebtedness was as complicated as an ever-changing Congress and thirteen independent, sovereign sub-debtors, all compelled to anticipate resources which were never realized and to sustain an ever-falling credit by increasing the burdens which bore it down, could make it. Its evidences were the currency of the country; and they came, in time, to be held by all sorts and conditions of men, from the poorest soldier up to the richest banker. These had acquired them at every conceivable rate of value and depreciation, from par to a hundred, or a thousand for one. The most that the old Confederation Congress and the States could do during the war and for some time after its close, was to settle with their creditors, consolidate the debts, and issue new certificates of indebtedness for the accruing interest and the depreciation. With all this, however. Mr. Gallatin had nothing to do. But when the new federal government was formed, in 1789, it by the Constitution and laws early enacted, was in duty bound, assumed the payment of all those multiform debts, so far as they were incurred for the general cause. The mode adopted for their security and payment, was almost as complicated as had been their forms of creation. The foreign debt, unpaid, had to be provided for by loans. The States and the domestic creditors were subjected to what was called the Funding System, devised by Alexander Hamilton, Secretary of the Treasury under President Washington, Mr.

Gallatin, though not in Congress at the time this system was adopted,—in 1790-'92, advocated the plan, but stoutly resisted some of its leading details.

To make the reader thoroughly understand the old debts of the country, and the system adopted for its funding and payment, would be a task as hopeless as its accomplishment would be uninteresting. Suffice it to say here, that the funding system consisted in subscriptions to a national loan, the subscribers paying therefor in some one or more of the various adjusted evidences of debt, and taking in lieu thereof certificates of government stock, payable or redeemable in installments, bearing interest and transferable. In this way the home debt became a marketable commodity which its holders could sell, and the government, as well as others, could buy, before, or when due. By one of the provisions of the system, 21,500,000 dollars of stock was authorized, to absorb the debts of the States, without having previously ascertained their amounts with accuracy; leaving the amounts of surplus, or deficiency, of State debts, beyond or below the amount allowed of the stock to each State, to be otherwise thereafter provided for. To this Mr. Gallatin was opposed, as doing injustice to some of the States, and more than justice to others. He was for having each State's share of the debt first settled, and then give to each a correspondent amount of stock. But he was reconciled to this upon the ground that the measure was necessary to give immediate relief to some of the States, whose people were groaning under unequal and oppressive taxation. The relief consisted in enabling them to pay their taxes in the State scrip which was convertible into stock. But the most objectionable feature of the funding system adopted, in Mr. Gallatin's estimation, consisted in its not providing for full and entire payment of the principal and interest of the debts it was designed to fund. These it cut up into equal parts—giving to one part six per cent. interest, to another three, and to another no interest for ten years. This seeming injustice received a plausible advocacy in the increased value which the funding gave to the debts, and in the well known fact that the holders had acquired much of their amounts at prices greatly below their standard value. But Mr. Gallatin looked upon it as repudiation. His Genevan education was against it. He could not see that the precedent inability of Congress and the States to sustain the credit of their paper, and to pay the interest thereon, was any excuse for now disowning portions of their liabilities. Congressional action was beyond his reach. But being in the Legislature of Pennsylvania, he advocated successfully the payment by the State, in a mode satisfactory to creditors, of all those portions of interest on her debts, which were unprovided for in the national loan.

Early in his congressional service, Mr. Gallatin saw, as he thought, that the statesmen of that era, even those of his own political party, did not understand and appreciate the true principles of finance applicable to our government, and to its indebted condition. This induced him, in 1796, to give his views to the public under the modest title of "A Sketch on Finances." This little treatise greatly elevated him in the esteem of the republican party; not because it enunciated any new system, or developed any hitherto undiscovered principles of finance, applicable to our fiscal affairs. It claimed no such distinction. It advocated a sinking fund into which all the accumulated surplus revenues should fall, to be sacredly applied to the payment of the public debt. But there was nothing new in this. That fund had been already established. That it had not been very productive was the fault of the times and not of those who administered it. The sketch was, in part, a very distant echo of the popular complaints of extravagance and unequal taxation; and it sounded a little louder and in clearer notes than had heretofore been given out from the high places of power, the pleasing calls for retrenchment and reform. The unpretending dissertation was, nevertheless, one of real merit and utility. It presented the true financial policy of the country at that period in bold relief, and in vivid colors; and advocated, with peculiar force of argument and appeal, the necessity of keeping up the widest possible margin of excess of revenue beyond expenditures, so as therewith to pay off, as fast as it came due, or faster, the public debt, without a resort to new loans. He fought the dogma that a national debt was a national blessing, and contended with all the earnestness of resisted truth, that the payment of interest by nations, as well as individuals, was a burden upon progress and a tax upon industry. Now-a-days all this is looked upon as very obvious statesmanship. But then it required strong advocacy and clear elucidation to render it acceptable to the people and their representatives: so deeply had they become imbued with the errors of European system, and the loan expedients of our Revolutionary era.

The policy and purposes, thus advocated by Mr. Gallatin, became banner pledges of the republican party in the great struggle of 1800; not that the Federalists disowned them, but having been long in power, without acquiring the prestige of their fruitful application, they could not rally under them so successfully as did their adversaries. The consequence to Mr. Gallatin was, that when his party succeeded to power in 1801, he was regarded by both parties as the embodiment and exponent of a new, progressive financial system which had now to be inaugurated and enforced; and therefore he must be, and was, as already stated, called to the helm of the Treasury Department.

Of course Mr. Gallatin persisted steadily in the policy which he and his party had so earnestly advocated—the utmost practicable increase of revenue, and the utmost practicable entrenchment of expenditure, postponing all minor calls upon the Treasury, however loud and tempting, to the one grand leading purpose of a rapid extinguishment of the national debt. Happily for his success and fame, all branches of the government, legislative and executive, seconded and sustained his efforts. Moreover, the business of the country had just begun to recover from the deep depression into which it had sunk during the Revolution, and the ten or fifteen years which ensued. The public debts had all been funded, and the sources of revenue established. It was conceded that all this was wisely done; and, except in a few minor details, they were not disturbed. The revenue from duties on foreign goods had risen from less than three millions, in 1791, to over ten millions and three quarters in 1801. The aggregate of all the revenues—customs, internal duties, direct tax, postages, public lands and miscellaneous, rose from less than four and a half millions, in 1791, to nearly thirteen millions in 1801; while the expenditures, which in 1791 were about one million and three quarters, or nearly forty per cent. of the revenues, rose, in 1801, to less than five millions—about the same proportion; but leaving about nine millions to go to the debt. The revenues of the first period of eleven years and nine months, from April 1st, 1789, to January 1st, 1801, were a little over sixty-five and a quarter millions, while the ordinary expeditures were nearly thirty-seven millions—leaving less than twenty-eight and a half millions to go to the debt—not half enough to pay its annual interest. In the next period of eleven years and nine months, from January 1st, 1801, to October 1st, 1812, the aggregate revenues were nearly one hundred and fifty millions and a half, and the gross ordinary expenses a little over seventy-one millions—leaving a surplus applicable to the debt of over seventy-nine millions. Mr. Gallatin had therefore full coffers whereupon to base his operations. Wherein, then, it is asked, consists his merits as a financier? We answer, in husbanding and rightly applying the resources at his command, and devising for Congress and executing when enacted, measures for their augmentation; and, above all, in resisting by argument and influence any undue diversion of the revenues to other objects than the sure and rapid reduction of the debt.

The public debt, on the first of April, 1801, was, in round numbers, 80,000,000 (eighty millions) dollars—its annual interest, $4,180,000. The purchase of Louisiana from Napoleon, in 1803, added $15,000,000 to the principal, and about the same time an agreement, by Jay's treaty of 1794, to pay over three millions to British subjects came due. Thus the debt was increased to about ninety-eight and a half millions, and its annual interest to about five and a quarter millions. With these resources and liabilities Mr. Gallatin so managed the finances as to reduce the principal of the debt on the first of April, 1812, to a little over forty-five millions, bearing an annual interest of only $2,220,000. He achieved this great result by inducing Congress, early in his official career, to set apart an annual appropriation of $7,300,000 for the payment of interest and gradual reduction of the principal; which was increased to $8,000,000 after the purchase of Lousiana. He was ably seconded in this course of policy by President Jefferson, and upheld in it by Congress.

But the smooth, deep current of financial fullness upon which Mr. Gallatin had sailed so long, was destined soon to be broken by the shoals and storms of war. The restrictive systems of France and England had blighted our blooming commerce; and our government was impelled to corresponding commercial restrictions, which made sad inroads upon our revenues. The aggregate revenues which, in 1808, had risen to over seventeen millions, fell in 1809, to less than eight millions, and were destined to still further depression; while the expenditures, which never in Mr. Jefferson's administration exceeded six and a half millions, came to more than double that sum in 1812. Of course new loans had to be resorted to, to meet this deficiency, and the still growing deficiencies which war must inevitably create. At the close of the war, the public debt had swollen to $120,000,000.

Mr. Gallatin, as well as other statesmen of sagacity, saw, years before it came, the imminent danger of war. And when appealed to to allow a fund to accumulate to meet, or provide munitions to encounter the shock, he resisted it; saying, "sufficient unto the day is the evil thereof," and if you have the funds you will squander them:—let us put our trust in the patience and patriotism of the people, to bear the burdens of privation and taxation when the emergency arises:—in the mean time let us get ready for new, by paying our old debts.

It is well known that Mr. Gallatin was not an adviser of the war, which public opinion, springing from wrongs too grievous to be borne, forced upon President Madison and the country. His voice was aye for peace. War would not only arrest his darling scheme of getting out of debt, but would increase its amount to an extent which would perhaps weigh down our national energies for a century. Hence he was the last of his cabinet colleagues to consent to war. But patriotism demanded the sacrifice, and he yielded; and while it lasted no man bent his energies more devotedly to sustain it than he did.

When called upon officially a few months before the war opened to give his views of the expedients to raise revenue necessary to meet the new order of things, he had the moral courage to recommend, among other things, a resort to taxation on stills and the distillation of spirits from domestic products—in others words, to the odious Excise. This drew upon him the maledictions of many of his old political friends. What, said they, can you devise no adequate plan of revenue without including those execrable expedients of Hamilton and Wolcot? His old Pittsburgh meeting proceedings, of August 21, 1792, were trumped upon his "budget," wherein he declared that "internal taxes upon consumption, from their very nature, never can be effectually carried into operation, without vesting the officers appointed to collect them with powers most dangerous to the civil rights of freemen, and must in the end destroy the liberties of every country in which they are introduced!" This was a most terrible **argumentum ad hominem.** When his letter proposing this tax was read in the House, so indignant and mortified were many of his political adherents, among them his friend Findley, of Westmoreland, that they refused to vote for it being printed. Let us not, said they, give any countenance to a letter containing propositions which will not probably be agreed to by Congress, and which can serve only unnecessarily to alarm the people! Congress, however, did adopt the propositions—the people were not alarmed—nor were their liberties destroyed.

In his letter he says, "there is not any more eligible object of taxation than ardent spirits." He proposed, however, to vary the tax from what it was in the time of the Insurrection, so as to divest it as much as possible of its odious inequalities, by laying the tax upon spirits distilled from foreign materials, (molasses, &c.,) according to the quantity distilled; and that distillers of fruit and domestic grain, &c., should pay a specified tax per annum. It was so enacted.

The other plans and subjects of revenue which he proposed, and which Congress substantially adopted, were, a direct tax upon lands, &c., (1) to yield $3,000,000—taxes upon refined sugars—licenses to retailers of foreign merchandise, and liquors, foreign and domestic—upon sales at auction, upon carriages, and a stamp tax. These and loans, aided by the tariff and the public lands, sustained the war and paid the interest of the debt. "Sweet peace restored," the recuperative energies of our people enabled the Government, within twenty years, and without the aids of either direct or internal taxes, to pay off the debt of two wars—"the money consideration of our independence and liberties."

Although the National Road from Cumberland to Wheeling was the fruit of a compact between the United States and the State of Ohio, upon her admission into the Union in 1802, Mr. Gallatin was the originator of its plan of construction, the most magnificent and expensive of any turnpike ever built in this country.(m) It was undertaken, its route, as far as Brownsville, fixed, and partly constructed, during his administration of the Treasury Department; to which, in those days, such work pertained. He was opposed to the circuitous route adopted—having urged a more direct course, through Greene county and by way of New Geneva. But the President, (Jefferson,) under the mighty influences brought to bear upon him, decided in favor of Brownsville and Washington—whether wisely or not, is a question not worth while now to consider.

In March, 1807, the Senate of the United States called upon Mr. Gallatin, as Secretary of the Treasury, to prepare and report to them at their next session "a plan for the application of such means as are within the power of Congress to the construction of

---

(1) Pennsylvania's share of this tax was $365,479. Fayette county had to pay $4,500; Greene, $2,130; Washington, $6,920; Westmoreland, $5,440; Allegheny, $5,210; Philadelphia city, $79,500—county, $38,230, &c., &c.

(m) This great work was begun in 1806—not much done on it until after the war (1815), and completed to Wheeling about 1822. It cost, originally, nearly $1,700,000; which (131 miles) is an average of nearly $13,000 to the mile. The eastern section, from Uniontown to Cumberland, (63 miles,) cost about $14,000 per mile; the Western Section not so much. The Pennsylvania Rail Road from Harrisburg to Pittsburgh was constructed (single track) at an average cost of $39,000 per mile, inclusive of the great tunnel.

roads and canals, with statements of works of that nature which may require and deserve the aid of Government, and which have been commenced—the progress made upon them and their means and prospects of being completed, with such general information as he shall deem material to the subject." In obedience to this requirement, he, in March, 1808, submitted a most elaborate and able report, covering some seventy pages, containing a full response to every branch of the inquiry. The report is a detailed statement of all the works of that nature then completed, in progress, or projected in the several States of the Union; and suggests numerous new undertakings of a national character; recommending a gradual appropriation of twenty millions to their construction. Among the work recommended were four roads from the Allegheny, Monongahela, Kanawha and Tennessee rivers, to the Susquehanna, Potomac, James and Santee; none of which were ever made but the second. Other works he proposed to aid by loans or subscriptions of stock. He exhibited on these points none of those constitutional scruples which have borne so heavily upon the more enlightened (?) judgment of modern statesmen. However its orthodoxy may now be regarded, the report is, even yet, a model of lucid conciseness and expansive statesmanship.

It is well known that Mr. Gallatin was friendly to a re-charter of the United States Bank, a bill which Mr. Madison vetoed in 1811, but signed another in 1816. He never regarded it as that

"Monstrum horrendum, informe, ingens, cui lumen ademptum"

which modern sages have found it to be; but looked upon it as a safe, necessary and useful fiscal agent of Government, and regulator of the exchanges and the currency. He even withstood all the lights and denunciations which more recent discussions poured upon the subject; and in the calm retirement of his matured life gave his views to the world in an extended treatise, entitled "The Currency, &c." It was read only as the opinions of a statesman of the old regime, unillumined by the light of latter day luminaries, in whose effulgence the people have rejoiced, and the Government grown strong.

Mr. Gallatin was, however, never the advocate of a Protective Tariff. He had no objection to "incidental" protection; but his theories and recommendations never went beyond revenue. This accorded with the uniform tenor of his financial schemes—the utmost attainable increase of income, so as thereby the more speedily to extinguish the public debt. His free trade proclivities were fixed, yet he did not obtrude them in his State papers. Once, when a private citizen of New York, he did unfold them to Congress in the form of a memorial, from the Philadelphia "Free Trade Convention," of which he was a prominent member. It was tauntingly flouted by Southern nullifiers in the faces of the friends of protection, which provoked Mr. Clay, their great champion, to visit upon its author his most indignant denunciation.(n)

We pass now from the field of Mr. Gallatin's fiscal displays to another. It is not 'for us to attempt an estimate of his financial character. His long continuance in that department, and the eminent success which crowned all his efforts, warrant the laudations which were showered upon him while in office, and which followed him into his latest retirement. He won his honors well and wore them long.

In common with other officers of the ship of state, Mr. Gallatin hailed with delight the first gleamings of the star of peace through the murky clouds of war. And when, in the spring of 1813, the Emperor Alexander I of Russia, offered his friendly mediation to the two belligerent nations, the President promptly selected Mr Gallatin as one of the negotiators; this, without allowing him to let go his hold upon the helm of the Treasury. John Quincy Adams being then our resident minister at St. Petersburg, the President, in April, 1813, in the recess of the Senate, appointed Mr. Gallatin and James A. Bayard, of Delaware, to join him there as joint plenipotentiaries to sign a treaty of peace with Great Britain, under the proffered mediation; and also to negotiate and sign a commercial treaty with Russia. When the Senate convened, in June, 1813, the President sent in his nomination of the three Envoys. Thereupon quite a dignified quarrel sprang up between

---

(n)"But, Sir, the gentleman to whom I am about to allude, although long a resident of this country, has no feelings, no attachments, no sympathies, no principles in common with our people. Nearly fifty years ago, Pennsylvania took him to her bosom, and warmed and cherished, and honored him. And how does he manifest his gratitude? By aiming a vital blow at a system endeared to her by a thorough conviction that it is indispensable to her prosperity. He has filled, at home and abroad, some of the highest offices under this Government, during thirty years, and he is still at heart an alien. The authority of his name has been invoked; and the labors of his pen, in the form of a memorial to Congress, have been engaged to overthrow the American system, and to substitute the foreign. Go home to your native Europe, and there inculcate upon her Sovereigns your Utopian doctrines of free trade; and when you have prevailed upon them to unseal their ports, and freely admit the produce of Pennsylvania and other States, come back, and we shall be prepared to become converts, and adopt your faith."
Henry Clay's Speech in the U. S. Senate, February 2, 1832.

the President and the Senate, they deciding to interrogate him rather closely as to why he sent Mr. Gallatin, and what became of the Treasury in the meantime; and he refusing to be interrogated. The result was, after much deliberation, that the Senate refused, by a vote of seventeen to eighteen, to advise and consent to Mr. Gallatin's appointment, on the ground of incompatibility of the two offices of Secretary and Minister. Mr. Adams was confirmed by a vote of thirty to four, Mr. Bayard by twenty-seven to six. Mr. Gallatin had gone on the mission, and it does not appear that the President recalled him.

England, however, rejected the Russian mediation, but offered to treat for peace, untrammeled, at Gottenburg, in Sweden. Thereupon, on the 9th of February, 1814, the President appointed Mr. Gallatin one of the commissioners, the Senate thereto consenting; George W. Campbell, of Tennessee, having been at the same time nominated to be Secretary of the Treasury and confirmed. The seat of the negotiations was subsequently moved to Ghent, in Belgium, where Messrs. Adams, Bayard and Gallatin were afterwards joined by Henry Clay and Jonathan Russell, who, as joint Plenipotentiaries, negotiated the terms of peace with Lord Gambier, Sir Henry Goulbourn and William Adams, and on the 24th December, 1814, signed the treaty which terminated the war as soon as known. The news of it reached New York on the 11th February, amid the rejoicings over the victory at New Orleans. Thus was peace born in the arms of victory.

Mr. Gallatin had now entered upon a long career of diplomatic service. In 1815, he, with Messrs. Clay and Adams, negotiated and signed at London a commercial treaty with Great Britain. Thereupon he returned home for a short period, in company with Mr. Clay. From 1816 to 1823, he was our Minister resident at the court of France. This was a most interesting period in the history of that long convulsed and ever changeful nation, and of all Europe. Waterloo had sealed up her fate for fifteen years, and her capital, long the abode of terror, had now become again the seat of gaiety, and the center of attraction to civilized Europe. The long banished elite of England had returned, or rushed thither anew, to revel in its cheap luxuries of sense and intellect. In such a conjuncture of teeming events it behooved our Republic to be well represented. Mr. Gallatin was wisely assigned to a court where now for a while the greatest diplomats of Europe resided. We had also claims upon that nation of grave and perplexing importance for outrages upon our commerce committed by virtue of the Berlin and Milan decrees of Napoleon; and although it was too soon for a Bourbon to respond fully for those depredations, yet Mr. Gallatin was enabled to pave the way for their ultimate recognition and payment. During his residence at Paris he was twice deputed by our Government upon special missions, to the Netherlands in 1817, and to England in 1818. He returned to the United States with his family early in 1824, and for a while again took up his abode at his old home in Fayette, in a new and splendid mansion which he had procured to be erected preparatory to his return.

In 1824, there were four prominent candidates for the Presidency of the United States, Jackson, Adams, Clay and Crawford. The machinery of National Conventions had not yet been devised, by which to combine sectional influences and crush out the pretensions of unavailable aspirants. Mr. Gallatin's long absence had not estranged him from his old political friends; and, upon his return, many of them, especially in Virginia and Pennsylvania, run up his name as a candidate for the Vice Presidency, in connection with William H. Crawford, of Georgia, for President. For a long time Mr. Gallatin regarded the movement as only complimentary, or experimental, and took no public notice of it. Gradually it became more and more earnest and imposing; and the cry of constitutional ineligibility was raised against him, because not "a natural born citizen of the United States." Those who raised this clamor were actuated less by a wish that "none but Americans should rule America," than by motives of envy or selfishness. Certain it is that the Constitution gave no ground for the objection; for, having been a citizen at its adoption, in 1789, he was as eligible as if "to the manner born," that carefully prepared instrument presenting the singular incongruity, in the early years of its operation, of permitting a man to become President or Vice President who could not be a senator!(o) Mr. Gallatin had the good sense to silence the distracting agitation by publicly withdrawing from the canvass.

The dignified retirement of Mr. Gallatin, at the home of his younger days, was honored, in May, 1825, by a visit from his "long tried, his bosom friend," La Fayette. On the 26th, the "nation's guest" was most honorably received at Uniontown by the people

---

(o) We well recollect the witling (or witless) newspaper effusions of the day upon this question—illustrated by a proposition to run Albert Gallatin, of Switzerland, for Vice President, along with Joseph Buonaparte, of Spain, then residing in New Jersey, for President.

of the county which wears his illustrious name. On this great occasion, Mr. Gallatin, with signal appropriateness, made the reception address. On the Thursday following, (May 28th,) the General and suit, well accompanied, were driven to Mr. Gallatin's residence, where a most sumptuous and abundant entertainment was provided, not only for the special guests, but for the thronging multitude who rushed thither to greet them. It was a truly gala day at the stately mansion and verdant lawns and groves of "Friendship Hill." Who that was there can ever forget the "feast of reason"—and other good things, and the "flow of soul"—and champagne? The like of which old Springhill had never seen—may never see again.

But Mr. Gallatin was not allowed long to enjoy his retirement—if indeed it was an enjoyment. For there appears to be a witchery in the excitements of public life which few who have largely shared them are ever willing to resign until driven to it by having attained the topmost round of ambition's ladder, or by the decrepitude of age. He was still in the vigor of a green old age, and in the maturity of experienced statesmanship. There were questions of serious import yet to be settled with Great Britain, springing out of all the precedent treaties with that power, from 1783 to 1818—the North-east and North-west boundaries, the fisheries, the navigation of the Mississippi, captured slaves, &c., with all of which Mr. Gallatin was well acquainted—better, perhaps, than any other statesman then at command. To consummate their adjustment, as far as attainable, Mr. Adams, in 1826, called him from his Springhill home, and sent him as Minister Plenipotentiary to London. His mission was eminently successful as to all those subjects; although, as to some of them, subsequent events showed that his negotiations still left room for further disputes. He returned to the United States in December, 1827, but never again resumed his residence in Fayette county. For a short period he took up his abode in Baltimore, where, we believe, two of Mrs. Gallatin's sisters, Mrs. Few and Mrs. Montgomery, then resided. He soon afterwards removed to the city of New York, and they with him; where he spent the long remnant of his life, not, however, in stately ease and idleness, as we shall presently see.

Although the sun of Mr. Gallatin's official career had now set, he continued to shed a long and brilliant twilight. In 1828-'29, at the instance of President Adams, he prepared the celebrated argument on behalf of the United States, to be laid before the King of Holland, the chosen umpire between us and Great Britain on the troublesome question of the North-east boundary. This umpirage having proved unavailing, the subject continued to occupy the active mind of Mr. Gallatin during subsequent years. In 1840 he published an elaborate dissertation upon it, in which he treated it historically, geographically, argumentatively and diplomatically; in all of which he exhibited an acuteness and fullness of knowledge never expended upon a similar question before or since. When this protracted and portentious controversy came to be finally adjusted between Mr. Webster and Lord Ashburton, in 1842, these labors of Mr. Gallatin—so full, so clear, so conclusive, contributed greatly to the satisfactory arrangement embodied in the treaty of Washington.

Soon after Mr. Gallatin's settlement in New York, he became the President of the National (not United States) Bank, one of the largest banking institutions of the commercial metropolis. Indeed, we believe the charter was procured with the special view of putting him at its head, and thereby adding the weight and wisdom of his financial character to the monetary power of that "mart of nations." And perhaps no one event added more to its growing greatness than the speedy resumption, in May, 1839, of specie payments by the banks of New York, after the general suspension of 1837. To this masterly achievement of policy and right, Mr. Gallatin gave his most earnest advocacy.

Mr. Gallatin continued, almost to the close of his life, to keep a watchful eye upon public affairs. When the Mexican war was sprung upon the nation, in 1846, his attention was at once arrested by the grounds upon which it was begun, and the pretensions and purposes of its continuance. It involved questions worthy of his mind and pen; and being adverse to the continuance, if not to the commencement of the war, he hesitated not to make an open avowal of his views in an extended discussion of the whole subject entitled "Peace With Mexico," published in 1847. His opinions, as to the grounds of the war, correspond with those of Mr. Benton, and as to its further prosecution, with those of Mr. Calhoun.

The closing years of Mr. Gallatin's life were spent chiefly in scientific and literary labors, partaking of an antiquarian and historical character. He became President of the New York Historical Society, and of another association denominated Ethnological, or pertaining to the original races or divisions of mankind; taking great interest in the objects of both. Among his contributions to the former, after the North-east boundary question had, in 1842, become a subject of history, was his Essay on Mr. Jay's map, which related to part of his celebrated treaty of 1794. Long prior to this, in 1836, he had published a "Synopsis of the Indian tribes in the United States, east of the Rocky Mountains, and in the British and Russian possessions,"—a work of wonderful labor and research. And he closed his life amid labors upon a similar work relating to the Indians of Mexico.

Mental labor and writing had become so much a habit of his life as to be an aliment of his existence. His is a rare case of a man who has spent his life in sedentary labors, and amid the excitements of politics and diplomacy, being able to preserve his mental and bodily health beyond four-score years. In writing to his friend, Judge Brooke, of Virginia, on the 4th of March, 1848, he says:—"Although you were pleased in your favor of December last, to admire the preservation of my faculties, these are in truth sadly impaired. I cannot work more than four hours a day, and I write with great difficulty. Entirely absorbed in a subject which engrossed all my thoughts and feelings," &c.—alluding to his ethnological labors. He adds:—"But though my memory fails me for recent transactions, it is unimpaired in reference to my early days. * * * I am now in my eighty-eighth year, growing weaker every month, with only the infirmities of age. For all chronical diseases I have no faith in physicians, consult none, and take no physic whatever."

But his "throwing physic to the dogs" does not quite solve the phenomena. Were we allowed to hazard an additional solution, it would be the unimpassioned, imperturbable structure of his mind, which rescued his most earnest pursuits and labored efforts from that cerebral excitement which generally superadds mental debility to physical prostration. He was eminently a man of thought and calculation, and not of feeling or impulse. The friends he had, he grappled with the hooks of steel; but they were hooks of cold, intellectual steel. He was always calm and self possessed, shut up in his own rich resources, keeping out the fear of failure and a wish for help by his own confident ability to succeed. Just as the student who is conscious of having his proposition in geometry at his finger's ends, will with an examination prize at stake, go through the exercises of the blackboard, without becoming either flushed or pale; and will sit down with as equable a pulse as if in a morning ride. Another proof of his serene equanimity, was his unvarying vivacity and extraordinary conversational powers. This may seem somewhat paradoxical; but if scrutinized, it will be found accordant to all the principles of sound intellectual pathology. Those endowments indicate a smooth, healthful flow of mental action, exempt from the undercurrent of passional elevation or depression. The attractiveness of their display, gave to Mr. G. much of his unbroken success:—the mental habitude from which they sprung, added years of health to his prolonged usefulness. He was, moreover, always at ease in his pecuniary affairs, and his domestic relations were uncommonly harmonious. Corroding care had no closet in either his heart or his household.

To his other studies Mr. Gallatin had added that of theological science. In youth he had imbibed Unitarian views of the character of Christ; but he avowed, in maturer years, his conviction of the errors of that belief. He was an admirer of the republican simplicity of the Presbyterian Church polity, but not of some of its doctrines. He was, he said, an Arminian Presbyterian. We believe he never became a visible member of any branch of the church militant; but, in the later years of his life, he worshiped at the Presbyterian church in New York, of which the Rev. Erskine Mason, D. D., (new school) is pastor.

Mr. Gallatin left two sons, James and Albert, and one daughter, Frances, wife of B. K. Stevens, Esq., to inherit his great fame and ample estates. They reside, in elegant ease, in the city of New York and vicinity, James having succeeded his father in the presidency of the National Bank. These are the children of his second wife—his first having been childless. She, however, adopted the fatherless child of a poor woman,—a boy, whom in regard for her memory after her death, Mr. Gallation educated, for which he, in return, assumed his benefactor's name. In early life he sought his fortunes in the West, but found, we believe, an untimely grave.

We will attempt no resume of the character and achievements of the subject of this extended memoir. If there be such a thing as a "self-made man," rising from untoward beginnings, and climbing unaided to the loftiest seats of fame and usefulness, Mr. Gallatin was one, of the highest order. Perhaps Longfellow chants truly in his Psalm of Life—

> "Lives of great men all remind us,
> We can make our lives sublime."

Mr. Gallatin died at the residence of his son-in-law, in Astoria, Long Island, on Sunday, August 12th, 1849, in the eighty-ninth year of his age.

[APPENDIX TO CHAPTER VII]

LIST OF SETTLERS IN FAYETTE

AND IN CONTIGUOUS PARTS OF

GREENE, WASHINGTON & WESTMORELAND COUNTIES, IN 1772:

COPIED FROM THE OFFICIAL ASSESSMENT ROLLS OF BEDFORD COUNTY FOR 1773.

In 1772, and until the erection of Westmoreland in 1773, Bedford county embraced all of South-western Pennsylvania.

All of what is now Fayette county, east of a straight line from the mouth of Redstone to the mouth of Jacob's creek, composed two townships, Springhill and Tyrone, between which the division line was Redstone creek, from its mouth to where it was crossed by Burd's Road, thence Burd's Road to Gist's, thence Braddock's Road to the Great Crossings. That part of Fayette which is west (or north-west) of the line from the mouth of Redstone to the mouth of Jacob's creek, was included in Rostraver township; which then embraced all of the "Forks of Yough" to the junction.

All of Greene and of Washington counties, which were then supposed to be within the limits of Pennsylvania, and lying west of Fayette, seem to have been included in Springhill.

We give the entire lists for Springhill, Tyrone and Rostraver.(a)

SPRINGHILL TOWNSHIP.

John Allen,	John Artman,	Samuel Adams,
William Allen,	Ichabod Ashcraft,	Robert Adams,
John Armstrong,	John Ally,	
Edward Askins,	John Allison,	George Boydston,

(a)As a curiosity, and to contrast the eastern part of Allegheny county, including Pittsburgh, &c., with Fayette county, in 1772, and with herself and city now, we give the names then on the roll for Pitt township, in all 79, viz: John Barr, Jacob Bausman, Col. Bird, Richard Butler, Wm. Butler; John Cavet, Jas. Cavet, Wm. Cunningham, Wm. Christy, Geo. Croghan, John Campbell; Wm. Elliott, Joseph Erwin; Mary Ferree; Thomas Gibson, Elizabeth Gibson; Samuel Heath; Thomas Lyon, Wm. Lyon; Jas. Myers, Eleazer Myers, Wm. Martin, Aeneas Mackay, Robt. M'Kinney, Jno.M'Callister, John M'Daniel, Thos. M'Camish, Thos. M'Bride, Charles M'Ginness, Lachlan M'Lean; John Ormsby; Wm. Powell, Jonathan Plummer; James Royal, Jas. Reed, Wm. Ramage, Peter Roletter, Andrew Robeson; John Sampson. Robert Semple, Samuel Semple, Geo. Sly, Devereaux Smith, Joseph Spear, John Small; Wm. Teagarden, Wm. Thompson, Benjamin Tate; Rinard Undus; Conrad Winebiddle, Conrad Windmiller, Philip Whitesell. Inmates.—Andrew Boggs, Charles Bruce; John Crawford, John Crawford, Joseph Closing, David Critslow; Jacob Divilbiss; Wm. Edwards; Geo. Kerr, Wm. Kerr; Wm. Owens; Geo. Phelps, Ab'm. Powers; Jas. Rice, Henry Rites, Jacob Ribold; Abrm. Slover, Charles Smith; Christian Tubb, John Thompson. Single Freemen.—Richard Butler, Wm. Butler; Geo. Croghan, Moses Coe; Ephr'm. Hunter; Geo. Kerr; Wm. Martin; Hugh O'Hara; Alex'r. Ross; John Sampson, Alex'r. Steel, John Thousman; Jacob Windmiller.

Peter Backus,
Brazil Brown,
Jas. Brown, (Dunlap's creek,)
Thomas Brown, (Ten Mile creek,)
Joseph Brown,
Samuel Brown,
Adam Brown,
Maunus Brown,
Thomas Brown,
John Brown,
Walter Brisco,
Peter Baker,
Nicholas Baker,
James Burdin,
John Burris,
Robert Brownfield,
Edward Brownfield,
Empson Brownfield,
Charles Brownfield,
Jeremiah Beek,
Charles Burkham,
Henry Beeson,
Jacob Beeson,
Alexander Buchanan,
James Black,
John Barkley,
Nicholas Bauk,
Thomas Banfield,
Thomas Batton,
William Brashears,
Joseph Barker,
Lewis Brimet,
James Branton,
Henry Brenton,
John Braddock,

Michael Carn,
George Craft,
Wm. Case,
Adam Cumbert,
John Craig
Joseph Caldwell,
James Crooks,
William Campbell,
John Carr,
John Carr, Jr.
Moses Carr,
William Cochran,
George Conn,
Nicholas Crowshoe,
Anthony Coshaw,

Wm. Crawford, Capt.
Wm. Crawford, Quaker,
Wm. Crawford,
Josias Crawford,
Oliver Crawford,
Richard Chinner,
Peter Cleam,
Jacob Cleam,
John Casteel,
George Church,
Michael Cox.
Joseph Cox,
Michael Catt,
Abraham Cills,
Anthony Cills,
William Conwell,
Jehu Conwell,
Michael Cresap,
William Colvin,
George Colvin,

Peter Drago,
John Drago,
Samuel Douglass,
Jeremiah Downs,
Augustus Dillener,
Edward Death,
John Death,
Owen David,
Jesse Dument,
William Downard,
Jacob Downard,
Henry Debolt,
George Debolt,
Henry Dever,
Lewis Davison,
Andrew Davison,
William Dawson,
Jacob Dicks,
Lewis Deem,

Henry Enoch,
John Evans,
Richard Evans,
Hugh Evans,
Edward Elliott,
Michael Franks,
Jacob Franks,
James Fleeharty,
John Fisher,
James Frame,

Nathan Friggs,
Henry Friggs,
Hugh Ferry,
James Flannegan,
David Flowers,
Thomas Flowers,

Thomas Gaddis,
Samuel Glasby,
William Garrat,
John Garrard,
John Garrard, Jr.
William Goodwin,
Joseph Goodwin,
Thomas Gooden,
John Glasgo,
Fred'k. Garrison,
Leonard Garrison,
Jacob Grow,
Zachariah Gobean,
John Griffith,
Hugh Gilmore,
Robert Gilmore,
Thomas Gregg,
Charles Gause,
Daniel Goble,
Nicholas Gilbert,
Andrew Gudgel,

Henry Hart,
David Hatfield, Jr.
John Hendricks,
Henry Hall,
John Hall,
Adam Henthorn,
James Henthorn,
Jas. Henthorn, (the less.)
John Henthorn,
Charles Hickman,
Aaron Hackney,
Martin Hardin,
Benjamin Hardin,
William Hardin,
John Hardin, Jr.
John Harman,
Geo. Huckleberry,
John Huffman,
John Harrison,
David Hawkins,
James Herod,
William Herod,
Levi Herod,

SPRINGHILL.

Henson Hobbs,
Samuel Howard,
William House,
Philemon Hughes,
Thos. Hughes, (Muddy creek,)
Thomas Hughes,
Owen Hughes,
John Huston,

Hugh Jackson,
David Jennings,
Aaron Jenkins,
Jonathan Jones,
John Jones,

Thomas Lane,
Absalom Little,
Samuel Lucas,
Thomas Lucas,
Richard Lucas,
Hugh Laughlin,
David Long,
John Long,
John Long, Jr.
Jacob Link,

Aaron Moore,
John Moore,
Jno. Moore, (over the river,)
Simon Moore,
Hans Moore,
David Morgan,
Charles Morgan,
William Masters,
John Masterson,
Henry Myers,
George Myers,
Ulrick Myers,
Martin Mason,
John Mason,
Alexander Miller,
John Messmore,
John Mene,
Daniel Moredock,
James Moredock,
Adam Mannon,
John Mannon,
John Marr,
William M'Dowell,
John M'Farland,
Francis M'Ginness,
Nathaniel M'Carty,

Samuel M'Cray,
James M'Coy,
Hugh M'Cleary,

Tunis Newkirk,
Barnet Newkirk,
Peter Newkirk,
James Neal,
George Newell,
James Notts,
James Notts, Jr.
Charles Nelson,
Adam Newlon,
Bernard O'Neal,

Jacob Poundstone,
Frederick Parker,
Philip Pearce,
Theophilus Phillips,
Thomas Phillips,
Adam Penter,
Richard Parr,
Henry Peters,
John Peters,
Christian Pitser,
Ahimon Pollock,
John Pollock,
Samuel Paine,
John Wm. Provance,

Ieronemus Rimley,
Casper Rather,
Telah Rood,
Jesse Rood,
Daniel Robbins,
John Robbins,
Roger Roberts,
Jacob Riffle,
Ralph Riffle,
William Rail,
David Rogers,
Thomas Roch,
Edward Roland,
William Rees,
Jonathan Rees,
Jacob Rich,

Thomas Scott,
Edward Scott,
Andrew Scott,
James Scott,
John Smith, (Dunlap's creek,)

John Smith,
Robert Smith,
James Smith,
Philip Smith,
William Smith,
Conrad Seix,
Isaac Sutton,
Isaac Sutton, Jr.
Jacob Sutton,
Lewis Saltser,
Samuel Stilwell,
William Spangler,
John Swearingen,
William Shepperd,
John Swan,
John Swan, Jr.
Thomas Swan,
Robert Sayre,
Stephen Styles,
Samuel Sampson,
Joseph Starkey,
David Shelby,
Elias Stone,

Obadiah Truax,
John Thompson,
Michael Tuck,
Abraham Teagarden,
George Teagarden,
Edward Taylor,
Michael Thomas,

Henry Vanmeter,
Abraham Vanmeter,
Jacob Vanmeter,
John Vantrees,
John Varvill,

David White,
James White,
George Williams,
David Walters,
Ephraim Walters,
David Wright,
George Wilson, Esq.
James Wilson,
John Waits,
John Watson,
George Watson,

Joseph Yauger,
Telah Yourk.—305.

THE MONONGAHELA OF OLD.

Inmates—(Boarders not heads of families.)

Richard Ashcraft,
Ephraim Ashcraft,
Samuel Adams,

John Bachus,
William Burt,
John Beeson,
Samuel Bridgewater,
Coleman Brown,
William Brown,
Bazil Brown,
Benjamin Brashears,
Richard Brownfield,
Benjamin Brooks,
Alexander Bryan,
William Bells,

Gabriel Cox,
Israel Cox,
Samuel Colson,
Joseph Coon,
Robert Cavines,
John Cross,
Edward Carn,
Christian Coffman,
John Curley,
Nathaniel Case,
John Crossley,
Christopher Capley,
George Catt,
John Chadwick,
Jonathan Chambers,
John Cline,

Benajah Dunn,

Zephaniah Dunn,
Timothy Downing,
Jeremiah Davis,
James Davis,

Thomas Edwards,
Bernard Eckley,

James Fugate,

John Guthrey,
William Groom,

Captain John Hardin,
William Henthorn,
William Hogland,
Edward Hatfield,
John Hawkins,
Samuel Herod,
John Hargess,
Thomas Hargess,

Joseph Jackson,
Jacob Jacobs,

John Kinneson,
Thomas Kendle,

William Lee,
Andrew Link,

Elijah Mickle,
William Murphy,
John Morgan,
Morgan Morgan.

Samuel Merrifield,
John Main, Jr.
William Martin,
John Morris,
Jacob Morris,
George M'Coy,
John M'Fall,
Alexander M'Donald,
William M'Claman,

John Pettyjohn,
Baltzer Peters,
Richard Powell,
Thomas Pyburn,
John Phillips,
Thomas Provance,

Thomas Rail,
Noah Rood,

William Spencer,
Alexander Smith,
John Smith,
Francis Stannater,

John Taylor
William Thompson,

Jonah Webb,
John Williamson,
Alexander White,
Benjamin Wells,
Michael Whitelock,

Jeremiah Yourk,
Ezekiel Yourk.—89.

Single Freemen.

John Brown,
Joseph Batton,
Isher Budd,
David Blackston,

Hugh Crawford,
John Crawford,
Francis Chain,
William Cheny,
Daniel Christy,
James Chamberlain,
James Carmichael,
James Campbell,

John Catch,

John Dicker,
John Douglass,
Edward Dublin,

Elias Eaton,
Alexander Ellener,
Samuel Eckerly,

Thomas Foster,
Jacob Funk,
Martin Funk,

Joseph Gwin,
Bartlett Griffith,

John Holton,
Abraham Holt,
John Holt,
Joshua Hudson,
John Hupp,

Cornelius Johnson,

Josiah Little,

TYRONE.

William Marshall,
James Morgan,
Hugh Murphey,
George Morris,
Joseph Morris,
David M'Donald,
Abraham M'Farland,
John M'Gilty,

John Notts,
Philip Nicholas,

James Peters,
Isaac Pritchard,
Jonathan Paddox,
Ebenezer Paddox,

Noble Rail,
Nathan Rinehart,
Samuel Robb,
James Robertson,
Philip Rogers,
Total 452

John Shively,
Christopher Swoop,
Ralph Smith,
John Sultzer,

William Teagarden,
John Taylor,

John Verville, Jr.
John Williams.—58.

TYRONE TOWNSHIP.

Jonathan Arnold,
Andrew Arnold,
David Allen,

Andrew Byers,
Christopher Beeler,
Henry Beeson,
John Boggs,
Thomas Brownfield,

Bernard Cunningham,
Daniel Canon,
Edward Conn,
George Clark,
George Clark, Jr.
John Cherry,
James Cravin,
John Clem,
John Cornwall,
John Castleman,
William Crawford, Esq.
Valentine Crawford,
William Collins.

George Dawson,
Edward Doyle,
Joshua Dickenson,
John Dickenson,
Thomas Davis,

Robert Erwin,

Thomas Freeman,

James Gamble,

Reason Gale,
Thomas Gist, Esq.

Charles Harrison,
William Harrison,
Ezekiel Hickman,
Henry Hartley,
James Harper,
Joseph Huston,
William Hanshaw,

John Keith,

Andrew Linn,
David Lindsay,
John Laughlin,
Samuel Lyon,

Alexander Moreland,
Augustine Moore,
Edmund Martin,
Michael Martin,
Hugh Masterson,
Isaac Meason,
Philip Meason,
Providence Mounts,
William Massey,
William Miller,
Robert M'Glaughlin,
William M'Kee,

Robert O'Gullion,

Adam Payne,
Elisha Pearce,

Isaac Pearce,
George Paull,

Andrew Robertson,
Edmund Rice,
Robert Ross,
Samuel Rankin,
William Rankin,

Dennis Springer,
Josiah Springer,
George Smith,
Moses Smith,
Isaac Sparks,
William Sparks,
John Stephenson,
Richard Stephenson,
John Stewart,
Philip Shute,

Philip Tanner,
James Torrance,
Thomas Tilton,

John Vance,

Conrad Walker,
Henry White,
William White,
Joseph Wells,
John Waller,
Richard Waller,
Lund Washington,
George Young.—89.

Inmates.

Reding Blunt,
Zechariah Connell,
Peter Castner,

Smith Corbit,
Francis Lovejoy,
Agney Maloney,

Joseph Reily,
Edward Stewart,—8.

Single Freemen.

Robert Beall,		Patrick Masterson,
James Berwick,	Elijah Lucas,	Alexander M'Clean,
George Brown,		
	Francis Main,	Daniel Stephens,
William Castleman,	James Mock,	William Shepherd.—13.
	Thomas Moore,	
John Felty,	Total ....110..	

Uncultivated Lands.

George Washington, (*)	1500 acres.	Nicholas Dawson,	300	acres.
John A. Washington,	600 "	Sniveley's Administrators,	300	"
Samuel Washington,	600 "	Halvert Adams,	300	"
Lund Washington,	300 "	Joseph Hunter,	900	"
Thomas Gist, Esq.	600 "			

ROSTRAVER TOWNSHIP.

Benjamin Applegate,
Daniel Applegate,
William Applegate,
Thomas Applegate,

Alexander Bowling,
Andrew Baker,
Samuel Burns,
James Burns,
Ishan Barnett,
Morris Brady,
Samuel Biggon,
Samuel Beckett,

Edward Cook,

Andrew Dye,
James Devoir,
John Dogtauch,
William Dunn,

Peter Elrod,
Peter Easman,

Paul Froman,
Rev. Jas. Finley,

Samuel Glass,
Samuel Grissey,
John Greer,
James Gragh,

Christopher Houseman,
Thomas Hind,
Peter Hildebrand,
Joseph Hill,
Llewellen Howell,

Deverich Johnson,
James Johnson,
Jacob Johnson,
Joseph Jones,

John Kiles,
John Kilton,

Andrew Linn,
William Linn,
Nathan Linn,
Frederick Lamb,

John Miller,
Oliver Miller,
Abraham Miller,
Alexander Miller,
Alexander Morehead,
Alexander Mitchell,
John Mitchell,
Jesse Martin,
Morgan Morgan,
Robert Mays,
Daniel M'Gogan,
James M'Kinley,

Robert M'Connell,

Ralph Nisley,

Dorsey Pentecost,
Benjamin Pelton,
David Price,
John Perry,
Samuel Perry,
Joseph Pearce,
John Pearce,
James Peers,
Andrew Pearce,

Edward Smith,
Samuel Sinclair,
Henry Speer,
John Shannon,
Michael Springer,
Richard Sparks,
William Sultzman,
Van Swearingen,

William Turner,
Philip Tanner,

Joseph Vanmeter,
Jacob Vanmeter,
John Vanmeter,
Peter Vandola,

---

*See Chap. XIV.—"Washington in Fayette."

ROSTRAVER.

Adam Wickenhimen,
David Williams,
George Weddel,
John Weddel,

James Wall,
Samuel Wilson,
James Wilson,
Isaac Wilson,

John Wiseman,
Thomas Wells,

James Young.—88.

Inmates.

Benjamin Allen,
Nathaniel Brown,
Benajah Burkham,
John Bleasor,

Samuel Clem,
Thomas Cummins,

Benajah Dumont,

Samuel Davis,
Thomas Dobin,
Hugh Dunn,

Peter Hanks,
Joseph Hill,

Joseph Lemon,

William Moore,
John M'Clellan,
Felty M'Cormick,

Martin Owens,

Abraham Ritchey,

Peter Skinner.—19.

Single Freemen.

William Boling,
Jesse Dumont,
John Finn,
Isaac Greer,
Moses Holliday,

Peter Johnson,
Ignatius Jones,
Thomas Miller,
Jacob M'Meen,
Baltser Shiling,

Levi Stephens,
Cornelius Thompson,
Robert Turner.—14.

Total 121

CHAPTER VIII.

MASON AND DIXON'S LINE.

Its peculiarities—36 deg. 30 min.—Slavery—Colonial Titles—New England and Virginia at 40 deg.—The Dutch Dynasty—Delaware born at Swaanendael—Maryland granted—The Swedes—The Dutch conquer them—The Duke of York conquers the Dutch—His Domains—William Penn—Pennsylvania granted—Where was 40 deg.—Disputes with Lord Baltimore begin—Penn buys Delaware—Boundary Negotiations—The King halves the Peninsula—Delaware stands alone—Death and Character of Penn—New Lords—Concordat of 1723—Agreement of 1732—Boundaries agreed upon—Strife renewed—Parties go into Chancery—Quibbling—Border Feuds—Cresap—Temporary Line—Lord Harwicke's Decrees—Final Agreement of July 4, 1760—Gains and Losses of the Parties—Retributive Justice—Pennsylvania ahead—Connecticut controversy—The Lines run—Mason and Dixon—Lines around Delaware—the Great Due-West Line—Slow progress—Indians about—Halt at the War-path—The Corner Cairn—How the Line was marked—The Visto—Instruments used—Measurements—New Troubles—All quiet—Distances and Localities—Re-tracings in 1849—Errors and Certainties—Mutations of Boundary and Empire—Is the History of the Line ended? Not yet.

The southern boundary of Pennsylvania exhibits several striking peculiarities. Its eastern end consists of a considerable arc of a circle, which, springing from the river Delaware, connects itself with the latitudinal part of the line by a deep, sharp indentation, or notch, so as to resemble what in architecture is called a bead. From the initial point of the latitudinal line, near the circle, it stretches away to the west, through field and forest; intent only upon preserving its course, without being deflected by either the channel of a river or the crest of a mountain. Climbing obliquely the summit of the Alleghenies, it turns its back upon the fountains which feed the Atlantic; and, rushing down into the Ohio Valley, stoops in its pathway to drink of the crystal waters of the Youghiogheny. Rising refreshed, and with its eye still fixed to the West, it hurries on, regardless of the intersecting line of a sister sovereignty; and, stalking across the Cheat and the Monongahela, stops amid the Fish creek hills, within half a day's journey of the river Ohio; as if exhausted by the rugged route it has traversed, and unable to reach that great natural boundary, recognized by every other State than Pennsylvania which its current laves.

Upon a closer inspection it will be seen that it is equally regardless of the established lines of admeasurement upon the earth's surface; conforming to neither of the limits of a degree of latitude, nor to any of its easily-comprehended parts; and this, without being forced into its anomalous position by any object, or obstacle of nature. For at neither end does it terminate, nor in any part of its extended course does it touch, upon any prominent natural landmark. It is wholly, in every part, and in all its forms, an artificial, arbitrary line, without a model, or a fellow upon the continent.(a) And yet it is perhaps more unalterable than if nature had made it: for it limits the soverignty of four States, each of whom is as tenacious of its peculiar systems of law as of its soil. It is the boundary of empire.

Whence came these peculiarities—this palpable disregard of the plain provisions of nature and science for the divisions of dominion? Is this singular line the result of compulsion, or of compact—of noisy strife, or of quiet agreement? How old is it—what its ancestry—whence its name? These, with many other curious questions which spring from the subject, take hold upon the past, and find their solution only in history. Strange subject too, for history, is a line, defined to be "length, without breadth or thickness." Yet this line has a history of a hundred years' duration, spreading out over more than half the old thirteen States, and sinking deep into the very foundations of their being. It abounds in curious conflict of grant and construction, in bold encroachments upon vested rights, in artful remedies for inconvenient limitations. Kings, lords and commoners, English, Swedes and Dutch, Quakers and Catholics, figure conspicuously in the narrative, with dramatic effect. Upon much of the disputed margins of the line have been enacted scenes of riot, invasion, and even murder; which want only the fanciful pen of Scott or an Irving to develop their romantic

---

(a) In some respects, the celebrated 36 deg. 30 min. resembles Mason and Dixon's Line; with which political writers and declaimers sometimes confound it. But it has neither the beauty, the accuracy, nor the historic interest of our line. It is, or rather was intended to be, the southern boundary of the States of Virginia, Kentucky and Missouri; but it has been most bunglingly run, as a glance at a United States map will show. Beginning correctly, on the Atlantic, at Currituck inlet, by the time it gets to the western confine of North Carolina —to which it was run before the Revolution—it is some two miles to the south. Its extension was resumed in 1779-80; and after correcting the first error the surveyors run into a greater one, for at the Tennessee river they are some ten or twelve miles too far to the north. When afterwards extended to the southwest corner of Missouri the surveyors drop down to the true 36 deg. 30 min. and run it out truly; except the deviation, west of the Mississippi, to take in the New Madrid settlement. West of the south-west corner of Missouri, this line of 36 deg. 30 min. has a history which it is too soon yet to write.

interest. In the strife and negotiations which led to its establishment, endurance and evasion were put to their highest tests: in tracing it, science achieved one of its most arduous labors. In intricacy and interest, if not in importance, the subject is inferior to none in Amercan history. We regret that we can give to it here only a condensed exposition. That which, without undue expansion, could fill a volume, must here be limited to a brief statement of why, when and how the line was established, accompanied only by such illustrative details as have interest to us who stand upon its western end. It will be seen also that the subject is an indispensable preliminary to the boundary controversy with Virginia, to which we will introduce the reader in our next chapter. And although the two subjects are as inseparable as the lines to which they relate, they are sufficiently distinct to allow them to be separately considered. We take up the oldest first.

Some inconsiderate reader may be disposed to turn away in disgust from a further perusal of this sketch upon the assumption that Mason and Dixon's Line can have no other history than a diatribe upon the stale subject of slavery. To give instant relief to such an one, we promise to say not one word upon that subject. Historically, the line has nothing to do with human bondage. True, in the course of human events it has come to pass that it has long been the limit, to the northward, of the "peculiar institution;" and were it not that the "pan-handle," like an upheaval of schist through a stratum of free old red sand-stone, mars its continuity, it would, by direct connection with the Ohio, form, with it, an unbroken barrier to the desolations(b) of slave labor, from the Delaware to the

---

(b) We use this term in no harsh or political sense. Except in the culture of the great Southern staples of cotton, sugar, rice and tobacco, slaveholders themselves regard slave labor as unprofitable, and mourn over its desolations. Wasteful and imperfect tillage and depreciation of intelligent white labor, are its unavoidable tendencies. Hence the Southern avidity for new lands in the West, wherein to plant the "institution." Experience has shown that outside appeals and arguments, drawn from the right and wrong of the "relation," will never sever the South from slavery. Nor will climate effect the cure. Interest—loss and gain, are the great solvents before which it will crumble and dissolve. Whenever it can acquire no more virgin soil upon which to spread itself—whenever its peculiar staples can be as well produced by free labor, or find substitutes in the products of free white labor—then will slaveholders become the advocates of "abolition." Until then, the policy of the North is to let them alone; and firmly, but kindly, to resist any further enlargement of their territorial or political dominion. For they seek to acquire and maintain political ascendancy only to preserve and advance their interests. Happily, there is yet room enough for all—white and colored, native and foreign. Let each have their proper rights and places; and if we cannot agree, let us not quarrel, about their distribution.

Mississippi. But it was established for no such purpose, and when established, negro slavery existed upon both sides of it. That it has ceased to exist on one side and not on the other, are fixed facts, attributable to influences which we are not here called to consider. We have to treat of transactions that reach further back upon the track of time.

The discovery of America, in 1492, was a great event in the annals of human progress. And yet it seems to have come too soon; for it required the lapse of another century to render it available for any real good to the mass of mankind. In the meantime, however, mind was becoming emancipated, and separate portions of the New World were being appropriated by the nations who were, in due time, to people its wastes.

The mode of acquiring title to distinct parts of the American continent by the old European nations, had in it more of form than of fact, more of might than of right. It consisted in sending out some bold navigator, who, after sailing in sight of some hitherto undiscovered coast, or up some bay or river, upon whose surface had never before been cast the shadow of a ship, landed upon its shores, unfurled the flag under which he sailed, and with cross in hand, devoutly took possession for his country, to the exclusion of all other Christian claimants. In this consisted the vaunted Right of Prior Discovery—a kind of kingly "squatter sovereignty," or national pre-emption, founded upon a necessity for some limit to the land-greed of nations as well as individuals.

The domain of England in North America, conferred by the prior discoveries in 1497, of John Cabot, and his son Sebastian, extended, along the Atlantic coast, from N. latitude 58 deg. to 31 deg., or from Labrador to Florida. Her rights to the extreme latitudes of this range were, for a while, and very justly, too, disputed by France and Spain. She, therefore, wisely postponed asserting her rights to these, until after she had firmly seated herself within the temperate latitudes of her claim; which, although more southward than her own, were nearly isothermal in temperature, and congenial to the physical constitutions and industrial pursuits of her people. In due time she was thus enabled to crush out the pretensions of her rivals; and, in the meantime, to profit by their competition with her, and with each other.

The era of earnest effort in England to colonize America clusters within half a century around the year 1600. Other European nations awoke to like attempts within the same period and within the same latitudes; some of which will demand our notice in the sequel. We pass over the premature and ill-fated efforts of Gilbert Raleigh, from 1578 to 1588, under the patronage of Elizabeth; ill-fated because premature, not because ill-designed, so far as under the control of human will. Hence those early efforts were fruitless of aught else than disaster and discouragement, save that they afforded to that haughty queen the privilege of glorifying her "cheerless state of single blessedness" by giving the appellation of Virginia to the whole of her American possessions.

In 1603, Westminster Abbey received the remains of Elizabeth. The Tudor dynasty was now ended. Had our colonies been planted under their auspices, they would probably have grown into vast absolute feudalities. Happily for their fundamental adaptedness to become nurseries of civil and religious liberty, nearly all the Old Thirteen drew their charters from the prodigality, and their founders from the oppressed subjects, of the Stuart race of kings; who were as lavish of their distant domains upon "favorite courtiers, or troublesome subjects," as they were tenacious of power and prerogative at home. The set time for founding an empire of freedom had now come, and they were the appointed agents to effect it. Unwittingly, they became sponsors for foundlings, who within two centuries rose in independence, as if to avenge their dethronement upon the haughty House of Hanover. They gave away the soil of half a continent, which it cost them nothing to acquire, and with it the seeds of institutions which "were not the offspring of deliberate forethought, which were not planted by the hand of man;—they grew like the lilies, which neither toil nor spin."(c)

In 1606, King James I, of England, leaving ample margins at the North and the South for disputed dominion, granted eleven degrees of latitude on the Atlantic—from N. latitude 34 deg. to 45 deg., or from the southern point of North Carolina to the northern confines of New York and Vermont, to two companies of corporators; one of which, called the London Company, was to possess the South; the other, called the Plymouth Company, was to possess the North; with an intervening community of territory between

---

(c)Bancroft. The voluminous History of the United States by this eminent statesman and scholar, although invaluable for its fullness, richness and general accuracy, is lamentably deficient in defining the limits of the ancient colonial grants. Indeed, whoever wishes, from our most popular standard writers, to compile a boundary history, undertakes an arduous and perplexing labor. Generally, they are meagre, confused and conflicting.

them, from N. latitude 38 deg. to 41 deg. Virginia was the common name to both, but it was soon exclusively appropriated by the southern company, which was the most efficient. Under its auspices, in 1607, the first enduring English settlement upon the continent was planted at Jamestown. Even the Puritan Pilgrims who landed from the Mayflower, on Plymouth Rock, in cold December, 1620, sailed from Holland under a grant from this company.

In 1609, the same facile king, by a new or amended charter, greatly enlarged the privileges and territory of the southern company. He now gave it a front upon the Atlantic coast of four hundred miles, of which Old Point Comfort, the southern cape of James river, was to be the half way point:—"and from the seacoast of the precinct aforesaid up into the land throughout, from sea to sea, west and north-west:"—very ample limits, truly. Old Point Comfort is nearly upon N. latitude 37 deg. Hence, at 69½ miles to a degree, this enlargement had little effect upon the southern limit of the Old Dominion; but northwardly, it gave to her two degrees of latitude of what had before been common territory, and (making due allowance for the coast-line being the base of the triangle,) carried her about up to N. latitude 40 deg. This charter was revoked, or annulled, by the king, in 1624; but, except when portions of her territory were, by several subsequent grants, conveyed away to other favorites, to become the germs of other States, no further change was ever afterwards made in the boundaries of Old Virginia.

The old North Virginia Company was a rickety, short-lived concern. It accomplished nothing towards colonization. It, however, did one good thing. The southern company having, by maltreatment, driven from its service its father and defender, Captain John Smith, its northern rival gave him employment, and sent him out to explore and map its territory. He had proved his competency by having before performed similar labors upon the region around the Chesapeake. Having accomplished the work assigned him by the Plymouth Company, he returned to England in 1614; drew out a map and an account of his explorations, which he presented to the king's son, Prince Charles, who thereupon named the territory New England. Here ended the old North Virginia Company, whose territory was from N. latitude 41 deg. to 45 deg.

While the Pilgrim Fathers were on their ocean way from old to new Plymouth, in 1620, a new charter was granted by James I. to a new corporation, by the name of "The Council established at Plymouth, in the county of Devon, for the planting, ruling, ordering and governing of New England in America." Its territory was "all that part of America lying in breadth from 40 deg. to 48 deg. N. latitude, and in length by all the breadth aforesaid throughout the main land, from sea to sea:"—a grant which would have outlimited its southern rival,' had it not been that, ere this, the French had crept in, through the gulf and river St. Lawrence, behind them, and founded Canada. It, however, became the father of the New England States. From it the numerous colonies, of which they are now the aggregates, derived their territorial grants. Their charters of privileges and government they obtained directly from the throne. These grants were regarded as kind of sub-infeudations, carved out of the original grant; and, by 1635, had well nigh exhausted it. New England, however, was regarded as an entirety until after 1632, the year in which Virginia suffered her first dismemberment.

We have been thus particular in developing the foundations and territorial juxtaposition of these two old parent colonies, New England and Virginia, for the purpose of determining with precision at what point or line they united. The materiality of the inquiry will soon be apparent. Manifestly, their common boundary was the 40th line of north latitude. There we leave them together in peace, resting upon the bosom of Pennsylvania, while we go back to trace up the strife we are soon to contemplate.

Ere yet these two old parent colonies had solemnized their nuptials at 40 deg., in 1609, there sailed from the Trexel, in Holland, a well appointed ship, commanded by Sir Henry Hudson, an Englishman then in the employ of the Dutch East India Company. His object was to find a north-west passage to China. Driven out of the arctic inlets by ice and fogs, he turns his prow southward along the English-American coast, as far as the Chesapeake. Having studied Captain Smith's map of that region, he knew where he was. His object was discovery. He again steers northward. Keeping more closely to the shore, he discovered the Delaware Bay, into which he sailed; but its flat shores not suiting his taste, he repassed its capes without landing. Coasting along the sands of New Jersey, he discovered the entrance to the New York waters.(d) He enters and anchors within Sandy Hook. The forests

---

(d)Although Hudson was probably the earliest European discoverer of the Delaware, yet Verrazza'ni, who sailed under the flag of France, was in New York harbor before him, in 1524. The Delaware takes its name from Lord Delaware, Governor of the South Virginia Colony in 1609, who, it is said, perished off its capes.

and slopes of the Nevisink hills were inviting. The natives were kind and inquisitive. He had found the objects of his pursuit. Before he left he passed the Narrows, sounded his way up the river which now bears his name, beyond the Highlands, and, in a boat, went above Albany. Satisfied, he returned to England, and reported his discoveries to the Dutch. The next year, while in the service of London merchants, seeking the north-west passage, he perished in the great northern bay whose name is his only monument.

Holland, or more properly the States General of the United Netherlands, was then the most energetic maratime power of Europe. They quickly availed themselves of Hudson's American discoveries; and while Smith was exploring New England, they were seating themselves upon what are now the southern territories of New York and eastern New Jersey. Operating entirely by the agency of a corporation—the Dutch West India Company, whose chief aim was trade, they, for many years evinced no design to form any settlements beyond such as were convenient attendants upon traffic. They abode in strength upon the island of Manhattan, founding there, by the name of New Amsterdam, what has become the greatest commercial city of the New World. Gradually they assumed the form and functions of a colony. They spread themselves from Staten Island to Canada, and from the Connecticut to the Delaware, giving to their claim the name of New Netherlands. Although in the grant of New England, in 1620, there was an express exception of territory then in the possession of any other Christian prince or State, yet England and New England ever regarded them as intruders and omitted no opportunity of attack and annoyance. They, however, by policy and prowess, were enabled to maintain their possessions for half a century, "beset with forts, and sealed with their blood." They were there by sufferance; but in the pages of one of our richest American classics, and in the names of men and places upon both shores of the Hudson, they were there forever. It is, however, to one of the most thoroughly effaced vestiges of their power that our subject is most nearly related.

The Dutch continued to keep an eye to the shores of the Delaware. They built Fort Nassau on the Jersey side, at Gloucester Point, about four miles below Philadelphia. Cornelius May, one of their sea captains, divided his name between its capes, calling the stream South river, as they had called the Hudson, North river. Five years after the Virginia charter was revoked, and ere its northern latitudes had been re-granted or settled, in 1629, Godyn, a Hollander, bought from the natives a tract of about thirty miles front on the western coast of the Delaware Bay, between the southern limit of Kent county and Cape Henlopen:—not the cape now known by that name, but a headland fifteen miles further south, now called Fenwick's Island, where the southern limit of Delaware cuts the Atlantic. In 1631, he and his associates sent from the Texel, under the conduct of Devries, a trio of vessels, laden with men and women to the number of thirty, cattle, farming implements and seeds. They landed upon the desired coast, and there, near the present site of Lewistown, planted the colony of Swaanendael. Wheat, tobacco and furs were the objects of the settlement. At the end of a year Devries left it, begirt with the forests and the ocean, in peace and prosperity. The next year he returned, and found its site marked only by the blackened huts and bleaching bones of his countrymen. But this short-lived colony was the cradle of a commonwealth. The seed thus buried in blood and ashes, ere long germinated and grew into the State of Delaware—small for its age, but good for its size.

One of the Secretaries of State to James I. was Sir George Calvert, an eminent favorite with the court and the people, and whom the king created Lord of the Barony of Baltimore in Ireland. He resigned his office to embrace the Catholic faith; and his new-born zeal and love of colonial aggrandizement soon impelled him to seek for a grant of American territory whereto his religious brethren might flee from the rigors of conformity. His first resort was to Newfoundland; but failing there, he looked down into the more genial latitudes of Virginia. He had been a member of the old South Virginia Company, and hence looked for some favor in that quarter. This was in 1629. The Virginia Cavaliers, however, treated him rather cavalierly, and put at him the test oaths of conformity and allegiance. These he declined. He knew that the South Virginia charter was annulled, and that the unsettled wastes of her territory were subject anew to the royal grant. He saw that no settlements existed north of the 38 deg. and the Potomac. Its super-abundant water privileges and luxuriant forests were sufficient temptation to become its proprietary, without the incentive of revenge upon his old Virginia associates. He returned to England, and besought its investiture. It was well known there that not only the Dutch, but the Swedes and French, were preparing to send colonies into these central parts of the English dominion; but it was not known that any had yet been sent, or if Devries' voyage was known, it was unheeded. The Swedes had not yet moved, and the

French never did. England herself asserted the need of occupancy to perfect title to the wilderness. Hence these efforts of other nations stimulated the readiness of the king to yield to the solicitude of Lord Baltimore. The charter, drawn by Sir George himself with unprecedented wisdom and liberality, was prepared; but ere it passed the seals, he died; and his son, Cecil Calvert, inherited his Irish title and seigniory expectant in America.

In June, 1632, Charles I. granted unto his "trusty and well beloved subject," Cecilius Calvert, Lord Baltimore, all that part of the peninsula, or eastern shore of the Chesapeake, north of a line drawn eastward from the mouth of the Potomac through Watkins' Point and the mouth of the river Wighco, or Pocomoke, to the ocean; which line is nearly on north latitude 38 deg.;—"and between that bound on the south, unto that part of Delaware Bay, on the north, which lieth under the fortieth degree of north latitude, where New England terminates; and all that tract of land from the aforesaid Bay of Delaware, is a right line, by the degree aforesaid to the true meridian of the first fountain of the river Potomac, and from thence tending towards the south to the further bank of said river, and following the west and south side of it to a certain place," &c., to the beginning. The young proprietary grantee being of the same faith of his father and of Charles' aspiring Queen, Henrietta Maria, she named the grant Maryland.

At the date of this charter, save Claiborne's trading settlement upon Kent Island in the Chesapeake, which does not concern us here, the whole territory, within the confines of the grant, was a waste of woods and waters, uninhabited by a civilized man: and so it was recited to be, in the preamble—"hactenus terra incula." We will soon see what ominous import lay hidden in these unmeaning words. The obvious intent of this grant was to convey to Lord Baltimore the English title to all of the old revoked Virginia grant which was north of the Potomac and of the base line on the peninsula. It was intended to carry Maryland close up to New England, and full out to the Delaware. It can mean nothing else. No other grant, no settlement interfered. It was entitled to go to its uttermost bounds. The only real ambiguity that lurked in its descriptive terms was a latent one, of very considerable importance, which we will discover after a while.

The New England Company, as well as King Charles, had been outwitted in the charter which he, in 1629, gave to Massachusetts. It conferred privileges far in advance of the age. Thinking to undermine it, the Council at Plymouth in Devon, in 1635, surrendered its charter: and thus were all the unsettled latitudes of New England, south of the colonies which had been carved out of it, exposed to new grants and settlement. North latitude 40 deg. was no longer its southern limit.

New actors now come upon the stage. Gustavus Adolphus of Sweden had long meditated the planting of a Protestant colony upon the Delaware. But war diverted both his zeal and his funds. He fell, in defense of the Reformation, upon the bloody field of Lutzen. But his spirit remained in his Chancellor, Oxenstiern, who guided the helm of affairs during the minority of Queen Christina. Under his auspices, late in 1637, the first party of Swedes and Fins sailed for the Delaware, where they landed, at Cape Inlopen, early in 1638. We know that a much earlier date has been given to their advent; but later researches have disclosed the error, and thereby dissipated a favorite ground of attack upon Lord Baltimore's title to the Delaware shore, under cover of "terra inculta." Upon their arrival they bought from the natives rights to settle all along the western shore, up to Trenton Falls; and gave to their domain the name of New Sweden. The Dutch scowled upon them, but the terror of Swedish valor gave them protection. The new colonists grew rapidly in numbers and prosperity, built forts and churches, and were surpassingly successful in cultivating the soil, and in trade and favor with the Indians. In a few years the power of Sweden fell; and thereupon the envy of the New Netherlanders rose to resistance. In 1655, they sent into the Delaware a fleet of seven good Dutch ships, well manned, under the command of Governor Stuyvesant, who quickly reduced the Swedish forts and re-established the Dutch dominion. Annexing their conquests to the effaced colony of Swaanendael, they dated back their title, by relation, to the purchase by Godyn. It was this faction that overreached the title of Lord Baltimore. Had Leonard Calvert led the first settlers of Maryland to the Delaware coast of his brother's domain, the American confederacy would probably have had one little State less.

Charles I. was beheaded in 1649; and during the troubles which preceded that event, as well as during the supremacy of Cromwell, the Lords Proprietary of Maryland were less anxious about its boundaries than its existence. The Catholic colony grew slowly, and was weak. Hence no decisive efforts to dispossess the Dutch were made until after the Restoration, in 1660; and then it was too late. Possession gave confidence, if not power. And to all the arguments and entreaties of Lord Baltimore, the Dutch West

India Company answered: "We will defend our South river possessions even unto the spilling of blood."

Charles II. came to the throne of his father in 1660. Proud, profligate and prodigal, he cared less for the preservation of his dominions than for the gratifications of his passions. Alexander wept when he had no more nations to conquer—Charles II. sighed when he had no more distant territories to give away. He was justly caricatured in Holland with a courtesan upon each arm, and courtiers picking his pockets. This "screwed his courage to the sticking point," and he resolved to stick the States General in the extremities of their possessions. His first blow was at New Guinea, in Africa—then at New Netherlands, in America. But he must needs first give away the territory to be conquered. Finding no courtier greedy enough to take it, with its incumbrances, he, in March, 1664, granted it to his brother, the Duke of York, afterwards James II. Thereupon he sent out a squadron commanded by Col. Nicholls, who, with recruits from Connecticut, appeared in hostile array before the grim-visaged defenses of Manhattan; and, too easily, owing to intestine divisions, achieved a bloodless conquest of New Netherlands, upon the North river. The reduction of the South river dependencies, by Sir Robert Carr, quickly ensued. Governor Stuyvesant became an English subject. New Amsterdam became New York; Fort Orange, Albany; and Niewer Amstel, New Castle. In the vicissitudes of the war, the Dutch, in 1673, re-conquered their North river possessions; but only to be, the next year, again surrendered and confirmed by treaty to the English. And now the Anglo-Saxon dominion upon the Atlantic coast was unbroken from the St. Croix to Florida.

The westward limit of the Duke of York's grant was the Delaware river. New Jersey he granted to two favorites, Lord John Berkeley and Sir George Carteret, two of the proprietaries of the Carolinas. New York he kept for himself, retaining with it his conquests on the western shore of the Delaware; which henceforth, while he held them, were governed by deputy governors, resident at New Castle.

We are now ready to introduce the last great actor in this complicated boundary drama,—the immortal founder of Pennsylvania, William Penn. Assuming that our readers are familiar with his history and character, we will not pall them by any attempt at their rehearsal. Our subject is not a life, but a line. It sufficeth us here to know that, within five or six years before his purchase of Pennsylvania, he had become deeply interested in the ownership and settlement of West Jersey, and of East Jersey, too. This turned his attention to the yet ungranted territory lying directly west of New Jersey, and of which he had a "goodly report." Benevolence rather than ambition impelled him to its acquisition.

Except Georgia, which was founded so late as 1732, Pennsylvania was the last of the old thirteen British colonies to derive its charter from the crown. It is the only one also whose territory is not touched by the briny waters of the Atlantic. At the date of her title, all the sea coast claimed by England had been "taken up," and she was forced to take an inland position,—not a bad one, however, but one with which her proprietary grantee was at first greatly dissatisfied, and for which to provide a remedy, as he supposed, he was led into the controversy with Maryland, which we are now soon to consider.

The ostensible consideration of the grant of Pennsylvania to William Penn, was a debt for services and of gratitude to his father, Admiral Penn. But the son was not the less careful about the terms of his charter, because it was given in payment of an old debt. It would be insulting his intelligence, to doubt his full and accurate knowledge of all the grants of English territory in America, which we have noticed in this sketch,—their limits and their derivations. It is in evidence, upon most indisputable authority—nay, admitted, that when he petitioned for a grant of territory, in 1680, it was to lie west of the Delaware river and north of Maryland. It is also admitted that Lord Baltimore's charter was the model used by Penn, who himself drafted his charter for Pennsylvania. He thus had express notice that Maryland reached to the Delaware Bay, and took in all the land abutting thereon "which lieth under the fortieth degree of north latitude, where New England terminates." He thereby knew, or was bound to know, that New England did not terminate at any fractional part of the fortieth degree, nor at line 39 deg., its southern confine. For, a degree of latitude is not an indivisible line, but a definite space, or belt, upon the earth's surface, of 69½ statute miles. Nothing short of the northern confine of the fortieth degree would give to Old Virginia her complement of two hundred miles north of Old Point Comfort. And the New England grant was "from the fortieth degree, &c."

Great precaution and formality were used in acting upon Penn's charter. It was held up under consideration for nine months. The petition and original draft of the charter are not extant. It is known that the latter had to undergo many modifications. When presented to the king, they were referred to the Duke of York's secretary and Lord Baltimore's agents, in order "that they might report how far the petitioners' pretensions may consist with their boundaries." Both agreed to his proposals, provided his patent might be so worded as not to affect their rights. The Duke's commissioners insisted that Penn's southern line should run at least twenty miles northward of New Castle. At length the boundaries were adjusted so as to please all parties. And, after the articles had passed the scrutiny and emendations of the Bishop of London and Lord Chief Justice North, who shaped their church and governmental franchises, so as to eschew the "undue liberties" which had been granted to Massachusetts and to Maryland, the charter was approved by the Lords of Trade and Plantations, and prepared for the king's allowance. Penn's success depended upon concession and conciliation: resistance or pertinacity would have endangered all. And yet he obtained a wonderfully liberal grant, both of power and territory.

On the 4th of March, 1681, King Charles II. granted unto "our trusty and well beloved subject, William Penn, Esquire," the territory of Pennsylvania, (Penn's Woods,) by metes and bounds, as follows, viz:

"All that tract, or part of land in America, with the islands therein contained, as the same is bounded on the east by Delaware river, from twelve miles northward of New Castle town, unto the three and fortieth degree of north latitude, if said river doth extend so far northward, but if not, then by a meridian line from the head of said river to said forty-third degree. The said land to extend westward five degrees in longitude, to be computed from said eastern bounds. And the said lands to be bounded on the north by the beginning of the three and fortieth degree of northern latitude, and on the south by a circle drawn at twelve miles distance from New Castle, northward and westward unto the beginning of the fortieth degree of northern latitude, and then by a straight line westward to the limits of longitude above mentioned."

The partisian advocates of Penn's pretensions contend that this grant gave to Pennsylvania three degrees of latitude upon the Delaware, minus the circular-headed abscission around New Castle—that by the "beginning" of the fortieth degree, "unto" which the circular line, drawn at twelve miles distance northward and westward from New Castle, was to reach, was the southern beginning of that degree. The absurdity of this construction, when applied to the parallels of latitude as they now are, is apparent. By no geomertical use of the terms can a circle of twelve miles radius from New Castle reach either beginning of the fortieth degree, much less its southern confine, which is nearly fifty miles distant. Moreover, the circle was to come "unto" it by being drawn "northward and westward." The moment it began to go southward and eastward it must stop, and there the "straight line westward" must begin.

We cannot find that William Penn himself ever asserted this absurd pretense; or, that he was to have three degrees, of latitude, though his sons and their apologists did assert it most strenuously. The nearest that he ever came to it was to say that he petitioned for five degrees of latitude, (evidently from 40 deg. to 45 deg., the old northern limit of the North Virginia Company,) but when before the Board of Plantations, watching, not urging, his petition, "the Lord President turned to me and said, 'Mr. Penn, will not three degrees serve your turn?' 'I answered,' says he, 'I submit both the what and how to the honorable Board.'" He admits also that this inquiry was prompted by its being urged that Lord Baltimore had but two degrees, which must have meant, from 38 deg. to 40 deg.; for 38 deg. being fixed in his patent, by natural marks, if Maryland must stop at 39 deg.—the southern beginning of the fortieth degree, then she would have but one degree.

We may as well now disclose that latent ambiguity which lurks in Lord Baltimore's patent, but which becomes a patent one in William Penn's. Where, upon the ground, in 1632,, and in 1680, was that artificial line, marked "40 deg.," believed to be located? The answer to this question solves all the difficulty.

The knowledge of American geography, in those days, was very imperfect. It extended little beyond the great headlands, bays and rivers, which varied the outline of the Atlantic coast, and its immediate contiguities. But the high contracting parties, who dealt in conveyances which covered a continent, assumed that they knew all about it; and that capes, rivers, bays, islands and towns, must conform to distances in miles and in degrees of latitude. They were less precise in their use of terms which were to define the boundaries of independent sovereignties, than are people now-a-days in describing a town lot. The consequences of this headiness and heedlessness were conflicting grants and angry conflicts, memorable instances of which are now before us.

The only authoritative map, in 1632, of the localities upon which this strife grew, was that of the renowned Captain Smith, already referred to. And it would seem that some of the errors upon its face were continued down to 1681. It is very certain that one of them was. By that map, the transit of line 40 deg. across the Delaware was fixed about—a little below—where New Castle is. Penn says it was at Boles' Isle—but where that is we do not know. Others fixed it at the head of the bay—but that is very indefinite; for where the river ends and the bay begins is not agreed. Penn puts the bay thirty miles below New Castle: if so, his circular line could never attain "unto" it. Line 38 deg., the northern confine of the first South Virginia grant, was correctly fixed on Watkins' Point. The shortenings were between that and New Castle. The effect of this error—besides eighty years of angry strife—was to contract Maryland, and, as we shall see, correspondingly to widen Pennsylvania.

We have seen that the Duke of York insisted at first that Penn's southern line should be twenty miles north of New Castle. This was to keep clear of his Swedo-Dutch dominions. But, inasmuch as that would leave an indefinite ungranted vacancy north of 40 deg., the circle was introduced, and the radius shortened, to twelve miles, so as thereby, by a "northward and westward" sweep, and without coming any nearer the Delaware, to reach the "beginning of the fortieth degree," and leave no vacancy.

This collation of the facts and terms of the two grants solves all the mystery which hung around them for a century. It undoes the sophistry which claimed for Pennsylvania three degrees of latitude. The sophism consisted in assuming that as Penn's northern confine was to be line 42 deg.—the southern beginning of the forty-third degree, therefore, as the same words were used, his southern limit must be line 39 deg.—the southern beginning of the fortieth degree. But Penn must be considered as standing between these two confines; reaching with one hand to the southern beginning of the former degree, and with the other to the northern beginning of the latter. It matters not that, upon maps and globes, the degrees are numbered from the equator northward, so that 39 deg. is the beginning of the fortieth degree. Reverse the direction, and 40 deg. is its bginning; just as in surveying, the line which is north 39 deg. east, is, when reversed, south 39 deg. west.(e) In our next

---

(e) We adopt this view of the case with some hesitancy—not because we doubt its correctness, but because it stands opposed to the construction given to Penn's charter by nearly all the writers upon it whom we have consulted. Of these are Proud, (History of Pennsylvania,) Bancroft, (History United States, vol. ii. p. 362,) N. B. Craig, (1 Olden Time,) Darby, (History of Pennsylvania,) not to mention the sons of Penn, their agents, attorneys and Governors, in the controversies with Maryland and Virginia. The late James Dunlop, Esq., in his "Treatise upon Mason & Dixon's Line," (1 Olden Time, 530,)

chapter we will see, with complacent wonder, what mighty leverage there was in this pretense to give to Pennsylvania a most important addition to her western territory.

But we are getting into the strife before all the elements which engendered it are brought into action. We return to our narrative.

Penn was a favorite, but not a courtier, at the court of the Stuarts. Uprightness and benevolence can commend their possessors to influence, even with the most dissolute. Penn had laudable purposes—to his sect and his colony—to accomplish, by his complacency. That he was thrice imprisoned for conscience sake, and thrice discharged without guilt, is his triple shield against all the darts of envy and abuse which his traducers, from Fuller to Macaulay, have hurled against him.(f) His very innocency led him to boast of his influence. In the careless lapse of years which intervened, from the Duke's conquest to Penn's proprietorship of Pennsylvania, some tenantry of Lord Baltimore had settled upon the western shore of the Delaware, within his chartered limits. Penn, ere he had visited the localities, was led to believe they were upon his territory. In September, 1681, he wrote them a friendly general letter, warning them "to pay no more taxes or assessments

---

alone sustains our view, and he but scouts at the popular construction. We adopted it at first impression ourself; but research and reflection compelled us to the opinion we here, and elsewhere in this and the next chapter, enunciate. There is no disloyalty in it; for we consider it more to the honor of Pennsylvania and her illustrious founder, than the opposite construction. Why put him in the awkard predicament of wilfully overlapping a degree of Lord Baltimore's grant, when there is no need for it? and if he and his successors gained for Pennsylvania more territory than they contracted for, and gained it honestly, so much the better for them, and us who enjoy it.

(f)"From his early youth to old age, he was a man of mark, and lived constantly in the eye of the public; surrounded by enemies ever ready to put the worst construction upon his conduct. He went through the furnace without the smell of fire upon his garments; and left behind him a character for moral virtue upon which malice itself could fix no stain. * * * * That he was not habitually honest and upright is a historical proposition as absurd as it would be to say that Julius Caesar was a coward, that Virgil had no poetic genius, or that Cicero could not speak Latin. Nay, he was something more than an honest man. He was a philanthropist, who gave all he had and all he was, time, talents and fortune, to the service of mankind. The heir of a large estate, the founder of the greatest city in North America, the sole owner of more than forty thousand square miles of land, he never spent a shilling in any vicious extravagance; but his large-handed charities so exhausted his income, that in his old age he was imprisoned for debt. He had the unlimited confidence of a monarch whose favor an unscrupulous man would have coined into countless heaps of gold; but he left the court with his hands empty; and whosoever says they were not clean as well as empty, knows not whereof he affirms."—Judge Black's Address at Pennsylvania College, Gettysburg, September, 1856.

by any order or law of Maryland; for if you do it will be greatly to your own wrong and my prejudice; though I am not conscious to myself of such an insufficiency of power here with my superiors, as not to be able to weather the difficulty if you should." This kind monition and harmless boast was the letting out of the water of strife—partisans rallied to their leaders—the contest was begun.

When Penn's trusty kinsman, Markham, had landed his first emigrant party at Upland, his early care, under instructions from the king and the proprietor, was to confer with Lord Baltimore upon the interesting question of boundary. They met in the spring of 1682, and then first discovered, from a careful astronomical observation, what neither before knew, that the true line of 40 deg. was above the mouth of the Schuylkill. Lord Baltimore's eye dilated—Markham's fell. What was to be done? They parted in peace; and Markham reports the annoying discovery to Penn, in London.

Penn had wished and believed that his colony would take in the head of the Chesapeake, and be far enough down on the Delaware not to be locked up by ice and enemies. This discovery frosted his expectations, but did not freeze his energies. The Duke of York was his friend, and his West Delaware dependencies would give the desired outlet in that direction. True, the Duke had no title from the crown, and Baltimore had. But the Duke had possession. It was power against parchment; and Penn wisely concluded that power would prevail. A glimmer of light broke forth from the smouldering ruins of Swaanendael, which diffused itself all along the shore from the false Cape of Henlopen to the mouth of Christiana. Penn rejoiced in its light. He importuned the Duke to convey to him these unproductive possessions. The Duke yielded; and by two deeds, in August, 1682, invested Penn with all his titles to twelve miles around New Castle, and to all the coast below that to Henlopen. And now it was parchment and possession against parchment and right, with power as the preponderant in the unequal balance. "Without adopting," says an impartial historian,(g) "the harsh censure of Chalmers, who maintains that this transaction reflected dishonor, both on the Duke of York and William Penn, we can hardly fail

---

(g) Sir James Grahame, of Scotland, whose "History of the Rise and Progress of the United States of North America, till the British Revolution in 1688,"—two volumes octavo,—is exceedingly satisfactory upon our colonial titles and boundaries, especially those of purely English derivation.

to regard it as a faulty and ambiguous proceeding, or to regret the proportions in which its attendant blame must be divided, between a prince distinguished even among the Stuarts for perfidy and injustice, and a patriarch renowned even among the Quakers for humanity and benevolence."

Thus panoplied, Penn made his first visit to his Delaware domains, with "twenty-six sail" of colonists, in the autumn of 1682. He landed at New Castle, and after receiving livery of seizin of his newly acquired "territories," and the homage of three thousand people, he repaired to Chester, (Upland,) which now was his capital; for as yet Philadelphia had no existence. After transacting some governmental affairs, and paying his respects to the Duke's governor at New York, he repaired to Maryland, to confer with Charles, Lord Baltimore, about boundaries. The interview was friendly, but formal. It resulted in nothing, except to disclose more of the grounds of Penn's claim. One was, that Lord Baltimore's two degrees were to consist of sixty miles each:—another, that being to have only lands(h) "not yet cultivated or planted," (in 1631,)—**hactenus terra inculta,**—Delaware did not pass, for that it had been bought and planted by the Dutch; "but if it did, it was forfeited, for not reducing it during twenty years, under the English sovereignty, of which he held it, but was at last reduced by the king, and therefore his to give as he pleaseth." His lordship answered, "I stand on my patent." At a subsequent interview at New Castle, Penn offered to stand to **the 40th line,** provided Lord Baltimore would sell him some territory south of it on the Chesapeake, "at a gentlemanly price—so much per mile," in case he could not get it by latitude, so as to have a "back port" to Pennsylvania. His lordship offered to barter some territory in that direction, for the "three lower counties" on Delaware Bay. "This," says Penn, "I presume he knew I would not do, for his Royal Highness had the one-half, and I did not prize the thing I desired at such a rate." But his lordship was inexorable, and

---

(h)It is strange that Penn was not afraid to hazard the use of this pretense, for the very same words are in the preamble of his own charter; and the Delaware front of his grant, had, long before, been settled by Swedes, Dutch and English. He seems to have been aware of the frailty of his tenure; for, three days before he got his deeds for the "territories," he procured a release from the Duke of York of all his title to Pennsylvania. But if prior settlement rendered the grant void, the release could give it no validity; especially as the Duke himself had no other title than by conquest.

here friendly negotiations were suspended for half a century.(i) Lord Baltimore now assumed offensive attitudes. He first made forcible entry upon Penn's territories. His next resort was to the king. The matter was referred to the Lords Committee of Trade and Plantations, before whom both parties appeared. Pending the hearings, Charles II. died, and the Duke of York ascended the throne as James II. To him the committee reported in November, 1685. As might have been expected, the decision was against Lord Baltimore. It, however, decided but one of the questions at issue—the rights of the parties upon the Delaware Bay; leaving them still to find the "40th degree" as best they could. The order of the king in council, based upon the report, was, that that part of the Chesapeake and Delaware peninsula which is between the latitude of Cape Henlopen and 40 deg., be divided by a right line into two equal parts: that the eastern half should "belong to his Majesty,(j) (viz: to King James, who granted it to William Penn, when Duke of York,) and the other half remain to the Lord Baltimore, as comprised in his charter." Thus was Maryland dismembered. The little State, cradled at Swaanendael, could now "stand alone."

Except an ineffectual order from Queen Anne, in 1708, to enforce this decision, nothing was done under it. Both ends of the divisional line were in dispute, and until they were fixed, the execution of the orders in council was impracticable and useless. In the midst of these and other troubles, harassed by debt and persecution, his colony mortgaged to money lenders, and half sold to Queen Anne, in 1718, William Penn died. His grave is in England, but his monument is in the system of laws upon which he founded the commonwealth of Pennsylvania.(k) **Si monumentum quaeris circumspice.**

(i)Penn was here again in 1699-1701, and would doubtless have resumed, perhaps consummated, the negotiations; but he had no one to treat with— Lord Baltimore's province and government being then in the hands of a deputy of William of Orange, who had no love for any abettor of James II., as Penn himself had been made to feel.

(j)This, and Penn's admission to Lord Baltimore, in November, 1682, that his "Royal Highness had the one half" of the three lower counties—although Penn had absolute deeds from him for them—throws a cloud over the impartiality of that adjudication; and raises a suspicion that favor and interest had more to do with it than the **terra inculta** pretence upon which it was based.

(k)"With one consent the wise and the learned of all nations have agreed, that, as a lawgiver, he was the greatest that ever founded a State, in ancient or modern times. He was not the very foremost, but he was among the foremost to disclaim all power of coercion over the conscience. This alone, if he

Penn was almost as unfortunate in his will as in his charter; for it too gave rise to contention, as to whom his proprietary estates now belonged. After some ten years of doubt, it was finally settled that they went to his three sons, John, Thomas and Richard; the last named being a minor until 1732. All that was done relating to the strife, during this abeyance, was an agreement with Baltimore, by their mother and the mortgagees, in February, 1723, to keep the peace for eighteen months. In the meantime, the proprietorship of Maryland had descended to Charles Calvert, the second of that name, great grandson of the first proprietor.

A better spirit seems now to have actuated the parties. The protestant success was firmly fixed on the British throne; with whom, thus far, the Catholic proprietor had met with no more favor than from the Stuarts. The growing strifes along the borders were expensive, and retarded improvements. Policy, interest, and, we suppose, inclination, all called for a compromise; and as soon as Richard Penn was out of his minority, the call was responded to. Having procured from America a map of the localities, regarded as authentic, they, on the 10th of May, 1732, enter into a long agreement—covering ten or twelve closely written pages, by which they provide for the final adjustment of all their disputed boundaries. Its most remarkable features are, that it adopts the order in council of 1685, halving the peninsula; and supercedes all reference to 40 deg., or the 40th degree, by resort to fixed landmarks. The boundaries provided for by this important agreement, being those which subsist to this day, were to be ascertained as follows:

First. The map of the localities, printed upon the margin of the agreement, is that by which it is to be explained and understood. Second. Run a circular line at twelve English statute miles distance from New Castle, northward and westward. Third. Go down to Cape Henlopen, "which lieth south of Cape Cornelius," and, from its ocean point, measure a due west line to Chesapeake Bay; find its middle point, and plant a corner there.

---

had done nothing else, would mark the tallness of his intellectual stature. For, when the light of a new truth is dawning upon the world, its earliest rays are always shed upon the loftiest minds. * * * * His name is inscribed upon this mighty Commonwealth. Day by day it rises higher, and stands more firmly on its broad foundation; and there it will stand forever—sacred to the memory of William Penn." Judge Black's address, cited in note (f).

Fourth. From said middle point run a line northward, up the peninsula, so as to be a tangent line to the periphery of the circle, at or near its western verge; and mark the tangent point. Fifth. From said tangent point run a line due north until it comes to a point fifteen English statute miles south of the latitude of the most southern part of the city of Philadelphia, and there plant another corner. Sixth. From that fifteen mile point, run a line due west, across the Susquehanna, &c., to the utmost longitude of Pennsylvania. Seventh. That the red ink lines then drawn upon the map indicate the boundaries agreed upon: and, Eighth. That those lines when run and marked shall be the boundaries of the parties forever: provided, that if the due north line from the tangent point shall cut off a segment of the circle to the west, it shall belong to New Castle county.

The agreement then embodies mutual releases from each party to the other, of such portions of their chartered territories as were now relinquished. A joint commission to run and mark the lines is then provided for; the commissioners to begin their work in October, 1732, and complete it by Christmas, 1733. Default in continued punctual attendance by those of either party, so as to delay its consummation beyond the appointed time, was to avoid the agreement and work a forfeiture to the other party of £5000.

Commissioners to run and mark the lines were duly appointed. They met at New Castle, and began and ended in fruitless contention. Lord Baltimore's commissioners contended that the "twelve miles distance," at which the circular line was run from New Castle, meant its periphery, not its radius; and that the Cape Henlopen intended was the upper cape, opposite Cape May, the agreement to the contrary notwithstanding. Thereupon, the Penn commissioners happening to come one day a few minutes behind time, the Marylanders declared the penalty forfeited and the agreement avoided. "And now," says an excellent Maryland writer upon this subject,(1) "Lord Baltimore did what neither improved his cause nor bettered his reputation. Treating his own deed as a nullity, he asked George II. for a confirmatory grant according to the terms of the charter of 1632. It was very properly refused, and the parties were referred to the Court of Chancery.

---

(1) John H. B. Latrobe, Esq., of Baltimore, whose lecture upon Mason and Dixon's Line, read before the Pennsylvania Historical Society, November 1854, is a model of lucid and concise narration, as well as of eloquent and appropriate comment.

And here Lord Hardwicke decided in effect(m) that the true Henlopen was the point insisted on by the Penns; but the centre of the circle was the middle of New Castle, as near as it could be ascertained; and that the twelve miles were a radius, and not the periphery. This was in 1750. Other difficulties now arose. It was important to Lord Baltimore, if possible, to shorten the statute mile; and the mode his friends proposed was to measure it on the surface of the ground, and not horizontally. So Lord Hardwicke was again applied to, and horizontal measurements were ordered. This was in March, 1751. Still things were not clear. The shorter the line across the peninsula—its beginning on the Delaware side being fixed—the better for Lord Baltimore, for the nearer would the centre of it be to the ocean. And so here, again, his friends came to his aid, and insisted that Slaughter's creek—a channel separating Taylor's Island from the Chesapeake, gave the western terminus. But the Penns demanded that the line should be continued to the bay shore itself, from which the broad waters of the great estuary stretched, unbroken by headland or island, to the remote and dim horizon. And again was Lord Hardwicke referred to. But, in the mean time, Lord Baltimore died, and the suit abated. When it was revived, and the heir (Frederick) of Lord Baltimore was made a party, he refused to be bound by the acts of his ancestor. If, however, there was any thing that could equal the faculties of the Marylanders in making trouble, it was the untiring perseverance with which the Penns devoted themselves to the contest, and followed their opponents in all their doublings. And they had their reward."

It was in 1735 that the Penns called his refractory lordship before the High Chancellor. Sir William Murray, afterwards Lord Mansfield, was their counsel. The bill prayed specific performance of the agreement of 1732. Baltimore resisted its execution on the common ground of weak causes—fraud, and ignorance of his rights; choosing rather to be considered a fool than a knave. But the Chancellor reversed his position.

Pending this tedious judicial controversy, events of stirring interest occurred along the border, especially in the Susquehanna neighborhood. Lord Baltimore had in 1682-'3, for some purpose, run a due east line from about the mouth of Octorora creek to the

---

(m)Penn vs. Lord Baltimore. 1 Vesey, Sr., 144, and supplement.

Delaware, which is several miles south of the agreed line."(n) Thinking he meant this for his northern limit, Pennsylvania settlers had crowded down pretty close to that line, especially the Nottingham settlement, one of the oldest in Chester county. On the other hand, ere the precise import of the agreement of 1732 was known here, Governor Gordon, of Pennsylvania, had inadvertently given countenance to the idea that, west of the Susquehanna, Maryland was to go up to the true 40 deg., as compensation for the loss of Delaware. But long before this, as early as 1722, Marylanders had begun to "squat" all along the western shore of that river, even far above 40 deg. In 1730, the famous Col. Thomas Cresap (o)

(n) In the map printed on the margin of the agreement of 1732, (see copy prefixed to 4 Pa. Archives,) the head of Elk is put above New Castle, and the due east and west line from the corner, fifteen miles south of Philadelphia, crosses the Susquehanna at the mouth of Octorora. And it was proven that Lord Baltimore put that line on the map himself in red ink. Blood flowed from the blunder.

(o) The life of this renowned personage is a romance of realities. He was the father of Captain Michael Cresap, of Logan's speech celebrity, and elsewhere noticed in these sketches. The Colonel was an Englishman—came to this country before Gen. Washington was born, but as an acquaintance of the family. Having espoused the quarrel of Lord Baltimore with the Penns, he became its champion on the Susquehanna frontier. After the temporary line was run, in 1739, he had to leave. Being an Indian trader, he transferred his establishment within the confines of Maryland, where he failed in business. Thereupon he removed to Skipton, now called Old Town, on the Maryland shore of the Potomac, nearly opposite the junction of the North and South branches. Here Washington was his guest in March, 1748, when out surveying for Lord Fairfax. He acquired a large landed estate here and on the South branch. He was one of the old Ohio Company, and the commissioner for locating Nemacolin's road, from Wills' creek to the Ohio river. We find him at Skipton, in 1750, largely in the Indian trade; and, true to his hate of the Pennites, seeking to excite against them the enmity of the Indians. To this end he sent the messages that the Pennsylvania traders always cheated them in all their dealings; anl taking pity on them, he intended to use them better, and would sell them goods at less than cost, viz: "A match coat for a buck; a strowd for a buck and doe; a pair of stockings for two raccoons; twelve bars of lead for a buck," &c. This story we have on the authority of Barnaby Curran, "a hired man of Mr. Parker's," and one of Washington's "servitors" in his mission to the French posts on the Allegheny, in 1753. Col. Cresap was a contractor for army supplies to Gen. Braddock, and was much censured for tardiness and selling musty flour. In the perilous times which ensued upon the defeat of that General, Cresap was generous, brave and energetic in his contributions to the frontier defense. He made a fort of his house by stockading it; raised and equipped a company, commanded by his son Thomas, and kept up the struggle to the last. He mixed himself up in the disputes between Lord Fairfax and Lord Baltimore, concerning the western boundary of Maryland; making a map of the localities, which is yet extant. Ever ready to annoy Pennsylvania, he lent all his influence in favor of Virginia in the boundary controversy of 1770-'74, as we will see in the next chapter. The last took a position at the "Blue Rock" ferry, west of the Susquehanna, a little below Wrightsville, where he, for many years, was the head and front of the Maryland incursions and resistance. He became the right arm of Lord Baltimore and Governor Ogle in that quarter. He was licensed ferryman, surveyor, captain of the militia, &c. He built a fort, in and around which congregated some of the worst of "border ruffins." It was to counteract these encroachments that the manor of Springettsbury, in York county, of ten by twelve miles, beginning over against the mouth of Conestoga, was surveyed in 1722, giving birth to a dubious class of titles not yet wholly quieted. Many of the German palatines, which about this period flocked to Pennsylvania in hundreds, settled upon these lands. The Marylanders wheedled them to attorn to Lord Baltimore. Some complied; but, when they saw the trick, resumed their first allegiance. This incensed the Marylanders. They drove them off by armed force; and, under well guarded bands of surveyors, gave their lands to others. The Marylanders denominated the Pennites "quaking cowards;" and these retaliated by calling their assailants "hominy gentry." All sorts of outrages were perpetrated. Even the softer sex became furies in the strife. The deadly rifle told its aim on man and beast. The solemnities of sepulture became occasions for revenge; and rapine gloated in arrests and imprisonments. Fortunately for the peace of the two provinces, Governor Thomas Penn was at the helm in person. His policy was patience, under a confident hope of triumph in the august tribunal to which he and his brothers had appealed. Once only did he resort to magisterial redress. In a crisis of the conflict it became necessary to arrest Cresap on a charge of murder. The sheriff of Lancaster accomplished it by an armed posse, after firing his castle over his head. And while on his way to prison at Philadelphia, when in sight of the infant city, this compeer of Rob Roy Macgregor(p) said to his bailiffs, "This is a pretty Maryland town. I have been a troublesome fellow; but in this last affair I have done a notable job. For I have made a present of two

---

we hear of him is in January, 1775, as one of a Virginia committee to raise arms and supplies wherewith to begin the battles of the American Revolution. His hospitality was as unlimited as was his resoluteness and hatred of Pennsylvania. Hence the Indians called him the Big Spoon. We gather these particulars from various sources. having never seen the narratives of his relative, John J. Jacob, and of Brantz Mayer.

(p)There is more in this allusion than may strike the reader at first blush; for Rob Roy was flourishing about the same time—maybe a little earlier—in his raids upon the dukedom of Montrose. See introduction to Scott's "Rob Roy."

provinces to the king; and if the people find themselves bettered by the change, they may thank Tom Cresap for it." The meaning of this gasconade is beyond conjecture. Madness measures its achievements by the monstrosity of its own excesses. The provinces were yet safe to their proprietors.

So rife and rampant had these border feuds become, that, in 1737, the king and council had to interfere; and, in 1738, the high parties litigant came to an agreement to stay their further progress. The expedient was a temporary line. They agreed that, until the cause was decided, they would conform their grants and pretensions to an east and west line; which, east of the Susquehanna, should be fifteen miles and a quarter south of the latitude of Philadelphia; and, west of that river, fourteen miles and three quarters south of the same latitude. The king ordered these lines to be run and marked, and it was done.(q) This was in 1739. The western end of the line was the summit of the Cove, or Kittatinny mountain, near the western limit of Franklin county, then the western extreme of the Indian purchase of 1736. This ended the forays. Cresap, who had been liberated and thereupon had pitched in again, now withdrew. His occupation there was gone. We will hear of him again in another quarter. He seems to have been "born unto trouble," And yet his love of mischief was no vulgar propensity. He sacrified his own interests to appease his revenge, and exorcised personal quarrels that he might bring provinces within the circle of his sorcery.

We left the Lord Chancellor deliberating upon the length of the peninsular east and west line; and whether Frederick, Lord Baltimore, was bound by his father's agreement of 1732, or could overreach it by holding under deeds of family settlement made by more remote ancestors. Happily those deliberations were cut off by a compromise. For, on the 4th of July, 1760, the parties agree to celebrate their independence of judicial constraint by a new

---

(q)See map, in 1 Pa. Arch. 594, 558, &c. It was while measuring down these 15¼ miles, from the latitude of South Philadelphia, that the first dispute sprung up about horizontal measurement. The Marylanders insisted upon superficial. Some of the Penn surveyors had been over the ground before, and knew that about 20 perches would compensate for the difference. With this knowledge they procured the Maryland commissioners to agree to allow 25! So common is it for even honest (?) men, when engaged in controversy, to take advantages, which, under other circumstances, they would scorn. This line, west of Susquehanna, was run **ex parte**—one of the Maryland commissioners having to go home, and the other not choosing to go on without him. It was, however, fairly run.

compact or agreement, which was to end, and did end, all their controversies. The claims of the Penns were yielded to in every particular. The agreement of that date is an embodiment of the history of the dispute, and is a model of old fashioned artistic conveyancing, covering thirty-four closely printed octavo pages.(r) Substantially, it is but a recital of the old compromise of 1732, and of the events which had since occurred; and a full and absolute confirmation of that agreement, and assent to the judicial constructions which almost every part of it had received. Among its new provisions were stipulations by the parties respectively, that the Penns should confirm the titles of Lord Baltimore's grantees to lands east of the Susquehanna, any where north of the agreed line (fifteen miles south of the latitude of the southern limit of Philadelphia), but that west of that river such confirmation should extend only to lands within a quarter of a mile north of that line. On the other hand, Lord Baltimore was to confirm Penn's grants west of the Susquehanna, and south of the line indefinitely; but, east of that river, only to the extent of one quarter of a mile south of the agreed line; provided, in all cases, the lands were then (July 4, 1760,) in the "actual possession and occupation" of the grantees. This feature of the agreement has given rise to some litigation along the border.(s) The reader will remember that the temporary line of 1737-'9 had an offset of half a mile to the northward, at the Susquehanna; wherefore, is not disclosed. The agreement then provides for a speedy joint commission to determine, run out and mark all the lines between the parties, without let or hindrance; that the agreement itself shall be acknowledged and enrolled in chancery, and thereupon be humbly submitted to his Majesty in council, for his gracious allowance and approval. This done, the proprietories are at peace. Frederick, Lord Baltimore, goes upon a "tour to the east;" and

---

(r) It is the first document in 4 Pennsylvania Archives.

(s) See the Pennsylvania case of Stigers vs. Thomas, 5 Barr, 480; and again, in 11 Harris, 367, which originated in Fulton county, near Hancock, Maryland. The contest was between an old Maryland grant and survey, and a much younger Pennsylvania warrant, &c. In the first report of the case, the Maryland title prevailed, owing to an imperfect knowledge of the history of this dispute and of the agreement of 1760. In the meantime the publication, by Pennsylvania, of her Colonial Records and Archives, disclosed all the details of the strife, and the agreement itself. Eventually the Pennsylvania title triumphed. Judge Lowrie, in delivering the opinion of the court in the last case, inadvertently says the disputed territory was only half a mile wide. This is an error. It had a width of more than twenty miles.

the Penns remain in London to protect their private and provincial interests.

Before we proceed to run and mark the lines, let us pause a moment to take an account of the loss and gain of the parties, in the results of this long and perplexing controversy. Was the agreement of 1760, and its prototype of 1732, a compromise—a mutual concession of conflicting pretensions; or was it wholly a surrender by one party to the other? Maryland lost what is now the State of Delaware, that is certain; and, as we think, she was thereby unjustly shorn of her fair proportions. But that Calvert's loss was Penn's gain, is not so certain. He sought "water," but obtained gall—the bitterness of strife. He asked an outlet to the ocean for his "too backward lying province," and there was opened unto him and his sons an inlet to a sea of troubles. He purchased the Duke's appanage to New York, to make it an appendage to Pennsylvania; but, ere his title to it was settled, it set up for itself; and when the American colonies broke the bands of British dependence, it too became an independent State.(t) And so Delaware was lost to Pennsylvania. The judicious Scottish historian of our early settlements, already quoted, regards the loss of Delaware to Lord Baltimore as a retribution for his encroachment upon Virginia. May not the same punitive Providence be again traced in its ultimate severance from a State, all whose other foundations were in righteousness and peace.

We have before said that the consequence to Lord Baltimore, of the misplacement of the fortieth line of north latitude, in the maps of the Chesapeake and Delaware region, current at the date

---

(t) From 1682 to 1691, Delaware was, for all practical purposes, a part of Pennsylvania, each having the same charters of privileges, the same general laws, the same Governor and Assembly—in which each was equally represented; each having three counties—New Castle, Kent and Sussex, and Philadelphia, Bucks and Chester. In 1691, when Penn came under the ban of King William, Delaware affected to become jealous of Pennsylvania; and, although uniting in the same Assembly, had a separate Governor. In 1704, she set up a separate Assembly, under the same Governor. From 1755 to the Revolution, in 1776, she had both a separate Governor and Assembly; and in '76, became a State. She was always an undutiful child to the Penns; and had she only thought so, would no doubt have been as well cared for by Maryland—to which she naturally and rightfully belongs—as she ever was by the Penns, or by herself. But, one member and two Senators, in Congress, are no mean privileges, to a representative population—free and slave, of 91,000, when the ratio for one Representative is 93,420! But who complains? She has given us some great men, and may yet become the balance wheel of the Confederacy.

of his charter, was, to have the northern confines of his province considerably restricted. Had the calls of his patent been fully answered the Quaker City would inevitably have become, what Cresap called it, "a pretty Maryland town." On the other hand, had his lordship been forced down fully to the line 40 deg., as it stood in 1632, and, indeed, until his and Markham's discovery in 1682, Maryland would have been cut in twain in the region of Hancock, and Western Maryland would have lain so far "backward" as to be wholly inaccessible to its proprietor by either land or "water." If Penn had the advantage of Calvert in the misplaced position of 40 deg. in 1632, the latter had an available set-off in the requirement of Penn's patent of 1681, that the circular part of his boundary should reach the "beginning of the fortieth degree," by a northward and westward course. Here, then, was a most inviting call to compromise, which would doubtless have been much sooner responded to, had it not been for the successive disabilities, of Lord Baltimore's privation of his province by William and Mary, from 1692 to 1715 Penn's death in 1718 and the disputes as to his successors in the proprietorship, and the minority of one of them, until 1732. In this year, as we have seen, a compromise was agreed upon, which relieved both parties. Philadelphia was kept at the neighborly distance of fifteen miles from Maryland; and Lord Baltimore preserved a lane, of about a mile wide, at Hancock, for access to his iron and coal fields—then unknown and valueless —in the west. By this agreement, therefore, Maryland gave up not only her Delaware domain north of Henlopen—which was in effect taken from her by the royal order in council of 1685—but also a parallelogram of about nineteen and a quarter miles wide on her northern confines, extending from New Castle county to the "meridian of the first fountain of the Potomac." This alone exceeds one-third of her entire present area, territorial and aqueous. With Delaware added, it exceeds one-half. So Maryland has been largely the loser in this game of boundary. She is, however, quite a respectable sovereignty yet.

But how has Pennsylvania fared in the play upon 40 deg.? Evidently she has gained the parallelogram which Maryland lost; thereby restricting Lord Baltimore's two degrees of latitude to about sixty miles each,—"geographical," instead of "statute" degrees, as Penn wanted them to be in 1682. But she has also widened her own two degrees to about seventy-nine miles each. For in the adjustment of her northern boundary with New York, in 1774, and again in 1785, the true 42 deg.—the "beginning of the forty-third degree," was adopted; without any effort on the part of our northern neighbor to push us down to where that line of latitude was put in 1681—if indeed it had any location at that period. No hint was given or taken of the old misplacement of 40 deg.; and thus Pennsylvania was allowed to hold, on the north, by the rule which Maryland sought in vain to enforce against her on the south. The value of this item of fortunate territorial expansion by Pennsylvania, is greatly enhanced by the access to Lake Erie which was thereby obtained. But for this, the Erie triangle(u) would probably never have been a purchasable annexation to our chartered territory. Thus far, therefore, Pennsylvania has been largely the gainer by her boundary troubles. The loss of Delaware has been more than compensated. In our next chapter, we will see that her good fortune, or superior diplomacy, attended her to the last. To one, or both, of these influences do we of much of south-western Pennsylvania owe it that we are not now Marylanders or Virginians.

Although not within the scope of these sketches, we are tempted here briefly to notice the boundary controversy with Connecticut, which Pennslyvania had to sustain from 1760 to 1782.(v) It intervened to postpone the settlement of our northern limits for more than ten years from the time it was undertaken, in 1774, and until rival colonies had become changed to fraternal States.

The grant of Connecticut to Lords Say and Seal, and others, in

---

(u) The Erie triangle was within the chartered limits of Massachusetts, which claimed three-quarters of a degree of New York, immediately north of 42 deg. New York held it, we believe, under a purchase from, and alliance with, the Six Nations of Indians. Both having ceded their western territory to the United States—New York in 1782. and Massachusetts in 1784—the relative strength of their titles became an unimportant inquiry. The New York cession was of all west of a due north line from the northern boundary of Pennsylvania, through the extreme west end of Lake Ontario, or twenty miles west of Niagara river, to north latitude 45 deg.—thus taking in a considerable portion of Canada, to which her title proved rather unavailable. Pennsylvania first bought the triangle from the Indians, in 1789, for £1200, and then in 1792 from the United States for $151,640.25, continental certificates. This was done to get at the harbor of Presq'isle, at Erie, upon which the United States have since expended more than they got for it. The triangle contains 202,187 acres. See its history by Judge Huston in M'Call vs. Coover, 4 Watts and Sergeant's Reports, 151-164; and see 1 olden Time, 557.

(v) The controversy lasted much longer in litigation and legislation, but this year ended the boundary part of it. See Huston's Land Titles, 14; 4 Journals of Congress, (1782) 129-140; 4 Pennsylvania Archives, 679, &c., and other volumes, and Colonial Records, passim—indexed—Connecticut and Wyoming; Day's Historical Collections of Pennsylvania, "Luzerne County," and authors there referred to.

1631, by the New England Company, reached from the Atlantic to the Pacific, or "South Sea;" but, like its parent grant, there was excepted out of it any territory then in possession of any other Christian prince or State. This let in New York and New Jersey between her present western limits and the Delaware. So it was determined by a Board of King's Commissioners, in October, 1664. But Connecticut reserved her claims west of the Delaware, thereby covering nearly all the forty-second, or most northern degree of latitude, which is within the subsequently chartered limits of Pennsylvania, and extending westward indefinitely.(w) It is said that, when Penn's grant was pending, he had notice of this claim of Connecticut, but that the king and he gave no heed to it, upon the ground that eighty years of neglect to people or possess it, was to be considered as an abandonment. About 1753 Connecticut began to reassert her claim, and sent settlers into the Wyoming valley. Within the ensuing twenty years the Connecticut settlements upon the east or north branch of the Susquehanna, became numerous and formidable. Their descendants and enterprise are there yet. Pennsylvanians regarded their intrusions upon her territory with a jealous and angry eye. Conflicts ensued, personal, military, legal and judicial. Blood and treasure were freely expended. Our later colonial and early State annals, as well as our law books, are full of the controversy. At length, in 1782, under the old articles of confederation, the dispute was referred for settlement to a committee of Congress, who sat as a court at Trenton, New Jersey, in the fall of that year. The parties were fully heard by their proofs and counsel. Connecticut relied upon her ancient parchments. Pennsylvania planted herself upon the laches of Connecticut, upon her own charter of 1681, and upon a score or more of Indian deeds to the Penns.(x) It was contended that the royal grants gave but a pre-emption right; that the natives were the true proprietors; and, as the Penns had the Indian titles,

---

(w)Connecticut, in 1786, ceded all her western territory, north of 41 deg., and west of a due north line, one hundred and twenty miles west of the western boundary of Pennsylvania, to the United States. Her "Western Reserve," in the north-east corner of Ohio, was the one hundred and twenty miles westward of Pennsylvania, north of 41 deg. nearly. In 1800, the United States offered to give her the soil, or the proceeds of sales, of this Reserve, she surrendering the jurisdiction, which was agreed to.

(x)Connecticut had an Indian deed, also, obtained by one Lydius at Albany, in 1754; but it was pronounced surreptitious, illegal and fraudulent. It does not appear that it was relied on at the trial.

to which the commonwealth had succeeded,—by tacking these to the charter, the old abandoned pre-emption grant to Connecticut was "crushed out." The court so held. Its decision was unanimous in favor of Pennsylvania—the ever successful Pennsylvania, in all her boundary controversies. The way was now clear to fix and run a definitive line between Pennsylvania and New York; and it was done, in 1785-'6-'7, upon the line of north latitude 42 deg. We return now, from this digression, to run lines with Maryland.

Eight years of almost uninterruped labor were expended in running, measuring and marking these troublesome lines; and even then our line was unfinished. For, except around New Castle, and thence to the Susquehanna, the territories they traversed were dense forests, deep swamps and water courses, or rugged mountains; inhabited only by venomous reptiles and beasts of prey, with here and there the adventurous pioneer and roving Indian. Nor was geometrical science then the perfection that it now is. Its progress, if not so noisy as has been the march of material improvement over these then dreary wastes, has been not the less sure and surprising. In those days accuracy was a rare achievement; and, when its closest possible approximation was demanded, much time and experiment had to be disbursed. The delays were, therefore, wrought by real difficulties.

The commissioners on the part of each province having been duly appointed, and their surveyors selected, they met at New Castle, in November, 1760, and addressed themselves to their task in earnest. They worked with unwonted harmony. Indeed, so specific, upon every department of their labors, had been the decrees and agreements, that there was no longer even a loop hole through which either party could evade compliance. All that remained was to measure and mark the lines, as commanded. The commissioners were seven for each proprietary,(y) three of whom together were competent to act. The Penn surveyors at first

---

(y)On the part of the Penns they were Governor James Hamilton, Richard Peters, member and Secretary of Council; Rev. John Ewing, D. D., afterwards Provost of the University of Pennsylvania; William Allen, Chief Justice; Wm. Coleman, then a Justice; Thomas Willing, afterwards a Justice, and Benjamin Chew, afterwards Chief Justice of the Supreme Court. Edward Shippen, Jr., Prothonotary of the Supreme Court, was also a member of the Board part of the time. The Maryland gentlemen were Governor Horatio Sharpe, J. Ridout, Jno. Leeds, Jno. Barclay, Geo. Stewart, Dan. of St. Thos. Jenifer, and J. Beale Boardley. The commissioners seem to have entrusted the line, west of the Susquehanna, entirely to the surveyors.

chosen were John Lukens,(z) afterwards Surveyor General of the Commonwealth, and Archibald M'Clean, of York, eldest brother of the late Col. Alexander M'Clean, of Fayette. Two others were named, but never acted. Those of Maryland were John F. A. Priggs and Jonathan Hall.

The peninsular line, from Henlopen to the Chesapeake, was the only one which had been run under Lord Hardwicke's decree of 1750. This had been agreed to be correctly run and measured, and its middle point fixed at thirty-four miles three hundred and nine perches.(aa) It had also been agreed that the court house in New Castle should be the centre of the circle. Upon these data the surveyors proceed. Numerous "vistas" had to be cleared through the forests and morasses of the peninsula. Three years were diligently devoted to finding the bearing of the western line of Delaware, so as to make it a tangent to the circle, at the end of a twelve mile radius; and a close approximation only was then attained. The instruments and appliances employed seem to have been those commonly used by surveyors.

The proprietors, residing in or near London, grew weary of this slow progress, which, perhaps, they set down to the incompetency of their artists. To this groundless suspicion we owe their supersedure, and the introduction of the men, Mason and Dixon, who, unwittingly, have immortalized their memory in the name of the principal line which had yet to be run.

Charles Mason and Jeremiah Dixon(bb) were astronomers of ris-

---

(z) We believe that Mr. Lukens, who was an excellent officer, died in October, 1789, in Washington county, Pennsylvania; where, and in Beaver county, his descendants are yet found. He was the first Surveyor General of the Commonwealth, from April 1781, to his death. Col. Daniel Brodhead succeeded him.

(aa) The length of the west boundary of Delaware, from the middle point to the tangent point on the circle, is eighty-two miles, minus six and one-eighth perches.

(bb) Mason had been an assistant in the Royal Observatory, at Greenwich. Both, prior to their service in America, it is said, had been at the Cape of Good Hope to make observations of an eclipse of the sun. It is certain they were there in 1769, to observe a transit of Venus across the sun's disc. Dixon is said to have been born in a coal pit. He died at Durham, in England, in 1777. Mason died near Philadelphia, in 1787. He was probably the more scientific man of the two. From a careful study of their chirography and signatures, Mr. Latrobe infers that "Mason was a cool, deliberate, painstaking man, never in a hurry;" and that Dixon "was a younger and more active man, a man of an impatient spirit and nervous temperament; just such a man as worked best with a sober sided colleague." Their journal and letters, with a map of the lines, are preserved in manuscript at Annapolis. "Their letters are the merest business letters; their journal is the most naked of records." The

ing celebrity in London, in 1763. In August of that year they were employed by the Penns and Lord Baltimore to complete their lines. Furnished with instructions and the most approved instruments, among them a four feet zenith sector, they sail for Philadelphia, where they arrive in November. They go to work at once.(cc) They adopt the radius as measured by their predecessors; and, after numerous tracings of the tangent line, adopt also their tangent point, from which they say they could not make the tangent line pass one inch to the eastward or westward. So that if the proprietors had only thought so, the rude sightings and chainings of the American surveyors would have been all right. They thereupon cause that line and point to be marked, and adjourn to Philadelphia to find its southern limit, on Cedar, or South street. This they make to be(dd) north latitude 39 deg. 56 min. 29 sec. They then proceed to extend that latitude sufficiently far to the west to be due north of the tangent point. Thence they measure down south fifteen miles to the latitude of the great due west line, and run its parallel for a short distance. Then they go to the tangent point, and run due north to that latitude; and at the point of intersection, in a deep ravine, near a spring, they cause to be planted the corner stone at which begins the celebrated "Mason and Dixon's Line."

Having ascertained the latitude of this line to be 39 deg. 43 min. 32 sec.,(ee) they, under instructions, run its parallel to the Susquehanna—twenty-three miles; and, having verified the latitude there, they return to the tangent point, from which they run the due north line to the fifteen mile corner, and that part of the circle which it cuts off to the west, and which by the agreements, was to go to

---

Archives of Pennsylvania contain no counterpart of these. Even the agreement of 1760 was a long time lost but has lately been recovered. Certified copies have supplied the place of it and many others of our old Colonial papers. It is said that Joseph Shippen, Secretary to the Penn Governors, refused to give them up at the Revolution. Some have been recovered from his papers, and other sources. Those of Maryland and New York have been better taken care of. The original agreemnt of 1732 is nowhere to be found.

(cc)Their first care was to have an observatory erected on Cedar street, Philadelphia, to facilitate the ascertainment of its latitude. It was the first building in America erected purposely from which "to read the skies." It was rude and hastily constructed, for they used it in January, 1764.

(dd)The latitude of Philadelphia, at the State House, is 39 deg. 56 min. 59 sec.

(ee)More accurate observations make it 39 deg. 43 min. 26.3 sec—consequently it is a little over nineteen miles south of 40 deg., as now located.

(ff)This little bow, or arc, is about a mile and a half long, and its middle width 116 feet. From its upper end, where the three States join, to the fifteen

three dominions—an important point; and, therefore, they cause it to be well ascertained and well marked. This brings them to the end of 1764.

They resume their labors upon the line in June, 1765. If to extend this parallel did not require so great skill as did the nice adjustments of the other lines and intersections, it summoned its performers to greater endurance. A tented army penetrates the forests, but their purposes are peaceful, and they move merrily. Besides the surveyors and their assistants, the Messrs. M'Clean— Archibald, Moses, Alexander(gg) and Samuel, and others, there had to be chain-bearers, rod-men, axe-men, commissaries, cooks and baggage carriers, with numerous servants and laborers, men of all work and camp followers of no work. By the 27th of October, they come to the North (Cove, or Kittatinny) mountain, 95 miles from the Susquehanna, and where the temporary line of 1739 terminated. After taking Captain Shelby with them to its summit, "to show them the course of the Potomac," and point out the Allegheny mountain,(hh) the surveyors and their attendants return to the settlements to pass the winter, and to get their appointment renewed.

Early in 1766, they are again at their posts. They begin with an exhausted money chest, and having ascertained that the Penns had advanced £615 more than Lord Baltimore, they send to Governor Sharpe, at Annapolis, for £600 or £700, to be forwarded, "so that Mr. M'Lane may receive it at Fredericktown," the 24th of April. This obtained, they proceed. By the 4th of June, they are on the top of Little Allegheny mountain—the first west of Wills' creek. They have now carried the line about 160 miles from its beginning. The Indians, into whose ungranted territory they had deeply penetrated, grow restive and threatening. They

---

mile post, where the great Mason and Dixon's line begins, is a little over three and a half miles; and from the fifteen mile corner due east to the circle, is a little over three-quarters of a mile—room enough for three or four good Chester county farms. This was the only part of the circle which Mason and Dixon run—Lord Baltimore having no concern in the residue. Penn had it run and marked with "four good notches," by "friends Isaac Taylor and Thomas Pierson," in 1700-'1; but the trees are now nearly all gone, and it is hard to find.

(gg) See memoir of Colonel Alexander M'Clean, ante—Chap. VII. page 132.

(hh) From this summit, the path of the Potomac through the mountains, to the southwest, is distinctly visible; and the Allegheny crest—Big Savage— can be well seen. Old Fort Frederick, too, comes in for its share of the magnificent panorama. It was built in 1756, and its ruins are yet in good preservation, a little east of Hancock.

thought this army, though bannerless, meant something. Their untutoried minds could not comprehend this nightly gazing at the stars through gun-like instruments, and this daily felling of the forests across their hunting paths. They forbid any further advance, and they had to be obeyed. The artists return leisurely, and note, as they pass, the beauty of their "visto," which, they say, "from any eminence on the line, where fifteen or twenty miles can be seen, very apparently shows itself to be a parallel of latitude." They are pleased with their work.

The agents of the Proprietors now find that there are other lords of the soil whose favor must be propitiated. The Indians just at this time were deeply exercised upon some unsettled boundary questions between them and the whites, and were keenly sensitive to any anticipatory demarcations. The Six Nations, whose council fires blazed upon the Onondago and Mohawk, in Western New York, were the lords paramount of the territory yet to be traversed. To obtain their consent to the consummation of the line, the Governors of Pennsylvania and Maryland, in the winter of 1766-'7, at an expense of more than £500, procured, under the agency of Sir William Johnson, a grand convocation of the tribes of that powerful confederacy. The application was successful; and early in June, 1767, an escort of fourteen stroud-clad warriors, with an interpreter and a chief, deputed by the Iroquois council, met the surveyors at their camp at the summit of the Great Allegheny, to escort them down into the valley of the Ohio, whose tributaries they were soon to cross.

Safety being thus secured, the extension of the line was pushed on vigorously in the summer of 1767. Soon the motley host of red and white men, led by the London surveyors, came to the western limit of Maryland—"the meridian of the first fountain of the Potomac;" and why they did not stop there is a mystery, for there their functions terminated.(ii) But they pass it by unheaded, because unknown, resolved to reach the utmost limit of Penn's "five degrees of

---

(ii) There is some evidence that when Penn asked for his grant, he intended to go no further west than Maryland. It is the only one of the old royal grants which is limited by longitude. Its introduction was, perhaps, accidental, to square with his application for five degrees of latitude. He could as readily have had it to reach to the Pacific. The general south-westward bearing of the Appalachian range of mountains, may well have led the most knowing ones of that day to "guess" that "the meridian of the first fountain of the Potomac" might be much further west than it is. The prospect from the North mountain was very illusive. And yet one can hardly believe they would suppose that meridian to be west of the Monongahela, and within fifteen miles of the Ohio. In a letter from Governor Keith, of Pennsylvania, to Governor Spottswood, of Virginia, dated April, 1721, he says—"You very well know, sir,

longitude," from the Delaware; for so they were instructed. By the 24th of August, they come to the crossing of Braddock's road. The escort now became restless. The Mohawk chief and his nephew leave. The Shawnees and Delawares, tenants of the hunting grounds, begin to grow terrific. On the 27th September, when encamped on the Monongahela, 233 miles from the Delaware, twenty-six of the laborers desert, and but fifteen axe-men are left. Being so near the goal, the surveyors—for none of the commissioners were with them—evince their courage by coolly sending back to Fort Cumberland for aid, and in the meantime they push on. At length they come to where the line crosses the Warrior branch of the old Catawba war path,(jj) at the second crossing of Dunkard creek, a little west of Mount Morris, in Greene; and there the Indian escort say to them, "that they were instructed by their chiefs in council not to let the line be run to the westward of that war path." Their commands are peremptory; and there, for fifteen years, the line is stayed. It was afterwards run out by other hands, as noted elsewhere in these sketches.(kk) When completed, its terminus is a "cairn" of stones, on one of the slopes of the Fish creek hills, near the Broad Tree tunnel of the Baltimore and Ohio railroad. "And standing on the cairn, and looking to the east and north, a fresher growth of trees indicates the ranges of the vistas. But climb the highest tree adjacent to the cairn, that you may note the highest mountain within the range of vision, and then ascending its summit, take in the whole horizon, and seek for a single home of a single descendant of the sylvan monarchs, whose war path limited the surveys; and you will seek in vain. But go back to the cairn, and listen there, in the quiet of the woods, and a roll as of distant thunder will come unto the ear, and a shrill shriek will pierce it, as the monster and the miracle of modern ingenuity—excluded from Pennsylvania as effectually by the line we have described, as the surveyors of old were by the Indian war path—rushes round the south-western angle

---

that Pennsylvania, which is three degrees in breadth (?) and extends five degrees west of the river Delaware, must border upon his Majesty's dominion of Virginia to the westward of Maryland, and upon New York to the northward of New Jersey." This is the only avowed knowledge we have, prior to 1768, of Pennsylvania extending farther west than Maryland.

(jj)See ante—"Indian Trails, &c."—Chap. III.

(kk)See memoir of Col. Alexander M'Clean—ante. Chap. VII.; and Boundary Controversy," postea, Chap. IX.

of the state, on its way from the city which perpetuates the title of the Lord Proprietary of Maryland, to find a breathing place on the Ohio, in the "pan-handle, of Virginia."(ll)

Mason and Dixon with their pack-horse train and attendants, (mm) returned to the east without molestation, and report their discomfiture to the "gentlemen commissioners," who approve their conduct, and on the 27th December, 1767, grant to them an honorable discharge, but agree to pay them for a map or plan of their work, which they were instructed to prepare, and did prepare. The commissioners now address themselves to the erection of the required monuments, or stones, upon the lines, and at the corners and intersections around and near the "three counties of Delaware. This done, they, on the 9th November, 1768, made their final report to the Proprietaries; and here the labor upon these lines ends, in America, until after the titles of Baltimore and the Penns are wrested from them by the strong arm of revolution.

In conformity to the agreements and the decrees of the Chancellor, the lines were well marked. All the corners and intersections were ascertained by firmly fixing thereat "one or more remarkable stones," on which were graven the arms of the proprietors on the sides facing their possessions respectively. Along the lines, at the end of every fifth mile, a stone thus graven was planted, the intermediate miles being noted by a stone having M. on one side and P. on the other. Most of the stones on which the coats of arms were graven were brought from England. On the great due west line— Mason and Dixon's line proper, this mode of demarcation was used as far as the eastern side of Sideling Hill mountain 132 miles from the spring corner. But the difficulty of transporting the graven stones any further westward, compelled these surveyors to depart from the agreement, and to find their marks as they went along —no very difficult matter from Sideling Hill to the great Allegheny summit, they denoted the line by conical heaps of earth or stones, six or seven feet high, on the tops of all the ridges and mountains. From the summit of the Allegheny, westward, as far as they

---

(ll) Mr. Latrobe's lecture, before quoted. See ante, note 12.

(mm) Among these, besides the Messrs, M'Clean, were Hugh Crawford, the old Indian trader, who for his services, got a grant of part of Col. Evans' estate, (ante, Chap. VI. note 12), and Paul Larsh, of George's creek, father of Hannah, the wife of Joseph Baker, of Nicholson township, who was the widow of George Gans. See Larsh vs. Larsh, Addison's Reports, 310. Old John Tate, of Redstone, is said also to have been of the company.

went, similar marks were erected at the end of each mile, with a post inserted in each.

The "vista" of the line was opened twenty-four feet wide, by felling all the trees and large bushes, which were left to rot upon the ground. The monuments of the line were erected along the middle of this pathway, in the true parallel.

The instruments used by Mason and Dixon were an ordinary surveyor's compass, to find their bearings generally, a quadrant, and the four feet zenith sector which they brought from London, for absolute accuracy. The ferruginous character of much of the territory they traversed, forbid much reliance upon the needle. The sector enabled them to be guided by the unerring luminary of the heavens.

The measurements were made with a four pole chain of one hundred links, except that, on hills and mountains, one of two poles, and sometimes a one pole measure, was used. These were frequently tested by a statute chain carried along for that purpose. Great care was enjoined as to the plumbings upon uneven ground; and, so far as they have been since tested, the measurements seem to have been very true.

While the surveyors were in progress upon the line, the Proprietors humbly besought his Majesty, George III., to allow and approve their agreement of 1760, and the confirmatory decree of the Chancellor thereon, to the end that his Majesty's subjects inhabiting the disputed lands might have their minds quieted. His Majesty **deferred his approval until January, 1769,** after the lines had been completed and the final report of the commissioners made. Even all this, however, did not quite end the disturbances. Says Governor John Penn, in 1774:—"The people living between the ancient temporary line of jurisdiction, and that lately settled and marked by the commissioners, were in a lawless state. Murders, and the most outrageous transgressions of law and order, were committed with impunity in those places. In vain did persons injured apply to the government of Maryland for protection and redress." This, of course, refers to the little strip of a quarter of a mile in width along the southern confines of York, Adams, and Franklin. Thirty years had caused the temporary line to be deemed the permanent boundary—the common fate of accommodation lines between adjoining land owners.

Nor was this quite all. In 1771, Frederick, Lord Baltimore, died, and his heir was a minor under guardianship. And when, in 1774, Governor Penn, under stress of the "lawless state" of his south-western frontier, made proclamation of his purpose to extend and enforce his jurisdiction "quite home" to the established line, his young lordship's guardian was induced to ask the king to arrest the Governor's proceedings, upon the grounds that the Maryland proprietary had not capacity to concur in the ratification of the line, and that his subjects settled on the frontiers, knowing this, would resort to violence and bloodshed. The partisans of Virginia—who were now carrying on her boundary war with the Penns—had perhaps more to do with this groundless interference than had the friends of the infant Lord Baltimore. When the king was apprised that the line had been run, marked, reported and confirmed, in pursuance of Frederick's agreement, and all done in his lifetime, he "graciously" recalled his countermand of Governor Penn's proclamation. And now, finally, and, as we trust forever, Maryland and Pennsylvania are at peace. The two oldest and most contiguous sovereignties carved out of ancient New England and Virginia—the "North" and the "South," resume their primitive peaceful repose upon the line—this famous Mason and Dixon's Line—which is the agreed substitute for the ancient 40 deg.

The width of a degree of longitude varies according to the latitude it traverses—expanding towards the equator, and contracting towards the pole. In the latitude of our line, Mason and Dixon computed it at fifty-three miles and one hundred and sixty-seven and one-tenth perches. They consequently made Penn's five degrees of longitude from the Delaware to be two hundred and sixty-seven miles and one hundred and ninety-five and six-tenth perches. (nn) To their stopping place at the war path on Dunkard, they say, was two hundred and fifty-four miles one hundred and thirteen perches and seven and one-fourth feet. Hence they left, as they computed it, twenty-three miles and eighty-three perches to be run. It was subsequently ascertained that this was about a mile and a half too much—(oo) a discovery which created some inconvenience upon the western line of Greene county.

We have seen no evidence that Mason and Dixon actually measured the distance from the Delaware to where they began the due west

---

(nn) It seems it should have been only two hundred and sixty-six miles, ninety-nine and one-fifth perches; and so we say it was found to be by the surveyors of 1784, in our note (d) to Memoir of Col. Alex. M'Clean—ante, Chapter VII. But that is Col. Graham's estimate in 1849. We have not found what it was made to be, in 1784.

(oo) See note (d) referred to in note (nn), and note (pp).

line at the stone near the spring. But they, or some others for them, must have done so, for it is part of the five degrees of longtitude. They estimated it at fourteen miles forty perches and ten feet. The mile-stones upon the line are numbered according to their distance from the Delaware. This has created some confusion and misapprehension as to the length of the line. Our most approved State map—Barnes', of 1848—has them so numbered with great apparent accuracy; although not always coinciding with other notations of distance upon the line.(pp)

The line crosses the Cumberland, or National road, about three miles south-east of Petersburg; the Youghiogheny about three miles south of Somerfield; the Cheat at the north of Grassy run (the line ford); the Monongahela near the mouth of Crooked run.

The north-west corner of Maryland, upon this line, is near the road from Haydentown to Selbysport, or Friend's, about half a mile west of the intersection of Henry Clay and Wharton townships; being about one hundred and ninety-nine miles west of her northeast corner, and about fifty-four miles east of the south-west corner of Pennsylvania; or, one degree of longitude short of our western confine.

Very many of the marks and monuments upon the line have been removed, or have crumbled down; and its vista is so much grown up as to be hardly distinguishable from the adjacent forests. It should be re-traced and re-marked. Except in part of Greene county, all the original surveys of lands upon the line were made after it was authoritatively fixed. Hence, no inconvenience or trouble has yet arisen from its partial obliteration. But one of the best securities for peace between neighbors is to keep up good division fences.

(pp)The surveyors of 1739 made the distance from the Susquehanna to "the top of the most western of the Kittochtinny hills," (the North or Cove mountain,) only eighty-eight miles. The map shows it to be nearly one hundred.

The map makes the line cross the Monongahela at about two hundred and nineteen and a half, or two hundred and thirty-three and a half, from the Delaware, which accords with Mason and Dixon. But our Book of Official Surveys, made in 1786, shows the following mile posts east of the river, viz.: the two hundred and twenty-second on the south line of the old Samuel Bowen tract; the two hundred and twenty-first about half way in the south line of the old Robert Henderson tract; the two hundred and twentieth about the middle of the the south line of the John M'Farland tract—the Ferry tract. There was then a pile of stones in the line, on the river hill, near the south-west corner of the Bowen tract, and he is presumed to have known the marks. There is error somewhere. The line then (1786) bore south 89 deg. west.

Some trouble did grow out of a removal of some of the monuments upon the eastern part of the lines. Many years ago the "remarkable stone," which marked the south-west corner of Delaware, was dug up in one of the fruitless searches for the buried treasure of Captain Kidd; and at a later period the stone near the spring, which marks the north-east corner of Maryland, having been undermined by floods, and fallen, was taken by a neighboring farmer for a chimney piece, and a post planted in its place. Surmises sprung up that some others of the stones which defined the limits of the little State had been displaced. Many of the dwellers around the notch and circle seemed not to know to whom they belonged. These doubts and dilapidations induced the three states of Delaware, Maryland and Pennsylvania, in 1849, to create a joint commission to re-trace the lines in that vicinity, and replace the missing monuments. The commissioners procured Lieut. Col. James D. Graham, of the corps of Topographical Engineers of the United States, to execute the work. He, of course, had to review much of the labors of Mason and Dixon and their predecessors. Generally he found that remarkable accuracy characterized those early displays of geometrical science. The post near the spring was in the right place, and the courses all right. Some errors were, however, detected. Some of the miles had been made a few feet too long. The radius was found to be two feet four inches too short; and by some error in locating the tangent point, and the junction of the three States at the point of the notch, or bead, it was found that Maryland had got back from Delaware a little over one acre and three-quarters of what she had lost by King James' order, in 1685.(qq) Even these trifling errors prove the wonderful certainty of mathematical science. Col. Graham's labors wrought a change in the allegiance of several gentlemen residing near the circle, who had hitherto supposed themselves citizens of Delaware. A Mr. William Smith, who had been a member of the Legislature of that State, was found to be a full half mile within Pennsylvania; which also took in the old Christiana church by a hundred yards.

It is ever thus with all things terrestrial. Men change and are changed. Monuments crumble and are removed. Even "a thing of beauty is not a joy forever." Decay and renewals are the constant

---

(qq) See the curious and learned report of Colonel Graham, with other documents, in Senate Journal of Pennsylvania, 1850, vol. 2, page 475.

succession of human affairs and human structures. The marks of boundary cannot escape this destiny. No art, no care, can preserve them as they were. The limits of empire which nature establishes are not unvarying. Rivers change their channels—the soil of one State becomes the delta of another—and ocean takes away from continents, to be compensated by new islands in the watery waste. An assurance of permanency, and of enduring peace upon its borders, may be derived from the purely arbitrary origin of our line—that in its establishment Nature had no agency; for

> "Lands intersected by a narrow frith
> Abhor each other. Mountains interposed
> Make enemies of nations, who had else,
> Like kindred drops, been mingled into one."

To comprehend the subject of this sketch, we have had to course over more than three centuries of this world's history, halting here and there to gather up and arrange the events which relate to it. It is more than two hundred years since the seeds of strife were sown, of which the line is the harvest; and nearly a century has run since the surveyors were running its thread through the forests. Within these periods what great events have transpired. Civilization, science, freedom, religion and population have rolled their resistless tides over this continent. Empires have risen and fallen; dynasties have sunk into nothingness. Yet this line stands; and its story increases in interest as time grows older. Nor is its history yet ended. God grant that it may never have to be written of it that it severed this glorious Union! What is yet to be said of it now belongs to our next chapter; for "westward the course of empire takes its way," and with it goes its boundary controversies.

SUPPLEMENT.

BOUNDARY CONTROVERSY WITH VIRGINIA.

The further history of this celebrated line belongs to another of the controversies through which Pennsylvania has had to pass to establish her boundaries. We refer to that which the peculiarities of her charter and the stirring events in the south-western corner of the province, during the twenty years preceding 1774, brought to a head between her and Virginia, just as the great contest between the crown and the colonies was heading up to revolution, which pervaded the entire period of that eventful struggle, and terminated almost co-temporaneously with its successful close.

We cannot here narrate the events, or unfold fully the grounds of that once portentious strife. Its scope is too ample, and its amplitude too full of interesting and instructive teachings, to bear compression into what must be a mere appendage to the preceding sketch. The great subject to which it related was the extent and shape of our limits westward. We limit our design now to such an exposition only of its leading features as will fill out the history of our southern boundary. About four-fifths of the line was the result of a compromise to which Virginia was no party. North of 38 deg. and the Potomac, she had to be silent. But west of the "meridian of the first fountain" of that river, she lifted up her voice loudly against "northern aggression;" not, however, as we shall see, to her very lasting advantage.

As a colonial grant, Virginia never had any rights north of 40 deg. And upon her decapitation, by **quo warranto**, in 1624, she became a mere appendage of English empire, without any fixed boundaries, subject to having her limits impaired as often as it should please his Majesty to confer new grants out of her original domain. Maryland and North Carolina are thus derived. And yet, both as a colony and as a State, she has kept up continual claim to territory north of 40 deg. The "pan-handle" still rears its head above the 40th degree; and the doubtful recognition, since 1780, of her vaunted claim to the great territory north-west of the Ohio and east of the Mississippi, attests her pretentions in that direction.(a) With this we have here nothing to do. But we may well challenge her right to intrude within the limits of a specific grant, carved out of territory which she never owned. Indeed, she claimed that the extinction of her charter enlarged her bounds; that thereupon, she became keeper for the king of all contiguous territory not rightfully held by some other colony. It was upon this pretense that she assailed Pennsylvania. The posture was plausible enough during her colonial vassalage. But upon her revolt from her kingly allegiance— asserting existence as an independent State—she forfeited her viceregal prerogatives, and became shut up to the territory which, without encroachment upon her neighbors, she had settled and governed. And yet Pennsylvania had to contend with her in both these characters.

The site of Pittsburgh, and the Indian trade which centered there became early the objects of Virginia cupidity. Her efforts to acquire these brought on the French war of 1754-'63, in which Washington rose and Braddock fell. It was upon the laggard defense, and almost abnegation of ownership, of her ultramontane territory, by Pennsylvania, in the early stages of this war, that Virginia based her claim as the king's representative. She turned upon the sons of Penn the battery which he, in 1682, raised against Lord Baltimore's right to Delaware. The position taken was that the Penns, by suffering the French to conquer all west of the mountains, thereby rendering it necessary that it should be re-conquered by his Majesty's arms, had forfeited, to that extent, their chartered limits; and that upon its retrocession by France to the British king, in 1763, it became his again "to give as he pleaseth." The argument, when tested by the rules of right and the truth of history, turns out to be more specious than solid. It was soon superseded by other pretexts which were thought to possess greater potency.

The natural connections of South-western Pennsylvania were with Maryland and Virginia. These were greatly strengthened by the opening of the old Ohio Company's path, afterwards Braddock's road, from Wills' creek (Cumberland,) to the head of the Ohio, and

---

(a) We are aware that we are treading here upon tender ground. But, were this the place to do it, it could readily be shown that the postulate of Mr. Chief Justice Taney, in Dred Scott vs. Sanford—that "this immense tract of country was within the acknowledged limits of the State of Virginia," is an entire reversal of the truth of history. Her claim was only a claim, and so regarded by the old Confederacy Congress.

the events of the French war. The early settlers came almost wholly from middle Virginia and Maryland, upon the Potomac, bringing with them a hereditary dislike to Pennsylvania rule and manners, and squatting down upon what they supposed was Virginia territory. Hence when, in 1769, the Penns began to sell their lands at £5 per one hundred acres, and, in 1771, by the erection of Bedford county, extended over them the arms of government, with its restraints and taxes, repugnance soon rose to resistance.

At this opportune crisis Virginia, under the governorship of Lord Dunmore, late in 1773, interposed to assert her jurisdiction. The disputed territory was made the western district of Augusta county, with Fort Pitt as the seat of dominion. The invasion was at once both civil and military. Early in the same year Pennsylvania had erected the county of Westmoreland over all her western territory, with her seat of justice at Hannastown. At first the conflict was fierce and alarming. His lordship, finding a fit instrument of mischief in one Doctor John Connolly,(b) with numerous subordinates and a ready populace, held his usurped possession with unyielding tenactiy. Pennsylvania officers were contemned and restricted, her justices imprisoned, her jail broken open, and her courts broken up. Vagaries and enormities were for a while enacted, which find no parallel in any other period of our western history. To quell the tumult of the times, the Penns had recourse to negotiation; but without any other result than to disclose more fully the conflicting claims of the parties.

The reader will remember that the only fixed, natural landmarks named in the charter, by which to determine the form and extent of Pennsylvania, were New Castle town and the river Delaware. The latter was her eastern bounds; while the former was to be used as the centre of a circle of twelve miles radius, whose north-western segment was to connect the river with the "beginning of the 40th degree." Westward, the province was to extend "five degrees in longitude to be computed from said eastern bounds."

The Penns now claimed, for their western boundary, a line beginning at 39 deg., at the distance of five degrees of longitude from the Delaware, thence at the same distance from that river in every

---

(b) As an adventurer—tool to Dunmore—instigator of Indian war—Tory—prisoner—and in 1788, fomenter of troubles in Kentucky, the life of this renegade son of Pennsylvania is one of peril and mischief. The curious reader may trace him in Washington's Journal, 1770, Nov. 22—4 Pa. Archives, Index "Connolly"—1 Olden Times, 520—2 Ditto, 93—3 Sparks' Washington, 211, 269, 271—8 Ditto, 25—9 Ditto, 474, 485—Western Annals, 492.

point, to north latitude 42 deg., so as to take into the Quaker province some fifty miles square of North-western Virginia, west of the west line of Maryland. Dunmore scouted his claim and difficult-to-be-ascertained line. He insisted that our western boundary should be a meridian line run south from the end of five degrees of longitude from the Delaware, on line 42 deg.; which, said he, will throw the western line of Pennsylvania at least fifty miles east of Pittsburgh. This pretense was based, upon the belief that the Delaware continued to 42 deg. the north-eastward bearing, which changes to north-west at the eastern corner of Pike county—so little was then known of our interior geography. The next expedient by the Penns was to propose Mason and Dixon's line to the Monongahela, and thence that river to the Ohio, as a temporary boundary.(c) This, too, was rejected; his lordship saying that upon nothing less than his Majesty's express command would he relinquish Pittsburgh. Here negotiation ended; and violence and oppression continued their sway, until checked up by those absorbing interests.

The outburst of the Revolution, in 1775, and the fall of the Dunmore dynasty, produced a lull in the storm of inter-colonial strife. Partisans became patriots, and rushed with eagerness to repel a common foe.(d) For a brief period the civil jurisdiction of Pennsylvania seems to have been yielded. Military control was all that Virginia exercised. But this blending of incoherent pretentions could not long endure. It severed, as soon as the first intense fervors of revolution had cooled down, into an earnest struggle for independence.

And now Virginia behaved towards Pennsylvania with an inconsistency, if not cool vindictiveness, without precedent or palliation. On the 15th of June, 1776, her revolutionary convention, justly deprecating the conflict of jurisdiction in the disputed territory, proposed to Pennsylvania a temporary boundary, which, they said, "would most nearly leave the inhabitants in the country they settled under;" which boundary is as follows: from the north-west corner of Maryland to Braddock's road—by it to the Great Cross-

---

(c) As the Penns claimed it, not far from the true line; which would have left Pittsburgh about six miles in Pennsylvania.

(d) Among the most resolute of the Penn adherents were, Arthur St. Clair, then prothonotary, &c., of Westmoreland, afterwards Major General, &c., and Thomas Scott, afterwards first Prothonotary of Washington, and first member of Congress from Western Pennsylvania. Of the Virginia partisans were Dorsey Pentecost, afterwards Clerk of Yohogania county, first member from Washington in Sup. Ex. Council of Pa.; Colonel William Crawford, who was burned by the Ohio Indians in 1782; Colonel John Campbell, afterwards prominent in Kentucky; George Graham, Indian agent, &c.

ings of the Youghiogheny—down that river to Chestnut Ridge mountain—along its crest to Greenlick run branch of Jacob's creek —down it to where Braddock's road crossed—by the road and its continuation towards Pittsburgh to the Bullock Pens (a little northwest of Wilkinsburg), and thence a straight line to the mouth of Plum run (creek) on the Allegheny. East of this Pennsylvania was to rule—west of it, Virginia. The Pennsylvania convention, in September, 1776, very properly rejected this proposal; because, being very wide of her true limits, its adoption as a temporary line would be productive of more confusion than if it was to be final.

Ere the rejection of this preposterous proposition, the same Virginia convention that made it had, on the 29th of June, 1776, by her Constitution, expressly "ceded, released and forever confirmed unto the people of Pennsylvania, all the territory contained in her charter, with all the rights of property, jurisdiction and government, which might at any time heretofore have been claimed by Virginia." At this time she well knew, from Mason and Dixon's measurements and otherwise, that much of the chartered limits of Pennsylvania must fall west of the proposed line, while no Virginia territory could lie east of it. Nevertheless, during the further progress of the controversy she conformed her jurisdiction very nearly to this rejected line.

The next movement by Virginia was a bold stride at dominion. Assuming that Pennsylvania, as well as Maryland, should not reach further west than the "meridian of the first fountain of the Potomac," she, by an Act of her Assembly, passed in October, 1776, proceeded to define the boundary between her east and west Augusta districts; and having annexed some considerable parts of her now north-western counties, and all of Pennsylvania west of the aforesaid meridian, to the latter, divided it into three counties— Ohio, Monongalia and Yohogania. Nearly all of the last and much of the other two were composed of Pennsylvania territory. The last took in what are now the county seats of Washington, Fayette, Westmoreland and Allegheny, and all north of them. Under this law, justices' courts were regularly held—(e) senators and delegates to the Virginia Legislature chosen, and all other functions of government, civil and military, exercised, from 1776 to 1780. In the meantime Pennsylvania kept up her power, as well as she could, through her Westmoreland county organization, over the whole of

(e) The Yohogania courts were held in the upper story of a log jail and court-house, 24 by 16 feet, on the farm of Andrew Heath, upon the Monongahela, at or near where Elizabeth now is. We have seen its Minutes. It did a large and varied business.

her territory as she claimed it. There was literally an **imperium in imperio**, especially between Braddock's road and the Monongahela, which was perhaps the most densely settled portion of the disputed territory. West of that river, except here and there upon its western shore and the south-east corner of Greene, Pennsylvania did not venture. Nor did she ever intrude her functions south of Mason and Dixon's line.

The machinery of the new district counties worked badly, especially in its military movements, which at that warlike period were of primary importance. This, and a returning sense of justice, induced Virginia, in December, 1776, to propose an adjustment of the lines, as follows: extend the west line of Maryland due north to 40 deg.—thence due west to the limit of five degrees of longitude from the Delaware—thence northward, at five degrees distance from that river in every part; or, if preferred, at proper points and angles with intermediate straight lines, to 42 deg.:—thus cutting "a monstrous handle" out of south-western Pennsylvania—overlapping the ancient 40 deg., but yielding to the Penn claim of 1774, which Dunmore so stoutly resisted. There would have been some force in this claim of Virginia to go up to the true 40 deg., had her charter of 1609 not been recalled; for it bounded her on the north, not by a degree of latitude, as was Maryland, but by two hundred miles of coast-line north-ward from Point Comfort. But as between Penn and the king, in 1681, the 40 deg. of that day was the true limit of the grant. This offer was rejected also.

The disheartening reverses and exhausting efforts of the Revolutionary struggle, during 1777 and 1778, withdrew the disputants from any attention to their boundary troubles. For a while the strife stood still, except that its inconveniences and conflicts upon the disputed territory were as perplexing as ever. Brighter auspices dawned in 1779. Early in that year Pennsylvania proposed to Virginia a joint commission to agree upon their boundaries. The latter acceded. The commissioners met in Baltimore, and on the 31st of August, 1779, agreed upon the following boundaries:(f) "to extend Mason and Dixon's line due west five degrees of longitude, to be computed from the river Delaware, for the southern boundary of Pennsylvania; and that a meridian, drawn from the western extremity thereof to the northern limit of said State, be the western boundary of Pennsylvania forever."

(f)The Pennsylvania commissioners were, George Bryan, Rev. John Ewing, D. D., and David Rittenhouse; Virginia sent Right Rev. James Madison and Rev. Robert Andrews.

We know but little of what occurred at the meeting of these commissioners. A letter is extant from one of the Pennsylvania commissioners—Judge Bryan—saying that the Virginians offered to divide equally the 40th degree; but for what equivalent is not revealed.(g) There is a tradition, too, that the judge resisted an offer to extend Mason and Dixon's line to the Ohio. Doubtless this generosity on the part of Virginia was to be compensated north of that river. It is probable that, in this negotiation, the parties stood pretty much where they did in May, 1774—Pennsylvania claiming down to 39 deg., and to have her western line an irregular curvilinear parallel to the Delaware,(h) and Virginia claiming to stop her, on the south, at 40 deg. The idea of making our western boundary to be a straight line, or chord, subtending the irregular arc formed by the two extremes of five degrees from the Delaware, on the north and on the south, seems never, at any time, to have been claimed or proposed. A chancellor might have so decreed without any violence to the charter. One is almost tempted to regret that the Pennsylvania commissioners had not claimed to turn round at Fairfax's stone and ask for all of Virginia north of the 39 deg. They had as good ground for the whole as for part. And who knows but that a little more expanded pretentions in that direction might have induced the Virginians to give us the "pan-handle!" We must not, however, complain. They did exceedingly well. They probably did not know that there would be room there to turn(i) north of 39 deg. And it is fortunate that Virginia did not know that when Pennsylvania, in 1771, erected Bedford county, she expressly recognized the ex parte extension of Mason and Dixon's line, west of Maryland, as her southern boundary.

But the troubles were not yet ended. The agreement of the commissioners had to be ratified, and the lines to be run. Pennsylvania promptly assented to the "compromise" in November, 1779—as well she might, seeing that it expanded her western territory full half a degree without any equivalent loss on the south. Virginia, perhaps, seeing this, held back; and in December, 1779, sent into the disputed territory a court of commissioners to adjust land titles. No event in the whole controversy so aroused the ire of Pennsylvania as did this

---

(g) See 1 Olden Times, 451.
(h) The late Judge H. H. Brackenridge (Law Miscellanies, 254,) reverses this position of the parties. His views of the subject are palpably erroneous in other particulars; hence, very probably, in this also. If the parties stood as he places them, Pennsylvania got more than she claimed.
(i) It was at this date an open question whether Maryland would not begin her western line at the "first fountain" of the south branch of the Potomac.

attempt to dispossess her own settlers and adjudicate their lands to claimants who had defied her jurisdiction. A very determined intimation that a continuance of the intrustion would be repelled by force, led to its withdrawal. Thereupon, in June, 1780, Virginia ratified the agreement; clogging it, however, with a condition which protected all the rights to persons and property which her settlers had acquired prior to that date, providing that rights to lands should be determined by priority of title or settlement, and be paid for to Pennsylvania at Virginia prices, if acquired from her. Under these provisions many land titles in South-western Pennsylvania are laid by patents based upon Virginia certificates, and west of the Monongahela there are many Virginia patents. They conduced to many troubles and hardships. Pennsylvania foresaw that such would be their fruits; and, therefore, for a while withheld her assent; but at length, in September, 1780, declaring herself "determined to give to the world the most unequivocal proof of her earnest desire to promote peace and harmony with a sister State, so necessary during this great contest against the common enemy," assented to the unequal condition. And here this boundary controversy closed—the last of the series which Pennsylvania had to encounter.

It remained yet to run and mark the lines. This it was intended to do, in 1781, permanently; but the pressure of the "great war of liberty" compelled its postponement. The withdrawal of Virginia, in 1780, from the disputed and ceded territory, called for the erection by Pennsylvania, in 1781, of the county of Washington, comprising all of the State west of the Monongahela and south-west of the Ohio. This new organization imperatively demanded some ascertainment of its boundaries on its two Virginia sides. A promise of a jont effort to do this, by a temporary line, in the fall of that year, failed of accomplishment on the part of Virginia. It was run in November, 1782, by Col. Alex. M'Clean, of Fayette, (then Westmoreland,) and Joseph Neville, of Virginia, from the war path crossing of Dunkard to the corner, and thence to the Ohio. They were instructed to extend Mason and Dixon's line twenty-three miles, which proved to be about a mile and a half too much;—an error which occasioned some loss to certain Philadelphia gentlemen—the Cooks, and perhaps others, who, before the final running of the lines, had caused some land-warrants to be laid, abutting upon the temporary line, on the western border of, now Greene county. Less than twenty-three miles were wanting to complete the distance of the charter.

Pending these delays Pennsylvania had no little trouble with many of her newly-acquired Washington county citizens, who hated her rule and resisted their transfer. They asked Congress, under a provision in the old Articles of Confederation, to establish the curvilinear parallel with the Delaware, which would restore them to Virginia. Their petitions were unheeded. Whereupon they went deeply into a project for a new State, which was to include Western Pennsylvania, Ohio east of the Muskingum, and Virginia northeast of the Kenawha, with Pittsburgh as the seat of empire. It was a resurrection of the old "Walpole grant" of 1772.(j) So rife had the scheme become, that Pennsylvania had to counteract it by all her power, declaring it, by an Act passed in December, 1782, to be treason. In many other ways her authority was contemned, her laws resisted, and her officers defied and maltreated. Especially was this the case with her odious excise law. And in the resistance which it encountered is found the precedents for many of the excesses of the renowned Whiskey Insurrection." Gradually, however, and by the countervailing infusions of a more thorough Pennsylvania population, the disaffection receded; and nowhere, for at least half a century, has any people been more proud of their government, or more submissive to its requirements.

It was not until 1784 that Mason and Dixon's line was completed, upon astronomical observations, and permanently marked. The great difficulty—the nice point, was to fix its western termination. To do this, some of the most scientific men of that day were employed. On the part of Virginia they were the Right Rev. James Madison, Bishop of Virginia, Rev. Robert Andrews, John Page and Andrew Ellicott, of Maryland. The Pennsylvania Commissioners were John Lukens, Surveyor General, Rev. John Ewing, D. D., David Rittenhouse and Thomas Hutchins. They undertook the task from "an anxious desire;" they say, "to gratify the astronomical world in the performance of a problem which has never yet been attempted in any country, and to prevent the State of Pennsylvania from the chance of losing many hundred thousands of acres secured to it by the agreement at Baltimore." To solve the novel problem, two of the artists of each State, provided with the proper astronomical instruments and a good time-piece, repaired to Wilmington, Delaware—nearly on the line, where they erected an observatory. The other four, in like manner furnished and with commissary, sol-

---

(j) Concerning "Walpole's grant," see Sparks' Washington, 356-7, and 483—Sparks' Life of Franklin, 339—3 Journals of Old Congress, 359—4 Ditto, 23—4 Pa. Arch. 483, 579. On the New State project, see 3 Olden Time, 479, 537—Brakenridge's Law Miscell. 324, 438, 444, 565, 572, 637—10 Ditto, 40, 41, 163.

diers and servants, proceeded to the west end of the temporary line, near to which, on one of the highest of the Fish creek hills, they also erected a rude observatory. At these stations each party, during six long weeks of days and nights preceding the autumnal equinox of 1784, continued to make observations of the eclipses of Jupiter's moons and other celestial phenomena, for the purposes of determining their respective meridians and latitude and adjusting their time-pieces. This done, two of each party come together, and they find their stations were apart twenty minutes and one and an eighth seconds. The Wilmington Station was one hundred and fourteen four-pole chains and thirteen links west of the Delaware. Knowing that twenty minutes of time were equal to five degrees of longitude, they make allowance for said one hundred and fourteen chains and thirteen links, and for the said one and an eighth seconds, (equal, they say, to nineteen chains and ninety-six links), and upon these data they shorten back on the line to twenty minutes from the Delaware, and fix the south-west corner of the State by setting up a square unlettered white-oak post, around which they rear a conical pyramid of stones, "and they are there unto this day."(k)

There was no retracing of the line from the north-west corner of Maryland; nor was it measured from the end of Mason and Dixon's running to the cairn corner. All that was done was to connect these two points by opening vistas over the most remarkable heights and planting posts on some of them, at irregular distances, marked with P. and V. on the sides, each letter facing the State of which it is the initial. The corner was guarded by two oak trees; with notches in each, as watchers. It could not be too well secured; for it and the twenty-two miles from the war path, cost the State £1455 specie, equal to nearly $4,000, besides six dollars per day to each of the "astronomers!"(l) Their commissary was Col. Andrew Porter, father of ex-Governor David R. Porter. Being at the western end, some "thirty miles from any settlements," his duties were exceedingly onerous. And here, near the end of 1784, ends the history of Mason and Dixon's line.

The next year (1785) the western line, to the Ohio, and some forty or fifty miles beyond it was run and marked in like manner,

---

(k) See the Report in 10 Pa. Archives, 373, 374.
(l) They lived well. Among their "accommodations," ordered by the State, were 60 gallons spirits, 20 gallons brandy, 40 gallons Maderia wine, 200 pounds loaf sugar, a small keg of lime (lemon) juice, 6 pounds tea, 20 pounds coffee, 30 pounds chocolate, 20 pounds Scotch barley, &c.—"a ha'-penny worth of bread to this intolerable deal of sack."

with the addition of deadening the trees in the vistas between the hills. The Pennsylvania artists were Col. Andrew Porter and David Rittenhouse; those of Virginia Joseph Neville and Andrew Ellicott, the latter acting for Pennsylvania north of the Ohio, where Virginia pretensions ended by reason of her cession of the North-west Territory to the United States in 1784. It was completed to Lake Erie in 1786, by Col. Porter and Col. Alexander M'Clain. Its length is about one hundred and fifty-eight miles.

Thus honorably and successfully has Pennsylvania borne herself in all her boundary contests; never encroaching upon her neighbors' rights, yet always gaining by their intrusions upon her territory. Her uniformly calm, patient, persevering defensive policy, begun by her Proprietors and perpetuated in the Commonwealth, has added one-fourth to the area of her chartered limits. Setting out in her controversial career upon the maxium: "Be just and fear not," the fiercest assaults never provoked her to retaliate, nor did the boldest invasions ever compel her to yield. And although it would be unkind, if not unjust, to accuse her invaders of willful aggression, we may safely say of them, as did Lady Macbeth of her "thane:"

> "Wouldst not play false, and yet wouldst wrongly win."

In the ultimate accessions of both valuable territory and valuable population, with which Pennsylvania was compensated for the troubles they gave her, may be read an instructive lesson to all the States, in the present and coming time—never to encroach upon any of the rights of a co-equal Sovereignty. The redress of individual wrongs may be deferred to a future state of being, but the retributions which communities incur admit of no such postponement:

> "In these cases
> We still have judgment here; that we but teach
> Bloody instructions, which being taught, return
> To plague the inventor."

INDEX*

-A-

Abrams, (Judge) 93
  Henry 93
Ache, John 131
  Samuel 131
Adams, _____ 30
  John Quincy 145, 179, 180, 181,
    183, 192, 193, 194, 195
  Robert 82, 101
  William 193
Addison, (Judge) 141, 157
Adolphus, Gustavus 216
Alexander I 192
Allegre, (Mme.) 168
  (Mlle.) 168
Allen, _____ 57
  David 101
  John 94
  (Col.) John 168
  William 237
Allison, (Dr.) 32
  (Rev.) Francis 29
  John 92
Ames, _____ 179
Amherts, (Sir) Jeffry 82
Andrew, George 82
Andrews, (Rev.) Robert 254, 257
Angouleme, (Duchess of) 171, 172
Anne, (Queen) 225
Applegate, _____ 107

Armstrong, John 100
  (Col.) John 57
  John, Jr. 161
Arnold, Jonathan 99
Ashburton, Lord 196
Ashley, (Lieut.) 122
Ashton, Thomas 151
Austin, John M. 19, 20

-B-

Bache, _____ 167
Baddolet, John 136
Badolet, John 172
Bailey, Eli 22
Baker, (Mr.) 182
  Joseph 243
  Melchor 181
Baltimore, Lord 215, 216, 218-220,
  222-225, 227-232, 234, 239,
  240, 244, 245, 250
Bancroft, _____ 210
Barbour, James 183
Barclay, Jno. 237
Barrett, (Capt.) Lemuel 81
Bayard, _____ 179
  James A. 192, 193
Beale, Robert 99
Beall, (Col.) Robert 133

---

*This Index does not incorporate those names appearing in the alphabetical lists on pages 199-205.

Beatty, (Rev.) Charles 52
Beaujeau, (M.) 63
Beckett, (Capt.) Joseph 127
Beeson, _____ 100
  Henry 25, 35, 36, 66, 67, 133, 160
  (Gen.) Henry W. 19
  Isaac 79
  Jacob 102
  (Mrs.) Jacob 102
Bell, Edward 129
  James 162
Benton, (Mr.) 196
Berkeley, (Sir) John 217
Biffle, Jacob 98
  James 98
Biggs, (Capt.) John 122, 127
Bixler, _____ 19
Black, (Judge) 222, 226
Blackiston, _____ 22
  James 25, 99
Blackstone, James 119
Blaine, E. V. [16]
Blake, Nicholas 169
Blakeney, Gabriel 136
Bloomfield (see Brownfield)
Boardley, J. Beale 237
Botetourt, (Gov.) 89
Bourdelon, Louis 172
Bouquet, (Col.) Henry 27, 29, 81, 82, 83, 84, 86
Bowan, Jacob 38
Bowen, _____ 246
Bowman, James L. 38
  N. B. 30
Brackenridge, _____ 157, 176, 177
  Hugh Henry 178, 255
Brakenridge, _____ 257
Braddock, (Gen.) Edward 25, 26, 27, 30, 33, 35, 43, 44, 45, 48, 52, 55, 58, 59, 62-76, 80, 112, 229, 250
Bradford, _____ 176
  David 105
  David, Jr. 105
Bradstreet, (Col.) 83
Brashears, _____ 30
  Nacy 99
  Otho 99
Breading, (Judge) 100
  Clark 19

Brisco, Walter 99
Britt, Robert 23
Brodhead, (Col.) Daniel 238
Brooke, (Judge) 197
Brooke, Francis T. 169
Brown, _____ 87
  Abraham 110
  Abram 20
  Adam 79, 110, 111
  Bazil 32, 81
  Christopher 110
  Emanuel 79
  Manus 110
  Maunus 79, 111
  Richard 22
  Thomas 32, 79, 81, 92, 99, 110
  Wendell 50, 79, 109, 110
Brownfield, _____ 101, 110
  Basil 22
  Empson 93
  Isaac 27
  N. 28
  Robert 155
  Thomas 35, 93
  (Rev.) William 25, 102
Brubaker, _____ 33
Bryan, George 139, 254, 255
Bryson, Samuel 57
Bullitt, (Mr.) 131
Buonaparte, Joseph 194
Burd, (Col.) James 18, 27, 29-33, 53, 69, 70, 81
Burgoyne, _____ 57, 152
Burkham (see Burkon)
Burkon, Henry 93
Burton, (Lt. Col.) 57, 60, 65
Bute, John 19, 57
Butler, Richard 27, 149, 150, 151
  William 149
Byer, _____ 102
Byers, _____ 19

-C-

Cabot, John 209
  Sebastian 209
Cack (see Cook)
Cadwallader, Rees 81

Caldwell, _____ 100
  Joseph 100
Calhoun, _____ 146, 196
Calvert, _____ 233, 234
  Cecil 215
  Charles 226
  (Sir) George 214, 215
  Leonard 216
Campbell, George W. 193
  (Col.) John 252
Carnahan, (Rev. Dr.) 175
Carr, (Sir) Robert 217
Cartaret, (Sir) George 217
Carter, _____ 30
Cazenove, Anthony 172
Chadwick, John 129
Chalmers, _____ 223
Chaplin, John 102
  Thomas 102
Chapman, (Maj.) 57
Charles I 215, 216
Charles II 73, 77, 217, 219, 225
Charles, (Prince) 211
  Isaac 101
Cherry, Ralph 98
Chew, B. 98
  Benjamin 237
Christian, (Col.) 117
Christina, (Queen) 216
Christy, William 150
Claiborne, _____ 215
Clark, (Col.) 134
  (Gen.) 133
Clarke, (Col.) George Rogers 126, 127
  Samuel 25
Clay, Henry 146, 183, 192-194
Coburn, _____ 100
  (Capt.) 92, 93
Cock, Michael 107, 157
Coleman, William 237
Colley, _____ 30
Collins, _____ 149
  James 19
  (Capt.) Luke 81, 82
  (Maj.) Luke 130
Colvin, _____ 101
  D. C. 30
  William 30, 36, 81, 92
Conn, Gabriel 93
Connell, Zachariah 99, 101

Connolly, (Dr.) John 251
Contrecoeur, _____ 47, 49, 62
Conwell, William 107
Cook, _____ 256
  (Col.) 36
  (Col.) Edward 99, 101, 134, 135
  Hans 93
Cooper, (Dr.) 168
  John 93
Coover, _____ 235
Cope, Eli 30, 81
Corbly, (Rev.) John 101
Cornwallis, Lord 152
Cottom, John 20
Courtney, B. 29, 30
Craft, John 22
Craig, (Capt.) Isaac 127
  James 57
  John S. 148
  Neville B. 43, 221
  (Capt.) William 148
Craik, (Dr.) James 44, 57, 58
Crawford, _____ 22
  Hugh 30, 96, 243
  James 92
  John 118, 119, 125
  (Mrs.) John 131
  Josias 93
  Ophelia 118
  Sarah 118
  Valentine 118, 119
  W. H. 183
  (Capt.) William 88
  (Col.) William 37, 60, 85, 118-125, 129, 252
  William H. 194
  William, Jr. 119, 125, 127
  (Mrs.) William 121, 125
Cresap, _____ 81
  (Capt.) Michael 32, 81, 229
  (Col.) Thomas 26, 29, 32, 41, 229-231, 234
Crockett, (Col.) 127
Croghan, George 45, 57, 78, 84, 85, 90-93, 150
Cromwell, _____ 216
  William 80, 113, 115
Crooks, Thomas 36
Cross, James 99
Cumberland, Duke of 73
Curran, _____ 40

Curran, Barnaby 229

-D-

Darby,_____ 221
Davidson, (Mr.) 61
  John 40
  Thomas 107
Davis, Benjamin 99
Dawson, Benoni 99
  George 116, 138, 148
  John 116
  (Hon.) John Littleton 116
  Nicholas 116
Day,_____ 235
Dearth, James 99
DeBolt, Michael 87
Delaware, Lord 212
Delong, John 92
Desha,_____ 146
Devries,_____ 214
Dewitt, Ezekiel 93
Dickerson, Wm. 20
Dickinson, (President) 135
  John 158
Dinwiddie, (Gov.) 40, 75
Dixon, Jeremiah 238-244, 247, 253
Doane, Aaron 162, 163
  Abraham 162, 163
  Joseph 162, 163
  Levi 162, 163
  Mahlon 162, 163
  Moses 162, 163
Doddridge, (Dr.) Joseph 23, 36
Douglas, (Gen.) 57
  (Gen.) Ephraim 149-165
Douglass, (Gen.) 129, 135
  Adam 149
  Eliza 149
  Joseph 149, 152
  Sarah 149
Douter (see Douthitt)
Douthitt, Thomas 92, 93
Downard,_____ 110
Downs, Thomas 92
Drouillon, (M.) 46
Dumas, (Mr.) 63
Dunbar, (Col.) Thomas 56, 58, 60, 65-69, 74, 76
Dunkard,_____ 78
Dunlap,_____ 27
  (Rev.) James 105
Dunlop, James 221
Dunmore, Lord 251, 252, 254

-E-

Eckerlin,_____ 79
Edgar, (Mr.) 140, 176
Edmondstone, (Capt.) 82
Elizabeth, (Queen) 210
Ellicott, Andrew 257, 259
Elliott,_____ 153
  Daniel 149
  William 149
Enslow, Henry 93
  John 93
Evans, (Col.) 25, 113, 243
  Jesse 23
  Samuel 105
  (Col.) Samuel 96
Ewing, (Judge) 54
  James 20
  (Rev.) John 237, 254, 257
  Maria [15]
  (Hon.) Nathaniel [15]

-F-

Fairfax, Lord 52, 229
Fasenbaker, (Mr.) 54
Fauquier, (Gov.) 86, 87, 89
Few, (Mrs.) 195
  William 172
Findlay, William 143
Findley,_____ 175, 176, 180, 189
  William 64, 65, 70, 74, 108, 138, 140-145
Finley, Ebenezer 100
  Eli 100
  James 99, 100, 113, 142, 160, 170
  Robert 100

Fleming, (Rev.) Thornton 102
Flenniken, John 172
   R. P. 172
Forbes, (Gen.) 27, 29, 33, 63,
   75, 76, 112, 118
Fossit, Joseph 71
   Thomas 70, 71, 72
   Tom 35
Foster, John F. 25
Franklin, (Dr.) 52, 73, 167
Franks, John 19
   Michael 130
Frazer, _____ 115
Frazier, _____ 42
Freeman, _____ 25
   Edmond 99
Friggs, _____ 93
Froman, Paul 36
Fuller, _____ 222
Fulton, _____ 30

-G-

Gaddis, _____ 101
   Jacob 30, 118
   John 29, 118, 160
   (Col.) Thomas 22
Gage, (Gen.) 85
   (Lt. Col.) 57, 63
Galbraith, _____ 157
Gallagher, John 25
Gallatin, Albert 25, 140, 141,
   144, 166-198
   (Mrs.) Albert 171, 172
   Frances 198
   James 198
   John 166
Gambrier, Lord 193
Gans, George 243
   William 25
Garland, _____ 143
Gates, (Capt.) Horatio 57
George II 46, 227
George III 244
Gerry, Elbridge 147
Gibson, (Gen.) John 141
Gilchrist, _____ 102
   James

Gilchrist, John 142
Giles, William B. 179, 180
Girty, Simon 123, 124
Gist _____ 27-30, 40, 42, 45, 46,
   48, 49, 52, 55, 58, 60, 65,
   80, 81, 85, 87, 91, 93, 96
   Anne 115
   Christopher 40, 42, 44, 57, 66,
   79, 111-117
   Joshua 116
   (Gen.) Mordecai 116, 117
   Nathaniel 57, 66, 115-117
   Richard 115-117
   Thomas 36, 37, 79, 93, 112, 115,
   116
   Violet 115
Godyn, _____ 213, 216
Goe, William 18, 99
Goldsmith, _____ 146
Gordon, (Capt.) 27
Gordon, (Gov.) 229
Goulbourn, (Sir) Henry 193
Grable, _____ 30
   Joseph 99
Graham, (Col.) 245
   George 252
   Jacob B. 30
   (Lt. Col.) James D. 247
   William 96
Grahame, (Sir) James 223
Granger, Gideon 183
Grant, (Major) 44
Gratz, (Mr.) 151
Grayble, Joseph 36
Green, _____ 110
   Edward 157
Griffin, Charles 25
Gudgeon (see Gudgel)
Gudgel, Andrew 92
Guesse (see Gist)

-H-

Hadden, _____ 157
   (Misses) 25
   [James] 53
   Thomas 137
Halket, (Lt.) 72

Halket, Francis 57
  (Col. Sir) Peter 56, 58, 62, 64, 70, 72
Hall, Jonathan 238
Hamilton, ___ 179
  (Gen.) 143
  (Gov.) 48
  (Secretary) 144, 145
  Alexander 184, 189
  Daniel 178
  James 237
  John 25
Hammond, James 99
Hand, (Brig. Gen.) 120
Hardin, John 99
  Mark 99
  Sarah 99
Hardwicke, Lord 228, 238
Harmar, (Gen.) 128
Harper, ___ 146
Harris, ___ 93
  Samuel 28
Harrison, (Gen.) 129
  Battle 119
  Benjamin 119
  Catharine 119
  James 87
  John 87
  Lawrence 25, 92, 93
  Lawrence, Jr. 119
  Richard 93
  Robert 87, 99
  William 99, 118, 119, 121, 125
Hart, Henry 36
  William 135
Hastings, ___ 30
Hatfield, Samuel 27
  Wm. 30
Hatton, Adam 92
Hawkins, (Hon.) Wm. G. 131
Hayden, John 38
Headley, (Mr.) 69
Heath, Andrew 253
Heister, (Gov.) 141
Hellen, ___ 25
Henderson, Robert 246
Henrietta Maria 215
Henry, Patrick 168, 169
Henshaw, ___ 30
Henthorn, ___ 110
  James 102

Hickman, Ezekiel 93
Higgenbottom, Ralph 93
Higginson, ___ 110
Hill, (Col.) A. M. 20, 105
  (Rev.) George 105
  Jonathan 113
Hoge, John 141, 142
Hogg, (Capt.) 43, 44, 57
  George E. 61, 101
  William 33
Holmes, Sarah 131
Hook, Peter 102
Hooter, Michael 92
Hopwood, Moses 102
Hudson, (Sir) Henry 212
Hughes, James 129
Husten, Jane 148
Huston, (Judge) 235
  Joseph 54, 138, 148
Hutchins, Thomas 257
Hutton, Margaret 99

-I-

Ingman, John 88
Innes, (Col.) 44
Irvine, (Gen.) Jas. 152

-J-

Jack, (Capt.) 57
Jackson, ___ 25, 28
  (Gen.) 117, 183
  Andrew 180, 194
  Robert 96
Jacob, John J. 32, 230
Jacobs, Samuel 88
  William 80
James, (King) 247
James I 210, 211, 214
James II 217, 225
James, William 25
Jay, (Mr.) 196
Jefferson, Thomas 126, 145, 146, 181, 182, 188, 190

Jenkins, ____ 40
  Philip 162
Jennings, ____ 110
  Benjamin 93
  David 28, 102
Joh.is, David 36
Johnson, Andrew C. 19
  David 87
  Elizabeth 115
  Ezekiel 93
  Jet. (Jediah) 93
  (Sir) John 153
  (Sir) William 241
Johnston, (Sir) William 85, 91, 95
Jones, (Col.) 72
  John 22, 25
  William 22, 25
Jumonville, ____ 43-48, 51, 68
Junk, ____ 102

-K-

Kefover, Philip 181
Keith, (Gov.) 241
Keller, Daniel 149
Kennedy, ____ 157
Kidd, (Capt.) 247
Kincade, Samuel 99, 131
Kindell, ____ 110
King, Allen 149
Kirkpatrick, ____ 177
Knight, (Dr.) John 122-125
Krepps, (Mrs.) John S. 81

-L-

LaFayette, ____ 194
LaForce, (M.) 45, 46
Lane, John 125
  Presley Carr 125, 179
LaRochefoucald D'Enville 167
Larsh, Hannah 243
  Paul 243
Latrobe, (Mr.) 238, 243

Latrobe, John H. B. 227
Laughlin, Hugh 99
  John 99
  Peter 99
Leeds, Jno. 237
Lemes, Christopher 92
Leslie, Matthew 57
Lewis, (Capt.) Andrew 29, 43, 44, 48, 49, 57
Lewis, Freeman [15], [16]
  William 141
  William, (Esq.) 141
Ligueris, (M.) De 63
Lincoln, (Maj. Gen.) 152
Lindsay, Charles 93
Linn, Andrew 92, 99, 101, 155
  Andrew, Jr. 36
  Ayres 30
  Isaac 30
  William 92
Littell, William 105
Livingston, Edward 179, 180
Lochry, (Col.) 134, 181
Logan, ____ 32
Long, Robert 61
Louis XIV 39
Lowder, (Maj.) 127
Lowrie, (Judge) 232
Lukens, John 238, 257
Lyne (see Lyon)
Lynn (see Lyon)
Lyon, ____ 157
  James 93
  Mary 149
  Samuel 80, 115

-Mc-

McCall, ____ 235
McClain, (Col.) 135
  Alexander 154
  (Col.) Alexander 259
McClean, (Col.) 19, 159, 160
  (Mr.) 243
  (Col.) Alexander 96, 131-137, 238, 240, 242, 245, 256
McClean, Archibald 96, 131-133, 238, 240

McClean, James 92, 132
  Moses 96, 131, 132, 240
  Robert 88
  Samuel 132, 240
McCleery, Joseph 154
McClelland, John 105, 110
  William 102
McClung, (Capt.) 123
McClure, (Capt.) 131
McCormick, William 99, 118
McCoy, James 22, 27
McCulloch,_____ 35
  John 81
  Samuel 81
McCullough, John 32
McCutchen, (Mr.) 124
McDonald,_____ 110
  Angus 81
  James 157
McDowell, (Mr.) 140
  Robert 71
McFall, John 129
McFarland,_____ 25
  John 155, 246
McGlaughlin, Charles 105
  Robert 126
McKay, Daniel 93
McKean, (Gov.) 141
McKee,_____ 153
  James 118
McKibben, John 99, 100
McKown, Andrew 115
McLane, (Mr.) 240
McLean, James 93
  John 183
McMillan, (Rev.) John 100
McPeak (see McPeck)
McPeck, Daniel 36
McQuire,_____ 40

-M-

Macaulay,_____ 222
Macgregor, Rob Roy 230
Mackay, (Capt.) 43, 44, 48, 49, 50, 51, 53
  (Col.) Aeneas 151
  (Capt.) Alexander 86

Macon,_____ 146, 179
Madison,_____ 179, 180, 183
  (Mr.) 146, 147
  (Pres.) 182, 189, 191
  (Rev.) James 254, 257
Mansfield, Lord 228
Markham,_____ 223, 234
Marlow,_____ 59
Marshall,_____ 179
  Isiah 148
Martin, George 92
  Jesse 92
  John 81, 82, 93
  John F. 19
  Luther 32
Mason, Charles 238-244, 247, 253
  (Rev.) Erskine 198
  John 99
May, Cornelius 213
Mayer, Brantz 230
Meason,_____ 157
  (Judge) 117
  (Col.) Isaac 57, 61, 98, 99, 101, 115, 118, 119, 140
  (Hon.) Isaac 119
  (Gen.) Thomas 54
Meigs,_____ 183
Mendenball, Joseph 88
Mercer, (Lt.) George 43
  (Dr.) Hugh 57, 58, 98
Metcalf,_____ 100
Mifflin, (Gov.) Thomas 141, 157, 164, 165
Minor, (Hon.) John 131
  L. L. 131
Minter, John 22, 99, 118
Mitchell, Thomas 72
Monroe,_____ 183
  (President) 27
Montgomery, John 172
  (Mrs.) John 195
Montour,_____ 57, 78
Moore, (Col.) Andrew 23
  Auguetine 99
  Ebenezer 22
  John 33, 35, 69, 179
  Thomas 99, 101
Morgan, (Col.) 127
  (Gen.) Geo. 34
  John 34
  (Col.) Zachariah 127

Morris, (Gov.) 68, 69, 75
  Robert 172
  Roger 57
  William 19
Moser, Daniel (or William) 110
Mountz, P. Jr. 121
  Providence 99, 121
Muhlenburg, Fred. Aug. 140
Murphey, Jacob 30, 49, 79, 101, 102
Murphy, John 113
Murray, (Maj.) 86
  (Sir) William 228
Muse, (Major) 43, 48
Myers,_____ 162
  Martin 129

-N-

Napoleon 188, 194
Necker,_____ 166
Nelson,_____ 146
Nemacolin 26, 27, 41, 62
Neville, Joseph 134, 256, 259
Newman, Isaac 99
Nicholas,_____ 180
Nicholls, (Col.) 217
Nicholson, Hannah 171, 173
  J. W. 130
  James 105, 171
  James W. 172, 173
  John 155, 161
  Thomas W. 98, 105
Noble, Richard 99
Normanville, Sieur 59
North, Lord Chief Justice 219

-O-

Ogle, (Gen.) 141
  (Gov.) 230
O'Hara, (Gen.) James 151
Orme, (Capt.) Robert 55, 57-61, 64
Ormsby, John 150

Otos,_____ 179

-P-

Page, John 257
Parker, (Mr.) 229
Parkhill,_____ 102
Parks, Andrew 54
  Harriet 54
Parshall, (Mr.) 157
Parsons,_____ 183
Patterson,_____ 102, 123
Paull, Archibald 129
  George 80, 126, 129
  George, Jr. 118
  James 19
  (Col.) James 32, 80, 126, 128, 129
  James, Jr. 34, 57
  John 98, 129
  Joseph 126, 129
  Martha 129
  Thomas 129
  William 129
Penn,_____ 82, 97, 227-229, 232-234, 236, 239-241, 245, 250-252
  (Admiral) 218
  (Gov.) 86, 87, 89, 90, 95, 96
  John 92, 98, 226
  (Gov.) John 98, 244
  John, Jr. 98
  Richard 98, 226
  Thomas 98, 226
  (Gov.) Thomas 230
  William 77, 78, 217-226, 250, 254
Pentecost,_____ 101
  Dorsey 154, 252
Peters, John 92
  Richard 237
Peyronie, (Capt.) 43, 44, 57
Phelps, (Dr.) George 150
Phillips, (Col.) 155
  Isaac 71
  Theophilius 99, 142
Pickering,_____ 183
Pickett, James 101

Pierce, Isaac 99
  Philip 98
Pierson, Thomas 240
Pinkney,_____ 183
Pitt, William 75
Polk, (President) 125
Polson, (Capt.) 43, 44, 49, 57
Pontiac 56
Pope,_____ 99
Porter, (Col.) Andrew 136, 155, 156, 258, 259
  David R. 136, 156
  (Miss) Janet 138
  (Col.) Thomas 138
Potter, James 92
Poundstone, David 157
Pratt,_____ 162
Priggs, John F. A. 238
Prisser, Henry 92
Proud,_____ 221
Proudfoot, (Rev.) David 102
Provance,_____ 87, 93
  William Yard 88
Provence, John William 93
  William Yard 93
Pursley, Benjamin 93
Pusey, P. C. 79

-R-

Raleigh, Gilbert 210
Ramsay, James C. 100
Randolph,_____ 179, 180
  Edward 183
  John 143, 181
Rankin,_____ 30
Redick, David 140, 141
Renshaw, (Mr.) 157
Richason, Thomas 162
Rider, George 87
Ridout, J. 237
Riley, Dennis 19
Rist,_____ 26
Ritner, (Gov.) [15]
Rittenhouse, David D. 156, 254, 257, 259
Roberts, George 142
Robertson, William 98

Robinson, James 25
Rochambeau, (Count) de 167
Rodgers, (Capt.) 103
  Richard 92
Rodney,_____ 183
Rogers, Daniel 60, 119
  Philip 25, 103
Rohrer, James S. 87
Roletter, Peter 150
Ross,_____ 157, 176
  Alexander 149
  James 141, 171
  Robert 99
Rosse, (Maj.) William 119, 125
Rowan,_____ 100
Rowland, Jonathan 102, 160
Rush, Richard 183
Russell, Jonathan 193
Rutherford, (Capt.) 57

-S-

St. Clair, (Gen.) 131, 140, 141, 157, 158
  Arthur 130, 140, 252
  (Major Sir) John 57, 60, 67, 68
Sampey, James 54
Sample, Samuel 150
Sanford,_____ 250
Sargent, Winthrop 52, 55, 70, 74
Say, Lord 235
Schooly, William 81
Scott,_____ 110, 230
  Dred 250
  Thomas 35, 142, 145, 178, 252
Seal, Lord 235
Seaver,_____ 146
Seney, Joshua 172
Sergeant,_____ 235
Serre,_____ 167
Shain, Thomas 82
Sharp, Benjamin 117
Sharpe, (Gov.) Horatio 237, 240
Shearer, William 81
Shelby, (Capt.) 240
Shippen, (Col.) 27
  Edward, Jr. 237
  Joseph 31, 94, 239

Shirley, (Gov.) 69
  (Mr. Secretary) 62, 64, 73
  William 57
Sholly, Adam 87
Shryock, Henry 81
Shute, Phillip 35, 92, 93, 99, 113
Sitgreaves, _____ 179
Smilie, _____ 176
  John 98, 138-148, 155, 169
  Mary 148
  Robert 148
Smith, _____ 120, 151, 157
  (Rev. Doctor) 103
  (Judge) Charles 141
  Devereaux 149, 151
  James 33
  (Capt.) John 211, 212, 220
  Robert 101
  William 247
Snyder, (Gov.) 141
Southard, Samuel L. 183
Sparks, (Maj.) 57
  (Mr.) 53, 55, 120, 257
Spear, (Mr.) 150
Speer, _____ 92
Spencer, James 93
Spottswood, (Gov.) 241
Springer, Dennis 99
  (Maj.) Uriah 118
  Zadok 129
Stael, Madame de 166
Stanwix, (Gen.) 29
Steel, John 92, 93, 94
Steele, (Rev.) John 90
Stephen, (Capt.) 43, 57
Stephens, Benjamin 99
  Levi 135
  Samuel 102
Stephenson, Richard 99
Stevens, B. K. 198
  Samuel 20
Stevenson, _____ 22
  John 99
  (Col.) John 118
  (Col.) Richard 118, 125
  Robert 156
Stewart, _____ 40, 45, 80
  (Capt.) 64
  Abraham 70, 72
  Alfred 25, 103

Stewart, (Hon.) Andrew 53
  David Shriver 53
  (Lt.) Edward 127
  George 237
  William 40, 60, 113
Stigers, _____ 232
Stobo, (Capt.) 43, 50, 51
Stone, (Rev.) W. 101
  William 27
Storman, _____ 34
Strickler, Conrad 25
Stewart 138
Strong, (Justice) William [15]
Sturgis, Phineas 23
Stuyvesant, (Gov.) 217
Sute (see Shute)
Sutton, (Rev.) Isaac 101
  (Rev.) James 101, 137
  John 101
  Moses 101, 160
  Samuel 160
Swats, Henry 92
Swearingen, John 22, 100
  Van 22, 99, 100
  (Col.) William 105, 116

-T-

Taney, (Chief Justice) 250
Tanner, _____ 105
Tate, John 243
  Lee 100
Taylor, Isaac 240
Teagarden, Abraham 92
Ternay, (Admiral) De 167
Thomas, _____ 232
Thompson, Nace 100
  Smith 183
Thorn, Robert 82
Tilghman, (Chief Justice) 97
Todd, James [15]
  William 141
Tomlinson, _____ 43, 58
  Henry 102
  Jesse 35
Torrence, John 101
Trent, (Capt.) 28, 42, 48, 112
Tygard (see Teagarden)

-V-

Vail, ____ 28
Van Braam, (Capt.) Jacob 40, 43
    46, 51, 113
Vance, Hannah 118
    John 118
    Margaret 99
    Moses 118
Vankirk, Johnson 33
Varnum, ____ 179
Veech, David [15]
    David Henry [15]
    E. [16]
    James [15], [16], 102
Verrazzani, ____ 212
Vertner, Barney 150
Verval, John Jr. 92
Vervalson, John 92
Vickers, ____ 162
Villiers, Coulon de 28, 48, 49,
    50, 52, 80
Virgin, Rezin 99, 107

-W-

Waggoner, (Capt.) 57
    (Lt.) 43, 44
Walker, William 129
Wallace (see Waller)
Waller, James 92, 93
    Richard 36
Walpole, Horace 73
Waltzer, Frederick 79
Ward, (Ensign) 42, 47
Washington, George, 26, 28, 29,
    33, 40-45, 47-60, 62, 64, 65,
    68-70, 72, 74-76, 79, 80, 85,
    109, 112-121, 144, 145, 152,
    179, 180, 184, 229, 250
    John Augustine 41, 119
    Lawrence 41
    Lund 119
    Samuel 119
Watson, D. T. [15]
Watts, ____ 235
Wayne, (Gen.) 76, 140

Webster, (Mr.) 196
Wells, B. 144
    John 99
Whaley, (Capt.) Benjamin 126
    (Capt.) James
Wilcocks, ____ 98
William, (King) 233
William of Orange 225
Willing, Thomas 237
Wilson, ____ 120
    (Col.) 100
    (Judge) 141
    Agnes 131
    Alexander 19
    Elizabeth 131
    George 172
    (Col.) George 81, 100, 130, 131,
        172
    (Lt. Col.) George 151
    James 87
    Jane 131
    John 172, 157
    (Capt.) John 131
    Mary Ann 131
    Phebe 131
    Samuel 131
    Sarah 131
    William George 131, 172
Wirt, William 183
Wiseman, John 92
Wolcot, ____ 189
Wood, Isaac 79, 80, 115
    John 140
    Stephen 105
    William 157
Woodruff, Cornelius 34
Woods, (Mr.) 82
    John 28, 178
Woodward, Joshua 88
    Paul 162

-Y-

Yeldall, (Dr.) Anthony 157
Young, (Judge) 19
    Peter 92

www.ingramcontent.com/pod-product-compliance
Lightning Source LLC
Chambersburg PA
CBHW061438300426
44114CB00014B/1731